# Orval and Therese Epperson

Orval and Therese Epperson

Copyright ©2020 Winnie Carter

ISBN 978-1-7360368-0-8

All rights reserved. No part of this publication may be reproduced, distributed, or transmitted in any form or by any means, including photocopying, recording, or other electronic or mechanical methods, without the prior written permission of the publisher, except in the case of brief quotations embodied in critical reviews and certain other noncommercial uses permitted by copyright law.

Book design by StoriesToTellBooks.com

# Orval and Therese Epperson

# CONTENTS

## PART I THE EARLY YEARS — 1

Orval William Epperson — 3
Early History of Southwest Missouri — 6
My Mother's Siblings — 8
Oklahoma Territory — 10
Death of Lee Sellers — 14

## PART II HOME PLACE — 18

Home Place Timber and Crops — 20
Home Place Livestock — 25
Wintertime, the Smokehouse, and the Cellar — 29
Free Food from Nature — 34
Siloam's Sorghum Mill — 40
Fishing on the Farm — 42
Animal Traps — 44
Trust in God and Keep Your Powder Dry — 48
Bloodhounds — 51
Holy Terrors — 52

## PART III MIDDLE YEARS — 54

My Siblings — 55
My Education — 59
I Left Home at Fifteeen — 63
Train-Hopping and the Frog Hunt — 66
Fishing for Chickens — 69
Weekends in Anderson — 71
Sellers Drilling Well — 73
Fox Hunting and My Father Lost His Eye — 75
A Bachelor in Neosho — 77
Neosho Business Dealings — 80

## PART IV THERESE DEBROSSE — 83

I Fell in Love — 84
Therese Gertrude DeBrosse — 87
Therese's First Holy Communion — 93
Sisters, Blanche and Grace DeBrosse — 96
Therese's Education and Typhoid — 98
Therese's Double Cousin — 102

## PART V WORLD WAR I — 104

I Joined the Army — 105
My War Journal — 111
Postcards Back Home — 116
Couvertpuis, France — 129
Memoirs of France and 88th Division — 132
American Expeditionary Forces University — 135
Time to Go Home — 137

## PART VI THE MARRIED YEARS — 140

Therese Visits My Folks at Home — 141
Therese DeBrosse and Orval Epperson Marry — 144
344 South Hamilton Deeds — 148
Married Life and Children — 151
Our Son Billy — 161
Correspondence with Romere Martin — 175
Grandfather George Washington Epperson — 182
My Siblings and Parents Later in Life — 191
Our Children and Grandchildren
and Golden Wedding Anniversary — 196
My Investments — 200
Orval the Fisherman — 203

| | |
|---|---:|
| **PART VII THE LAST YEARS** | 211 |
| Mr. Banker at Bank of Neosho | 212 |
| The Maple Tree Poem | 217 |
| Orval and Therese Deaths | 220 |
| Research on Sellers and Sherer | 228 |
| Epperson Brief Family Lineage | 233 |

# PREFACE

My mother, Tirzah (Epperson) Federer, had asked me to help her research our family history. She found it fascinating and wanted it written down to be passed on to future generations. It had been her lifelong pursuit that was paused for several decades while she raised her eleven children. She died in 2015 and just before that she reiterated her appeal, "Winnie, please continue my research." Although I was overwhelmed by the request, not knowing how or when I could possibly accomplish this, a few years later I found myself with children grown and free time on my hands.

Around that same time, our dear cousin, Eppy (William Epperson Giles), son of my mother's sister, Joan (Epperson) Giles, sent an email to our Federer family. He had come across several drafts of stories that his mother had written. She, too, had died in 2015, a few months after our beloved mother.

These stories were precious, indeed. For you see, Joan recorded her father as he told the stories of his life during the long months he convalesced from cancer treatment, 1975-1976. Joan had traveled from her home in California to spend months living with Dede and Poppy in the small town of Neosho, collecting precious snippets of his early life on a Southwest Missouri farm in the 1890s, WWI stories, life with his cherished wife, Therese DeBrosse, and much more. Without Joan's painstaking work of recording and transcribing Orval's words, the story of his life would remain untold.

Furthermore, without the foresight of her son, Eppy Giles, who took the time to go through her papers and notes and forward them on to his cousins in St. Louis, this book would not exist.

Serendipity? Divine intervention? Two sisters in heaven urging us along to finish the book? I prefer to think Joan and Tirzah, along with their brother, Billy, who died tragically at the age of 22 during WWII, are having a wonderful time watching this play out. And of course, I hope that Orval and Therese are pleased with the outcome. We will have to wait to ask.

I would like to acknowledge my brother, James Robert (Jim) Federer for his help in researching our ancestry. Jim's research on our family lineage is extensive, going back to the 1500s, and without his help, historical data would be missing.

But, make no mistake, this book is the voice of Orval William Epperson, our grandfather Poppy. His Southwest Missouri humor, relaxed and intimate storytelling, earthy language, and matter-of-fact voice are unique to him and the era in which he grew up.

This is the story of Orval and Therese Epperson.

Winnie (Federer) Carter
September 2020

# PART I

# THE EARLY YEARS

*Orval William Epperson*

*Early History of Southwest Missouri*

*My Mother's Siblings*

*Oklahoma Territory*

*Death of Lee Sellers*

Orval William Epperson

# Orval William Epperson

I was born on a Tuesday, October 13, 1891, at Grandmother and Grandfather Sellers' farm, in a two-story house down on Indian Creek, just over the hill from Anderson, and deep in the rugged Missouri Ozarks. We called it Home Place. It was on a stretch of river called Indian Creek because at its banks, the great Indian rendezvous took place many years before. At the time of my birth, my mother, Emily Jane Sellers was 22 years old (1869-1951) and my father, William Stanley Epperson, was 23 years old (1868-1956). They married a little over three years later, on January 10, 1895, by the local ordained minister, M.G. Elliff, whose family owned Elliff's switch, the little spur off the railroad. The ceremony was held at the farm, near the bountiful waters of Indian Creek.

*January 10, 1895. Marriage License of William Epperson and Emma Sellers, State of Missouri, County of McDonald.*

The year I was born, Benjamin Harrison had become the President, railroads helped open up new territories. Montana, Washington, Idaho and Wyoming became the newest states. Wounded Knee Massacre had occurred, and both Yosemite National Park, and the sport of basketball were newly created.

The 1890's were marked by a severe economic depression with most of the nation living on farms or small towns. New machines for farming were invented during that time, but horse, oxen and people provided most of the power.

The county where I grew up was McDonald County (founded in 1849) in the furthest southwest corner of the Ozarks. It included Anderson, Ginger Blue, Noel, Pineville, Tiff City and a few others. Pineville, six miles away, named after the pine trees in the vicinity, was the county seat. It contained a 2-story brick courthouse, five stores, 1 hotel, 1 livery stable, 1 wagon shop, a fine grist and saw-mill, a weekly newspaper, a school house, and one Methodist Episcopal church. The log courthouse was burned down in 1863 by bushwhackers, destroying most of the records and deeds.

The nearest town to Home Place was Anderson, named after Robert Anderson, who in 1886 owned the only general store in town which housed the post office. On occasion, we would take a horse into town to trade supplies (eggs and butter for sugar), but rarely did we get any mail. Our entire world could be found in that small corner of Missouri.

Seneca, 22 miles north of Anderson, was in Newton County (established in 1833), and was named from a Native American word meaning, "keeper of the door," because it was the last town before entering Indian Territory to the west. It was also the town my mother's family settled as pioneers 53 years earlier.

Sixteen miles east of Seneca in Newton County, was Neosho, or Ne-u-zhu, an Osage Native American word meaning, "the meeting of clear cold water," and where I spend my adult life. The 1890 Newton County census stated the population was 22,108, and Neosho, the largest town in the county, claimed over 2,000 of those residents, a much bigger town than Anderson and Pineville combined, which had less than 200 total residents.

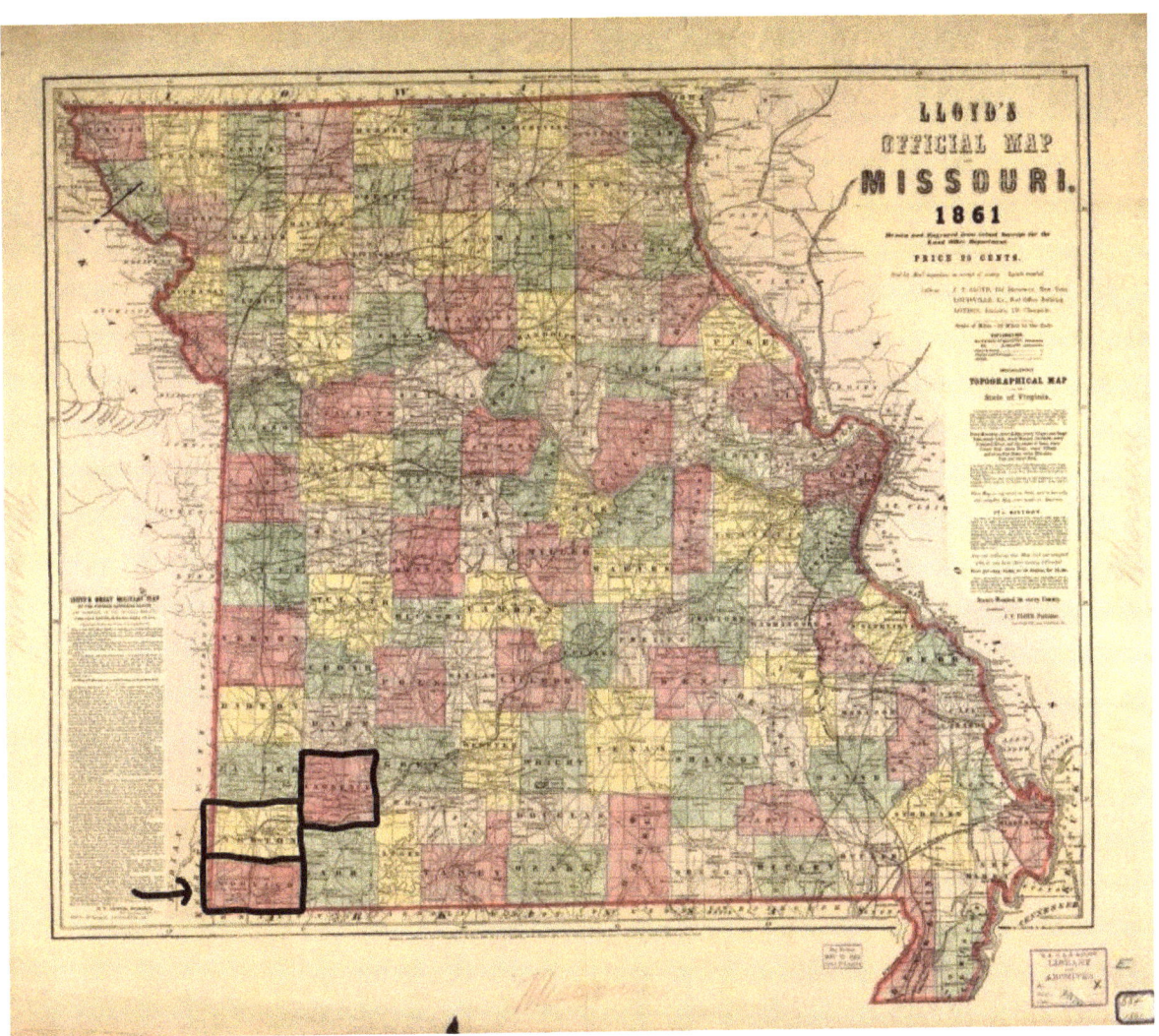

*Map of Missouri. McDonald County was where I grew up (arrow). Newton County (boxed) is directly above it and was where I spent my adult life. Just east is Lawrence County (boxed) where my future wife, Therese DeBrosse, was born.*

# Early History of Southwest Missouri

The word "Missouri" came from the Miami Indians meaning "canoe river." The Miami tribe called the Siouan people "Misuli's," that is, "people having canoes." The "L" sound was changed to the "R" sound by the white men, making it "Misuri," and finally "Missouri."

In the early years, southwest Missouri was called "Six Bulls" because an old settler from Tennessee, who in 1808, set out to hunt through the western wilds ended up living with the Indians. Long after his friends forgot his name, he returned in Indian dress, scarcely able to speak the language of his race. He related many adventures in the "country of six boils," the six springs that fed Indian Creek, Shoal Creek, Centre Creek and Spring River. His pronunciation of "Six Boils" sounded like "Six Bulls," and for many years southwest Missouri was known as "Six Bulls."

Among the earliest traditions gathered from the Indians who inhabited Indian Springs was of the healing fountains which were said to exist; the waters healed all manner of diseases, and large number of Indians came each year along with a few daring hunters to visit these secret fountains and told wonderful tales of the cures from the "Four Great Medicine Springs," including rheumatism and chronic eye sore. The springs all flowed from the solid rock within a few yards of each other and yet they differed in constituent elements and weight. These springs were known to be as health-giving as the Eureka Springs.

In 1897, Judges Sturges, wrote about the pioneer settlers in a book called, *History of McDonald County*:

> The early settlers of McDonald County were like those of all other localities located along the creeks and river bottoms. Here were abundant springs of pure, cold water, the streams were alive with fish and an abundance of game ranged near these water courses. The soil was extremely fertile, producing almost miraculous crops of all grains and vegetables, while the uplands called "barrens" or "flat woods," were considered almost worthless for agricultural purposes. Filled with a restless desire for pioneer life, the inhabitants of other states began to settle in these lonely valleys soon after the state was admitted into the Union. Here, in the solitude of the forests, with only the breeze whistling in the trees, the rippling of the water, the cries of wild animals and birds to wake the stillness, these men made their homes. Here many, many miles from any town or post office they reared their families, and here some of them have long ago found their narrow homes.

During the Civil War, 1861-1865, southwest Missouri was embroiled in conflict. Missouri was ravaged by the Civil War and was claimed by both the Union and the Confederacy with two competing state governments. It was a dangerous time to be alive in the lawless southwest Missouri, brothers fought against brothers, many people starved, and others hid out in the nearby caves after their property had been burned down and ravaged by bushwhackers.

The town of Neosho played a significant role during the Civil War because Missouri Governor Jackson, a southern sympathizer, set up a provisional government Capital in Neosho and its legislation passed a bill for Missouri's secession from the Union. Once the Civil War had ended in 1865, Missouri voted 60-4 to abolish slavery that same year.

Neosho grew into a prominent commercial center following the Civil War, with dozens of brick commercial buildings around the central courthouse square containing lumber yards, livery stables, general stores, and hotels. The nearest railroad station was located in Neosho. The Atlantic Pacific Railroad (A&P) and Kansas City, Fort Smith, and Southern Railroads (KCFS&S) had tracks going through Neosho by then.

Neosho was later nicknamed the "City of Springs" because of the local freshwater springs, and those springs were the perfect location for the Neosho Fish Hatchery, built in 1888, the oldest National Fish Hatchery System in the U.S. Seventy years later, Neosho was named the Flower Box City.

# My Mother's Siblings

My mother, Emily Jane Sellers, was the fourth child out of twelve, born to Emaline (Sherer) and Nathaniel Simmons Sellers.

Grandfather Sellers never had much money, but he was a hard worker, and must have enjoyed his downtime, especially at night, for they had twelve children. Matilda was the oldest, and then Mary, Margaret, Emily (my mother), Silas, Dan, Willy, Jim, Lon, Mae, Lawt and Maud. Willy had died at age one, before I was born. Silas died from cancer, at age 25, soon after he was married, and both Matilda and Margaret married young and moved away.

I was older than most of my cousins, and nine years younger than my closest uncle, Wilford Lawton, whom we just called Lawt. The two of us were good pals and shared many adventures together growing up.

There were plenty of children around Home Place, including me. My grandfather used to call me his "Little Jim Dandy," and my uncles called me "Skore," although I never knew why.

The menagerie of children ranged in ages, some even older than our aunts and uncles. One of my best pals living there was a little girl named, Mae Webb. She and another cousin, little Bessy Mitchell, were what we called, woods colts, or illegitimate children. Mountain talk described woods colts as, "ain't got no nown daddy," but my grandmother raised us all the same, and it was widely known that those girls belonged to my Uncle Dan.

Dan was known as the "Bull of the Woods" down around southwest Missouri. Everybody was familiar with his reputation. His woods colts would come and play with the rest of us, and except for legal recognition, were just like the other grandchildren. Grandmother loved us all the same, and their mothers, too. Mae's mother would come over often and Grandmother accepted her as one of her own. I understood there were more woods colts than Mae and Bessy, but those were the only two I remember.

In those days, people lived together for years sometimes without ever getting married. Dan didn't live with either of the girls' mothers. Maybe he was too comfortable at Home Place or maybe he felt he was needed there because Grandfather Sellers died while Dan was in his early twenties leaving him the oldest working man in the family.

Silas was actually the oldest son, but he had married in 1893, had one son, Roy, in 1894, and died at the age of 25, in 1896, the year after Grandfather died. He had cancer of the neck and I can still see those big lumpy sores disfiguring him.

Dan, years later, was finally pressured into adopting little Mae, although he never married her mother. He eventually married a woman and had children with her, but he was single a long time. By the time he married, little Mae was already married. Even though Dan had adopted Mae, his new family, either by will or by law, inherited everything, so, little Mae never got anything – except her name, Sellers. She was a nice girl. She came to Neosho one time to tell me her troubles. I took her over to Capt. Roark and he looked into things.

Aunt Maud was the closest in age to me, seven years older, and I remember her favorite treat was raw onions, slightly cooked bacon, and cornbread. She would sit and eat that concoction with tears rolling down her cheeks. Maud was also the last to leave home. She and Tom Roark had their house there at the southern edge of Anderson, near Indian Creek, all furnished, and ready to move into the night they were married. But the next morning, she appeared at Home Place bright and early, to the surprise of Grandmother.

"Maud, what are you doing here this morning?"

Maud wailed, "Oh Ma, I wanted to come home last night!"

Aunt Mary and Uncle Jeff Chapman (Jefferson Harrison Davis Chapman) lived in Anderson in a big place with four large columns in front, near the cemetery. I remember her well because my little cousins, Lois, Ethel, and Hubert Chapman spent almost as many nights at Home Place as I did. I would often take Hubert, who was six years younger than me, on fishing and frog hunting adventures.

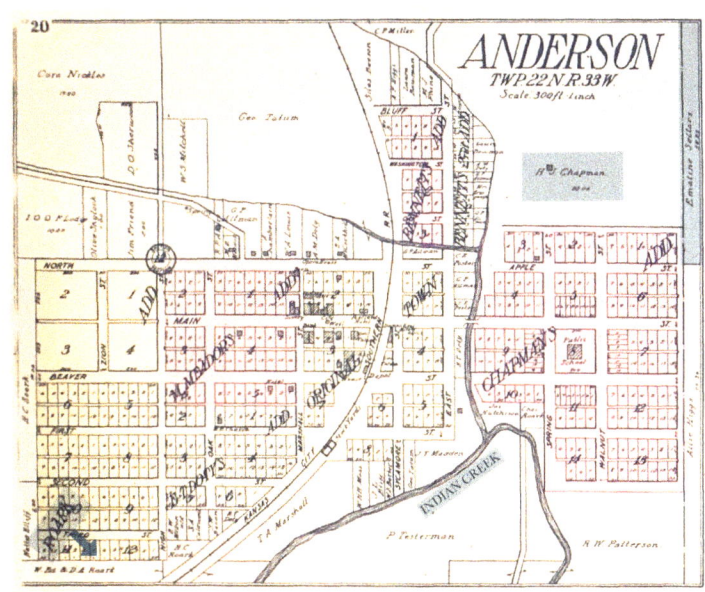

*Map of Anderson, Missouri. Aunt Mary & Uncle Jefferson Chapman (H.J. Chapman on the map) lived in a large house in the northeast corner of Anderson. A portion of my grandmother's extensive farm property began just east of them (highlighted Emaline Sellers). Aunt Maud & Uncle Tom Roark lived in the southwest corner of Anderson (highlighted with arrow). Indian Creek ran through a portion of the south end of town.*

# Oklahoma Territory

The early years of my life were spent living with my mother, and her family at Home Place. My father apparently took off west somewhere when he found out that my mother had become pregnant, and when he returned, the Sellers brothers may have persuaded him to do right, or he had a change of heart, because they eventually married. But for the first few years of my life, my mother was drummed out of her church because she was an unwed mother. It was terribly painful for her, and I was acutely aware of her pain even as a young boy. But soon after they married, the three of us moved to Adair, Oklahoma.

The Oklahoma Land Run was in 1889, two years before I was born, and it must have looked mighty inviting to my parents. If a settler could stay on an unassigned land for five years, and improve it, the land would be theirs, free and clear. My folks were not a part of that first wave to stake a claim, but around 1895, with a young son and a strong ambition, my folks set out for Oklahoma Territory. (Oklahoma Territory and the Indian Territory eventually merged into the State of Oklahoma in 1907.)

They put all our belongings in a horse-drawn covered wagon and started the journey south. Wagon trains traveled about 10 miles per day depending on the weather, terrain, and other factors. We rode in a covered wagon from Anderson, Missouri down to Siloam Springs, Arkansas, and stayed there for a while before moving on. I remember once down there around Siloam Springs getting stuck in the mud so deep that I had to leave my little boots in the muck and went barefoot the rest of the trip.

From there we rode west to Salt Creek, Oklahoma, then finally down to a little town called Adair, where our cattle could graze freely on the prairie. They called it Free Range.

Most of the settlers who moved in during the Territorial Days were either small farmers or cattlemen, and the two did not get along. Cattlemen claimed that farmers poisoned the waters where their cattle drank, and farmers claimed the cattlemen killed their dogs that protected their lands and farm animals. It was a contentious existence.

Herders would drive cattle into the prairie and often the animals would charge uncontrollably towards our fields to eat corn through the fence. We had little to spare, and so I would run towards them yelling and waiving my little straw hat in a circle over my head, to try to scare them off, but they would just look at me curious-like and bug-eyed, munching on the sweet corn until they meandered off at their own leisure.

We owned a big dog down there, sort of shepherd like. He was big enough for me to ride on his back like a pony, and he was a fierce protector of me and our property. We would send him out to the fields and he'd bring our cows home for milking. The grass was so tall he would jump above it from time to time to see where the cattle had gone. But one day our dog didn't come home and we found him ailing in the fields. We thought he was poisoned, probably from the hateful cattlemen, and he died soon after. It broke my heart.

During the three or so years, we lived in Adair, I spent most of my time with my mother in that one room farmhouse. I was very young, but curious. The walls of our house were wallpapered with newspapers, stuck on with corn flour starch. I would see the pictures and the writings, and asked my mother what they meant. That was how I learned my ABC's. She would show me the letters and words as she cooked, and I'd stare at them all day. It was in this manner that, when I returned to Anderson at the age of seven, I could do a little reading and writing, even though I had never been to school.

*Wallpaper made from newspaper*

## MOTHER HUBBARD AND MRS. VICKERS

My mother was known to wear a Mother Hubbard style dress; a long, wide, loose-fitting affair with long sleeves and a high neck. It was intended to cover as much skin as possible. All women in the west wore these daily gowns devised to free themselves from the constriction of corsets.

My mother was very cordial with all our neighbors in the Territory, and made friends easily. One was Mrs. Vickers, who had a son about my age, a six-years-old, named Henry. They would come to visit often, usually arriving about mid-morning and my mother, would have a few biscuits and some fried bacon left over from breakfast. She stored them with other leftovers in what we called the safe, a sideboard piece of furniture that was under lock and key, as it had prized cakes, pies, and other foods stored in it.

We could always tell when Mrs. Vickers and Henry were coming over because by the time they got within hearing distance, we'd make out Henry's cries, "I'm hungry!"

Once inside, his chant would change to, "Want meat and bread! Want meat and bread!"

Mother Hubbard's cupboard would soon be raided for the prized biscuits and bacon. Mrs. Vickers would make a feeble attempt at manners by grabbing the food from Henry's little fists, "Henry, you can't eat all of that!"

Then she would promptly tear off a larger piece for herself and have the insolence to ask for more.

My father soon put an end to that by locking the safe and taking the key to the fields with him, so that when Mother Hubbard went to her cupboard that morning for the usual biscuit and bacon mid-morning Vickers treat, it was effectively bare, locked up tight.

"Old Mother Hubbard, went to the cupboard to give a poor dog a bone. When she got there, the cupboard was bare, and so the poor dog had none."

Later, Mother declared, "I was never so embarrassed!"

*Emily Jane Sellers Epperson*

My father responded, "Embarrassed or not, there will be no more mooching."

That sort of broke Mrs. Vickers from her scrounging habit for a time. As I recall, her husband was just as capable of providing as anyone else. But she was pretty slow and sloven and probably too lazy to cook for her own family.

Another neighbor was Mrs. Large, who lived down the road and invited us over from time to time. She was very nice, nothing like Mrs. Vickers. One morning, she invited Mother and me over for watermelon. The road to her house ran right by the Vickers' place. Mrs. Vickers, of course, stopped us as we approached to learn where we were going.

"Wait! I will go with you!" she shouted.

She called Henry from play and sure enough they walked right along with us. Just as we came upon Mrs. Larges' house, Mrs. Vickers planted the idea, "Now Henry, don't you ask for no watermelon."

Immediately, Henry began, "Want watermelon! Want watermelon!"

When we got to Mrs. Larges' house, she said she didn't have any watermelon right then, but when the menfolk returned, they would go out and pick some. They would know which melons were ripe. But on and on Henry kept up his chant, "Want watermelon! Want watermelon!"

Mrs. Vickers, aka, Mrs. Moocher, then volunteered that she knew when watermelons were ripe enough to eat and that she could show us right then and there which ones to pick. We followed her out to the watermelon patch, where she picked up a melon, broke it open on the ground, scooped out the center with her hands, and began eating it right there on the spot. Once one watermelon was devoured, she picked up another one, and repeated the process, again and again. She and Henry gorged themselves on hot watermelon. That was the last time Mother ever let them go anywhere with us, which wasn't usually anywhere special.

One time, I recall, however, we did do something extraordinary. We went to a Ringling Brothers and Barnum Bailey circus. It was the first circus I ever saw.

The closest town that the Ringling Brothers visited was Vinita, Oklahoma, a half day's trip away. We hitched up the wagon with our two horses, Bert and Frank, and drove into town, just in time to see the circus parade, the first parade of any sort that I had ever seen, and it was a sight to behold. The parade had marching bands, circus wagons, clowns, performers, and exotic animals.

I was especially captivated by the large, majestic elephants. Those elephants were great big things, magnificent noble beasts, and they dropped tubsful of poop at a time. I was awestruck and fascinated. For an impressionable 6-year-old, that much poop was a big deal. The next time I saw an elephant was in Joplin, years later after we had moved back to Anderson, and even then I was still amazed by the volume of excrement those beasts produced.

*1900 Ringling Bros and Barnum & Bailey*

# Death of Lee Sellers

It was about that time when Grandfather Sellers died, killed in a logging accident. Grandfather was born in 1833 as Nathaniel Simmons Sellers, but was fondly known to everyone as Lee Sellers. We were still living in the Oklahoma Territory when we heard the news about his death.

*Logging in the Ozarks*

Missouri was in the midst of a logging boom, and sawmills produced lumber and railroad ties for a growing nation. Companies like the Missouri Lumber and Mining, and Ozark Land and Lumber, purchased land as cheaply as $1 an acre, and they clear it for wood.

Grandfather had the land (Home Place), and the laborers (his sons), and the knowledge (he had corded wood during the California Gold Rush), so he, too, went into the business of felling trees, using only hand tools and brute strength. To do so, my grandfather and uncles would saw down the large trees, wrap a chain around the logs, and have the horses pull the timber up to the top of the wagon, one after another until the wagon was full and overflowing.

But on that day, the chain slipped, and the logs rolled back down, crushing Grandfather.

The 1897 book, *History of McDonald County*, by Judges Sturges memorialized the death of Grandfather Sellers.

> DEATH OF LEE SELLERS
>
> Wednesday afternoon between two and three o'clock Lee Sellers, one of the most prosperous and highly respected citizens of this county met with a tragic death near his home on Indian Creek, about one mile east of Anderson.
>
> He and one of his sons were out in the hills loading a saw log. They had placed the rope around it and were rolling it up with the team, when the rope gave way and the log rolled over Mr. Sellers and mashed him so that he died in a short time.
>
> The children, some of whom reside in the Territory, have all been notified, and the burial will take place at the Beaver Springs cemetery today.
>
> The deceased owned a large farm on Indian creek about a mile east of Anderson and was well fixed for a comfortable life.
>
> He leaves a wife and several children.
>
> *McDonald County Republican*, February 22, 1895.

After the death of my grandfather, we made plans to leave Oklahoma, but it took a few years. The next large caravan traveling north to Missouri, left in 1898, and was led by a man named Todd Decker, who was a friend of my father. We joined the caravan, which had about four or five other wagonloads.

*Wagon Train*

All of our belongings, everything we valued, was heaped high into that wagon. The roads were not paved, just dirt worn down by travelers, and large potholes with deep grooves from wagon wheels. It was an uncomfortable journey, bumpy and hot. When it rained we were grateful for the cooling off, but the thick, sticky earth would suck up everything, wagon wheels, animal hoofs and all. There was nothing to do but push onward. Staying put would make it worse.

One night on the trail, there was a big rainstorm. I remember Mother and I both held down the tarpaulin over the wagon bed to keep the rain from soaking our belongings. As the storm raged on Mother pulled the tarp taut and urged me to do the same. I would tire out quickly and fall asleep, but Mother kept a vigilant eye and would nudge me to hold on tight; it would soon end.

My father had a good team of horses, the best in the caravan as it turned out. When we came upon a flooded area, we would get our own wagon across in good shape, but the wagons behind us would get stuck, bogged down by thick mud. So my father would unhitch our horses, Bert and Frank, and hitch them to the stuck wagons to help pull them out. He would then do the same thing for the next wagon in the caravan, and so on, one after another.

We had a cow or two walking behind us. Part of the way, my father walked along herding them and part of the time he would get in the wagon and ride with Mother and me. It took several days for the caravan to make the trip from Adair to Anderson, but it seemed like forever.

When we got back to Missouri, we moved into a small, one room house called Van Place about a mile from Grandmother's farm. It was called Van Place from the Van Winkle family, the previous owners. But no matter the name, that one room house was so small we nicknamed it Mouse House.

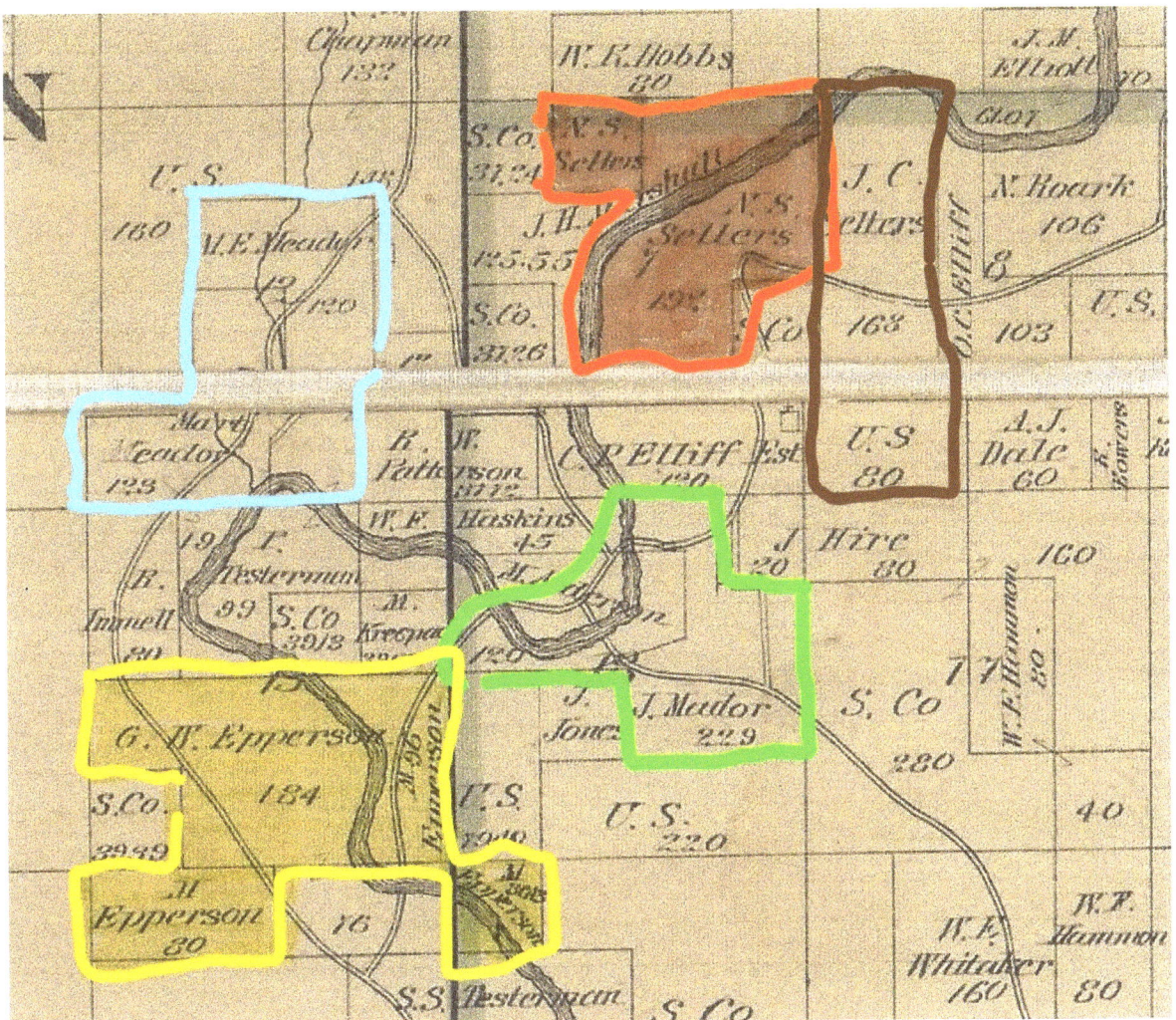

**Map of McDonald County, Missouri**

*1884 Map of McDonald County, Missouri. The highlighted property (upper right) of Nathaniel S. Sellers (N.S. Sellers) was a farm next to Indian Creek that I called Home Place. Nathaniel's brother, John Connaway (J.C. Sellers) owned the adjacent outlined land. It was said that J.C. Sellers built his house square with a compass by driving a stake in one corner and waiting until dark to line up the other stake with the North Star. When John and Nathaniel were young men they went out west to join in the California Gold Rush. The property of G.W. Epperson, my grandfather, (lower left) was the youngest son of Aphrey and Elizabeth (Hire) Epperson, and father to William Stanley Epperson (my father). The Epperson and Sellers families would unite with the marriage of my parents: Emily Sellers and William Stanley Epperson in 1894. The property of M.E. Meador, (directly north of G.W. Epperson) was Martin Meador, who was married to Sara Epperson (eldest daughter of Aphrey and Elizabeth, and older sister to G.W.). The property of J. Meador, next to G.W. Epperson's property, was Judge Joel Meador, who was a distant Epperson relative and the father of G.W. Epperson's 2nd wife, Lucinda Hannah Meador. Next to J. Meador was the property of Joel Hire (J. Hire) who was the younger brother of Elizabeth Hire, wife of Aphrey Epperson, and uncle to G.W. Epperson. Indian Creek ran from northeast to southwest and through the farmlands of N.S. Sellers down to the farmlands of G.W. Epperson.*

# PART II

# HOME PLACE

*Home Place Timber and Crops*

*Home Place Livestock*

*Wintertime, the Smokehouse, and the Cellar*

*Free Food from Nature*

*Siloam's Sorghum Mill*

*Fishing on the Farm*

*Animal Traps*

*Trust In God and Keep Your Powder Dry*

*Bloodhounds*

*Holy Terrors*

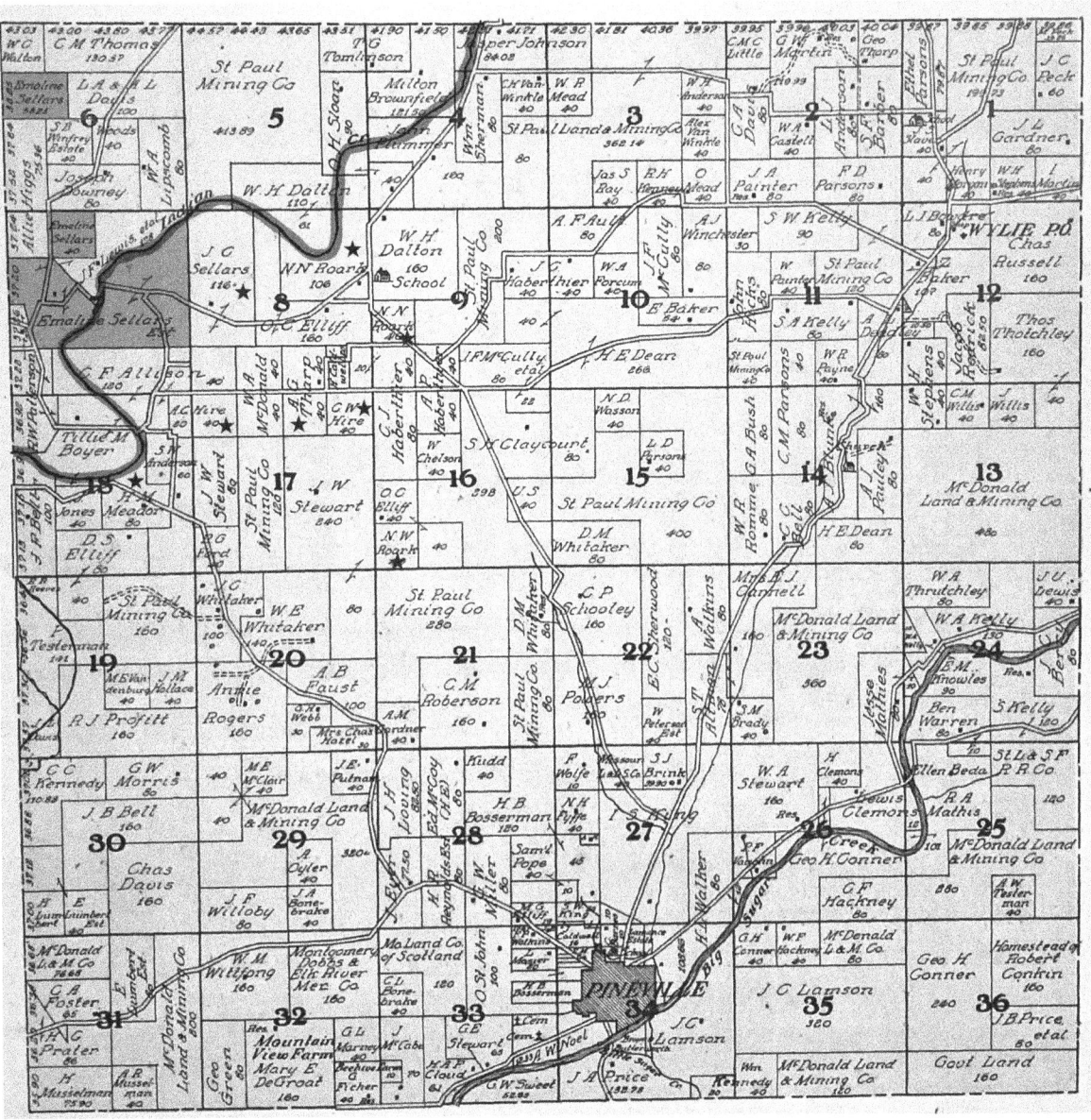

*1909 Map of McDonald County, Missouri, Township 22N, Range 32W. My grandmother Emaline Sellers est. farmlands (highlighted) were originally in the name of her deceased husband N.S. Sellers as seen on the 1884 map. Nathaniel's brother, J.C. Sellers farm property remained adjacent to Home Place. Indian Creek ran from the northeast to the southwest and directly through Emaline Sellers Home Place farm. Familiar family names appear (see stars), such as A.C Hire (Albert Curtis) and C.W. Hire (Charles Wilbur) both sons of Joel Hire, uncle to G.W. Epperson. A.G. Tharp (Philip Abraham Gilbert Tharp) was the son of G.W. Epperson's older sister Emily (Epperson) Tharp, and when Abraham (Abe) was a young boy he was bound as an apprentice to G. W. Epperson to learn the art and mysteries of farming. Much later, I (Orval William) would recall fondly eating many of his watermelons and cantaloupes for 5 cents each. Also nearby were the farms of H.M. Meador and several Roark family members.*

# Home Place Timber and Crops

My grandparent's Home Place, was a little more than half a section of land (1 section = 1 square mile, or 640 acres), but they owned several fields surrounding it, which were divided into 40 and 80 acre parcels, and scattered throughout the countryside. Much of it was rough land, mainly trees and pasture, but there was an access road to all of it, and Indian Creek ran through several parcels.

The property had plenty of good, hard, post oak trees, a slow growing oak that could thrive in dry, poor soil, and was resistant to rot, fire, and drought. The leaves of the post oak were distinctively shaped with three perpendicular lobes, much like a Maltese Cross. Because it was so hardy, it was the type of tree that my grandfather cut and sold for railroad ties. He and my uncles would chop the logs to size with broad axes, about one-foot square by eight feet long for regular ties, and fifteen feet long for switch ties. (Switch ties were cut longer because they had to extend from one track clear over to another, allowing freight cars to be switched off). Once cut they would take the ties to a flat car on a little spur off the railroad called Elliff's Switch, named for the owner, Jesse Elliff, who was the Lumber and Timber Dealer. When the car was completely loaded, Elliff would sell it to the railroad and put an empty car on the spur to be filled again. Not all of the wood was used for ties, though. Some logs were cut smaller and sold for cribbing in the local mines. A box crib or cribbing was a wooden structure used to support sub-surface mining as a roof support.

*Loading railroad ties to steam engine train. Building entrance and roof support for mines using wood cribbing.*

Home Place shared in the collective crop rotation with other tillable tracks. Wheat, corn, and oats were the main grains, but there was also timothy, millet, clover, and crops like tobacco, and sorghum. Timothy was a bunchgrass that grew two to four feet and promoted a shiny coat, good digestion, and healthy weight for the horses. Millet grew four to six feet, and produced a seed similar to oats. Clover was used for soil erosion prevention, and the blooms were excellent for honey bees. All three were considered grasses and used as hay for animal feed. (Hay is different than straw. The entire harvested plant including the seeds is hay. When seed heads are removed, the plant left behind is called straw, a hollow tube mainly used for animal bedding.)

*Horse drawn cultivator*

My father worked in the fields with horse and cultivator. The teeth in the cultivator would pierce the soil, stir, and pulverize it before he planted crops. Once the crops began to grow, he would cultivate the soil again to kill the weeds by uprooting them, but this time he did it in careful patterns so as to spare the plant but disturb the weeds.

When it came time to harvest, the wheat, oats, clover, and hay were cut, threshed, and stacked where they grew in the fields. The wheat was cut with a binder and bound into sheaves or bundles. The men would follow the binder, stack the wheat up on end, and spread out two or three stalks on top to keep the rain off until it was ready to thresh. When that time came, the threshing machine would thresh the grain out, and we'd put it into half-bushel measures and haul it off to our granary.

*Grain binder and threshing machine.*

Threshing machines were very large, loud and dangerous. We would continually feed the straw into it and watch while it beat the wheat grains out, removing the seeds from the stalks and husks. The machine had to be pegged to the ground so it would not detach from its tumbling shafts while operating. The loud sound of the spinning cylinder was a fearful roar.

We didn't own a threshing machine. It was very expensive, and only one person owned a thresher in the county. That was my grandfather George Washington Epperson. Owning a threshing machine implied some affluence, so when Grandfather George bought one, he saw to it that it was mentioned in the GoodSpeed Publication, a book that published personal biographies of prominent Americans.

Once threshed, the straw would go out on a conveyor belt to the grain bin. For weeks afterwards, we would test the wheat for the right temperature by sliding our hands into the middle of it. If it were warm, that meant that some of the grain was still green and moist and was probably molding, so we would have to stir it up to let air into it to dry. But the grain was usually dry enough when it was put up, so I don't remember losing too much to mold. Or mice, either. I guess our granary was mouse proof.

Every field on the property was used for cultivation. Pumpkins, squash, cantaloupe, muskmelons (similar to honeydew), and watermelons, were planted right in the corn field. They couldn't be stolen so easily that way. All during the summer, the melons were eaten as they ripened, and when the corn was harvested, it was eaten that way, too. Our melons and corn were never sold, and if there were too many to eat, they would be used as feed for the hogs and livestock in the winter.

We also grew strawberries. The strawberry patch was grown on Van Place, just across the creek from Home Place, and the popular destination was known as the Sellers-Epperson Strawberry Patch, long before Anderson became known as the "Strawberry Capitol of the World." But that glory was short-lived as competition proved too strong with western and southern states taking over the industry.

We tried to make sweet wine from the culls of the strawberries and blackberries, but the fermentation didn't work, turning into vinegar quickly. We could never figure out how to prevent that except to drink it before it reached the vinegar stage. We did, however, deliberately make homemade vinegar from apples culls. Apples that were too small, worm-eaten, or wasp-eaten were called downfalls, and these were pressed into cider, which eventually turned into vinegar.

Home Place had orchards that spanned six to eight acres; mostly apple, but also a few peach and plum trees. We never sprayed or pruned the fruit trees, birds kept the insects down most of the time. They were effective enough except perhaps in the Fall when the yellow jackets and wasps got to be too numerous for the job, and the birds couldn't keep up.

A big vegetable garden was on the farm, too, and it seemed to have a little bit of everything; tomatoes, peas, green beans, lettuce, cabbage, beets, radishes, parsnips, and lots of potatoes, both Irish and sweet. Grandmother would can vegetables and fruit from the garden, for winter eating. She put up tomatoes, peas, beets, and green beans that way. Berries, wild grapes, peaches, and plums were made into preserves. But in order to make the preserves, we would swap out what we had enough of, like a dozen eggs or a pound of butter, for some sugar at the store. For special occasions, we were treated to brown sugar, which we called "the trawling kind." That name had to have been a mispronunciation by one of us kids for "crawling" because when the brown sugar melted, it spread out slowly, like it was crawling along the table.

## THE BARN, TOBACCO, AND THE ROOSTER

The barn was the storage place for vine crops, like squash, pumpkin and such. Those that weren't keeping so well would be fed to the hogs, along with the corn. And of course, hay was stored loose in the barn loft.

To feed the livestock, we would push the hay down through a four foot opening in the loft rafters. It would land in the trough, a long narrow open container that the animals ate out of. There were horse stalls along either sides of the barn, so in order to miss those, we would sweep the hay through the narrow rafters to the front of the barn, and drop it into the trough as best we could.

I remember when Grandfather Sellers grew tobacco. It would grow so tall with blossoms at the top that attracted big, green tobacco worms. In order to kill them, he would have to nearly climb up the stalks, to pull down the large elephant leaves, and pluck off the worms. When the tobacco matured, he would cut it off at the ground, and hang it from the rafters in the barn loft to cure (dry out). If it were so dry that it crumbled, it was no good for rolling cigars, but if it were a bit damp, it was called case condition, and we would roll it around to make a twist at either end. Casing also included dragging the tobacco through a trough with sugar or licorice water. The excess was squeezed out, and it acted as base flavor for the tobacco.

The aim was to get a nice cased tobacco, but we used every part of the plant even if it were dry and crumbly. The leaves could be pressed into a pipe, and that was what my great-grandmother Elizabeth (Buzzard) Sherer would smoke. She would sit by the fire, rocking, and smoking her little clay pipe. She was also known to pick up small burning coals out of the fire with her bare fingers to light it.

Well, one time, Grandfather had tobacco stored in the barn loft, and a rooster took to roosting up there, and crapping all over it. So, Grandfather got one of the boys to crawl up into the loft after the rooster. In those days we had no flashlights, but we did have a "bullseye" lantern. This was an ordinary lantern where you could raise the globe up, light the kerosene soaked wick, then put the globe back down. On the front of it was a sort of magnifying round bulb. Grandfather was holding the lantern up, shining focus on where he thought the rooster might be hiding.

He was standing directly below the rooster, "There he is, right up there!"

A load hit Grandfather right in his face. That rooster emptied its entire bowels directly into Grandfather's mouth and whiskers. Spitting and furious, he ran out of the barn, and left the rooster to its own devices.

# Home Place Livestock

My grandparents kept about a dozen horses and colts for hauling and plowing, and twenty or thirty cows, about half dairy cows for milking, and the other half, cattle, for eating. Sheep, pigs, flocks of chickens, turkeys, geese, ducks, all lived on the farm. The pigs were raised mostly for lard, but later we had some Berkshire pigs that were good eatin'. The sheep were kept primarily for their wool.

The autumn was when we slaughtered animals for meat. It was just easier to store the meat afterwards when the outside temperature dropped. We would slaughter a cow and put the whole side of beef in salt water, cutting it into sections and storing it in crocks or barrels while it soaked in the briny solution to preserve the meat. It was then stored it in our smokehouse or cellar, whichever had the most room.

When the time came to cook the beef, it was moved into a barrel of water and soaked for a stretch in order to get the salt out of it. I guess it was what you would call corned beef, today, but back then, it was the only process we used for meat, without the help of modern refrigeration.

Corned beef, to me, meant that the cow had been raised partly on grass, and then put into an enclosure to fatten further on corn and mixed feed. That version of corned beef was done only on special occasions, and gave the meat streaks of fat, the marbled effect, which rendered it very tender.

*Spinning Wheel and the Stages of Wool*

We didn't eat our sheep, we raised them for their wool, and by carding it, made it suitable for clothing. Carding was when we disentangled and cleaned the sheep fibers by breaking up clumps and combing the fibers to produce a continuous web or "silver," suitable for spinning. The Sellers girls would then sell the wool after they carded it. There was a spinning wheel in the front room of Home Place that was passed down from generations before, but I don't recall Grandmother ever using it, or even my great-grandmother (Buzzard) Sherer.

## SELLERS-EPPERSON BERKSHIRE PIGS

The meat we raised on the farm was just for our own consumption. The Sellers and Eppersons raised Berkshire black and white pigs. We had several brood sows, which would have two or three litters a year, and each litter had about 10 to 12 piglets. We kept the ones we wanted and sold the surplus pigs. Occasionally, we kept a boar but usually we preferred to just bring one of our sows to a neighbor's farm for breeding.

*Berkshire pigs*

We had a frame built for the sow to back up into (helping the process along), especially if the boar were too big and heavy.

I remember once we put a sow in a wheelbarrow to haul her over to the neighbor's boar for breeding. Sure enough, when we returned the next day, she nearly jumped into the wheelbarrow anxious to return home.

When it came time to slaughter, we would strike the hog's head with an axe, take a knife to the neck to bleed it out (so as not to ruin the meat), and then place the beast in a big barrel (like a molasses barrel), full of boiling hot water, then souse it up and down in the boiling water so the hairs would soften and could be scrapped off more easily. Afterwards we would cut off the head at the neck and hang the hog by its hind feet, and remove its guts (heart, spleen, and intestines).

The next day, we would butcher the hog, leaving the bacon sides intact for frying up later, cook the brains for breakfast, and the rest was cut up in chunks and boiled. The head (after taking out the brains), the ears (after cleaning out the dirt), and the jowls (after boiling the chewiness out overnight), were what we called souse or headcheese, similar to scrapple. There was no dairy in this cheese.

Once the meat was boiled, we would mix sage and other seasonings with it, and pour the mixture into a mold. The marrow from the bones would supply enough aspic to hold the meat together. The souse was stored in the cellar, and when we wanted it, we would slice it and fry it up for breakfast.

My favorite treat to eat was the spleen. It was sort of like beef melt. Pork or beef melt was a term used in the market to avoid the rather anatomical description of spleen. It was about one-foot-long and three inches thick. I would score it, salt and pepper it, lay it on the burning coals, then promptly eat it. It was very tasty, high in protein, vitamins, and iron.

## SILVER-LACED WYANDOTTES

At one point while we were still living at the Van Place, my father decided to raise a heavier chicken, so he got a rooster and five or six chickens from Iowa, called silver-laced Wyandotte. The breed of chicken was named after the Indian tribe, Wyandot, who had befriended settlers in the east.

*Silver-laced Wyandotte*

The bird was somewhat round and fluffy with gorgeous feathers to keep it warm during the cold winter months. Roosters weighed 8.5 pounds and hens weighed 6.5 pounds and both lived six to twelve years. They were of good temperament, but were fairly dominant, often near the top of the pecking order. They would lay about 200 light to dark brown eggs each year. We would keep the fertilized eggs for raising more of our own Wyandotte chickens, but we would take the eggs from our other broods to the general store in Anderson, to trade for needed supplies.

Anderson was primitive back then with dirt roads, almost like a western movie set, and folks would travel into town when they heard the Eppersons dropped off eggs at the general store. They would ask the storekeeper to separate the Epperson eggs from the general run of eggs. They wanted to raise their own silver-laced Wyandotte chickens the cheap way, but they were fooled. We never took the Wyandotte eggs to the general store and as often as they tried, those folks never produced a single silver-laced Wyandotte. To get one of our prized birds would be impossible, and my father would laugh and say it was like "milking cold chickens."

*1907 Main Street in Anderson, Missouri*

# Wintertime, the Smokehouse, and the Cellar

In the winter when the plants were dormant, and the ground more visible, we would remove rocks from the fields, by lifting the big ones onto the wagon to be later thrown into the creek. That way the field could be mowed the next season without tearing up the blades. Over the years, that field finally got down to where the ground was in pretty good shape.

In the cornfields, there were many stalks left with a lot of shuck on them. So when cold weather hit, we would go through the fields, snap the corn off the stalks, and throw them in the wagon bed to be stored in the corn crib (a shed outside the barn).

For the part of the cornfields that we couldn't clear, we'd rent it out to local farmers who needed to feed their cattle. These fields had plenty of shucks and nothing to do but decay, so local cattle would graze on them until there were only little nubbins left. At other times we'd put a little fence around an area and turn steers loose to eat during the winter, selling the straw for $4 or $5 a stack.

Winter was the time, too, when we would make fence rails. Often in the spring, a leaf fire would get started and would burn the fence down, so we needed to have a supply of fence rails for quick repairs. We also spent winters making crates and cartons for the Strawberry Patch by stapling together old wooden slats. We had the time to do this when we couldn't be outside working in the fields.

The smokehouse was always full, especially during the cool months, and it was kind of a catch-all for many foods that didn't need quick access to the kitchen. After the slaughtering in the Fall, sides of bacon and ham were hung from the ceiling with a smudge of green hickory chips underneath, enough to make a fire, but not a blaze, so that smoke would rise to the top of the structure where the meat hung and flavor it. Mice weren't a problem in the smokehouse because the meat hung from the ceiling, and it was hard for them to get at it. However, gnats or what we called "little skippers" would lay eggs on the bacon, and we would have to scrape the eggs off every once in a while and put more salt on the meat to keep it sterilized.

Several barrels of other foods were kept in the smokehouse. Salt, for instance, and molasses, and pickles. We put up cucumber pickles ourselves in a salt solution. Some 'cukes from the garden were made with dill and some without. When we were ready to serve them, we'd soak the pickled 'cukes in plain water overnight to get rid of the brine, then slice them up into a vinegar solution for another 24 hours, then we'd spice them to our liking, sweet or sour.

The cellar, which was below the house, was another area where food was stored. It was cooler than the smokehouse, and things that needed extra protection were put there; sauerkraut, for instance. We made it ourselves by putting slices of raw cabbage between layers of salt, then pressing the whole thing down tightly with a heavy weight on top to keep the cabbage mashed down below the brine that formed.

Crockery churns of apple butter were stored there, too. We would leave the apple butter in the churn after processing and seal all around the edges, plugging up the hole in the top where the plunger pump was. That, for the most part, kept bugs and critters away.

The cellar proper had dirt walls, dirt floor, and a teepee type roof that allowed for some three to four feet of ventilation. We put a rod up there across the top of the cellar where the wind could blow through the window, and from it we hung onions, garlic, and red peppers, by their braided tails. This kept them from rotting. We also hung herbs, which had been grown around the edges of the garden, like mint, sage (for sausage), dill (for pickles), catnip (for tea), and horehound (for digestion and coughs).

*Caster bean plant*

Popcorn peanuts were raked with a pronged garden fork, vines and all, and hung from the pole with the goobers still attached to the root. Caster beans were hung there, too. They were planted mainly for their flowers and medicine; not for eating because the seeds and hulls contained ricin toxin. Castor oil, however, in small amounts was used as a laxative for constipation or to start labor in pregnancy, and it tasted terrible.

Root crops like carrots, parsnips, and radishes were also stored in the cellar, as well as Grandmother's canned goods. Of course, what wasn't eaten, or canned, or stored and could be traded for other things. We would trade our excess red plums and eggs for coffee and sugar.

*Goober Peas (popcorn peanut plant).*

Grandmother had many storage places on the farm. One was under the floor boards in the house, near the fireplace. There she had a box about three or four feet square filled with dry sand. Sweet potatoes were buried in it. When we wanted one, we would lift up that section of the floor boards, and dig out the potato.

It's hard to believe that there was once a time when no one paid much mind to the water we drank, the food we ate, or the air we breathed. We took things in stride. It was not simply a matter of ignorance or indifference as much as that we simply couldn't afford to live better. Grandmother would scrimp and cut corners to make ends meet, especially after Grandfather died.

We frequently ingested wasps and yellow-jackets from the damaged apples that were pressed for cider, unwittingly ate baby bees in the honey beebread, and unintentionally smoked rooster droppings that clung to the tobacco leaves. But all of this didn't seem to harm us.

Take mice, for instance, although known as one of the most common sources of contaminants, we didn't make much fuss about it then. Sure, the little rascals were everywhere; we were surrounded by pastures, orchards, and woodlands. But a trusty cat that was a good mouser, or a few snap-traps pared the population down somewhat, and the rest you just lived with, and they with you.

One of the favorite treats and retreats of mice in our house was the flour barrel, or the meal barrel. These barrels were kept in a little room close to the kitchen where they would be handy for cooking. We would put a burlap bag over the top of each barrel. Mice, of course, would chew a little hole in the bag and slip in to eat their meal. The slope of the barrel was such that once they slipped in, they couldn't get out. They were trapped.

The best way to deal with this was to simply pull the burlap bag back, grab the mouse by its tail, and squash its head between your fingers. That took care of the mouse. As to the droppings left behind, these were simply sifted out when it came time to use the flour.

We never went hungry, though. What with all the canning and storing, we ate just about as well as anyone. For breakfast, we would have fat bacon (we didn't raise hogs for lean meat), fried eggs, and big biscuits with sorghum and butter. Sometimes, we would take the melted bacon grease and mix it with sorghum and spread it on cornbread. It really hit the spot. If there were pies from the night before, that would be served at breakfast, too.

Even during the winter, the big meal was served at noon. A day on the farm was geared to whatever needed to be done that day, no matter the season, and we got up at dawn and went to bed at dusk, so the big mid-day meal provided energy for all that labor.

Supper, though, was pretty light. One of my favorite suppers was thickened milk. It was made by sprinkling flour into boiling milk. I remember when my folks and I lived at Van Place, my mother would do all of the milking (she had a more soothing touch with the cows than my father). Cow milking happened twice a day, seven days a week, on a regular schedule, at 6:00a.m. and 6:00p.m., and a cow would only give milk if she were relaxed and comfortable. When my mother would go to milk the cows for the evening, she would leave me at the house to watch the milk boil, and since I didn't stir it a lot, there were always little clumps of flour in it. But that did not matter much, it was still delicious.

## OLD TOM AND THE SORGHUM BARREL

We kept sorghum in the cellar in a barrel with a flappable lid. When one side of the lid was pressed down the other side would raise up. Mice weren't heavy enough to tip the lid open, but a cat was.

That must have been what happened to Old Tom, the patriarch of the whole cat tribe living on the farm. One day I looked down into the barrel and there were two glassy eyes staring back at me. Old Tom was as dead as could be in the half empty barrel.

I ran back and told Grandmother, "Old Tom's in the sorghum barrel!"

She came out, looked things over, then took Old Tom by the neck and raised him out of the barrel and let the sorghum drain off. She even used her fingers to scrape off a little more.

"Grandmother," I asked, "Are you going to use that sorghum?"

"Sure," she said, "All that's ruined is what's stuck to him."

That may not have been quite true, of course, because Old Tom could have fouled up the sorghum in any number of ways before he gave up the ghost, but we used it anyway, every drop.

Taffy was a special treat that Grandmother made for my little cousins and me. Mae and Bessie (Dan's girls), Hubert, Lois, and Ethel (Mary and Jefferson Chapman's kids), Reeta (Maud and Tom Roark's daughter), Roy Sellers (son of deceased Uncle Silas), and I would pester Grandmother until she gave in. We would dip a bucket into the sorghum barrel in the cellar and bring it back to Grandmother to cook. She would take out her pot and make the best taffy ever tasted.

While we sat and watched it boil, Grandmother made us clean up. She made us wash our hands with homemade lye soap which was strong enough to burn your skin off. We didn't want any more contact with it than what was necessary. Lye was made by pouring water over white wood ash and letting it drip into a container. Then you'd add fat scraps to the lye and boil it together. A pot of lye would make soap for nearly a year.

After washing, we would grease our hands with lard so as not to stick to the taffy. Then we would team up, each taking a side of the taffy and stretching it out until the sweet gooeyness got to the right consistency. Pulling taffy put air bubbles in it and made it light and chewy and so we pulled and pulled and pulled, stretching it until it was almost white no doubt, working dirt into it as well.

## THE APPLE HOLE

Of all the spots we stored food around Home Place, the one I remember best was the apple hole. Maybe it was because I was such a regular customer of it. Every day on my way home from school, I would reach in at arm's length and get an apple to sustain me for the half mile I had yet to go after passing Grandmother's house.

The apple hole was about 8 feet wide, 20 feet long, and 3 three feet deep. It was located in a nice place off the road, where water would drain easily from the teepee style wood roof, and had dirt piled high on the sides, so the overall pit was deep and safe from freezing.

But not just apples were stored there. Irish potatoes would be in one section, another might have turnips, and still another, heads of cabbage, or parsnips, or rutabagas. Each section had a way in from the outside, and I knew which board to move to get to the apples. They would be laid in between layers of straw with dirt piled on top, and on top of the dirt was the flat boards, about two feet wide, stacked teepee style to deflect surplus moisture and keep the apples somewhat dry. Occasionally, there would be a small snake in there which had crawled in to keep warm, but it would be dormant so it wouldn't bite. I never got a snake bite from the apple hole.

There were several sections of apples in the hole because we had grown so many in our orchards. One section would have Arkansas Blacks, a dark-red, nearly black, extremely hard apple, but as they matured the green-whitish course flesh would become crisp. Another section would be Grindstones, a flat, medium-sized greenish yellow apple with red stripes especially good for apple cider. Another section would have Pippins, a tart and astringent variety. But the biggest section were the ones we called Little Slicks, a very small apple that we wouldn't think of eating when they were picked because they were so hard and sour, but along towards Spring, after a long winter, they tasted better. Partly, I'm sure because of the diminished supply (they were the only apples left), but also because the apples themselves became more mellow. Still, you couldn't manage more than one or two at a time without the sour upsetting your stomach.

*Arkansas Black*

*Grindstone*

*Little slick crabapple*

# Free Food from Nature

Not everything on the farm was cultivated. Somethings were provided by nature, just for the picking, or shooting, or catching. In the Fall, there were nuts of all kinds; walnuts, hickory, hazelnuts, chinquapins (also called chinkapins).

The Ozark chinquapin, fondly called the Ozark chestnut, was a drought tolerant hardwood tree that had a single nut in each bur about the size of an acorn or hazelnut. As a child, I would stuff my pockets with chinquapins on the way to school, but now they are nearly extinct, due to the chestnut blight.

The chestnut blight began in 1904, killing American chestnut trees across the east, and the epidemic swept across the Midwest as the fungus jumped from chestnut to the Ozark chinquapin. The fungus attacked the top of the tree completely but allowed suckers to regrow from the base. When those fragile suckers began to grow to a certain height, the fungus would attack again and kill them off. The tree, once known as the chinquapin, is now little more than a shrub and blighted stump, found deep in the Ozark forest.

*Chinquapins*

But back in the day, you had to be careful of the chinquapin nuts. If you didn't heat them thoroughly in the oven to kill the worm eggs, they would soon be full of them and no good to eat. Kids frequently got worms from eating things like wormy chinquapins. I remember once feeling something in my bottom moving around. I reached clear down my pants and felt something quite unnatural. I shifted and moved about, thinking it would leave, but it didn't. I finally had to reach clear up into my bottom and pulled it out. It was a big red worm, about eight to ten inches long, and I promptly threw it on the floor and stomped on it. Vermifuge was the medicine we took to kill the worms in our gut, so they could be passed out.

There was plenty of wild fruit for the pickins'- blackberries, huckleberries, dewberries, paw paws, persimmons, and wild grapes (both summer and winter). The summer grapes were smaller than the cultivated kind, and the winter grapes were smaller yet, but still sweet. They grew in bunches around riverbeds and fields.

Blackberries were called brambles for good reason because their canes grew thorny and tangled if they weren't pruned. They grew wild, but Grandmother also had her own blackberry patch, which would get so thick, it would no longer produce fruit. We would have to cut out the canes every year, so that it would bloom again.

*Wild grapes, blackberries, persimmons, dewberries, huckleberries, Pawpaw tree fruit (hillbilly mango).*

Huckleberries were a variation of blueberries, bearing small red, blue or black berries. Dewberries, related to blackberries, were a small trailing bramble with fruit similar to raspberries but were purple to black in color.

The pawpaw tree, also known as the hillbilly mango, was the largest edible fruit tree around. It produced green-blackish fruit about three to six inches long. The flesh was pale yellow and full of dark brown seeds. The flavor was tropical like a combination of banana-mango-citrus with a floral yeasty aftertaste. Persimmons were a sweet, plump orange fruit that ripened in Missouri after the first frost.

There were wild greens; mustard greens, lambsquarters, wild lettuce, and poke. All of them were quite tasty, especially when wilted with hot bacon grease and vinegar, or boiled in a big pot and served with corn pone, or Indian pone, a type of cornbread made from thick malleable cornmeal dough, cooked in an iron pan over an open fire.

Mustard greens were coarse annual weeds that bloomed April through November in fields and roadsides. They were related to broccoli, cabbage, kale, collards and cauliflower. Lambsquarters were hardy weeds sometimes called pigweed, related to spinach, and grew in disturbed soil and roadsides. The young leaves of wild prickly lettuce, also called horse thistle, were bitter but edible, but as the plant matured, it was downright unpleasant to eat. The rich milky sap could be used as a diuretic, sedative for insomnia, relief from whooping cough, and cure for anxiety. Poke weed was a tall, smooth branching perennial with red stems and dark juicy berries that bloomed May through October. All parts were toxic if not cooked thoroughly at least twice in water. The dish was called poke salat. The berries were used as food coloring, ink, and dye, and was thought to have antiviral and antitumor properties.

*Mustard greens, prickly wild, pokeweed, and lambsquarter.*

## HONEYBEES

We had our own bees living in about half a dozen hives near Home Place, but there were also plenty of wild bees attracted to the orchards, clover fields, and wild flowers nearby. Bees loved sweet white clover, but not red clover, because the nectar was too deep in the blossom to reach.

Sometimes the wild bees would settle in one of our empty hives all on their own, but often we went looking for them. We might see a bee come up from some place along the creek where they were watering, or a bunch of them working on white clover as we walked along. It was hard to follow them because the tall trees could get right in the way of our sight. We might think they were taking off for their hive when they were just flying about to annoy us. We soon learned there was a better way to attract bees to our beehive.

We would take a strawberry carrier sweetened with a little honeycomb, or a few drops of anise (which had a good strong odor that could be smelled for a long way off), and walk around swinging it. We would go about a half a mile or so away from Home Place, otherwise we might have attracted our own bees. Once spotted, though, they were easy to track in an open field. Whenever bees were full of water or nectar, they would go up, circle once or twice, then take off in a "bee line," a certain straight direction. We would look up in the sky until we found the path they were taking and follow them, as they swooped, hovered, and landed in a tree, or hollow log, or even on the ground.

*White Clover*

Once we had the bees located, we would put a mark on their bee tree. Often times, you could find several bee trees, one after another, all on the same bee course, and we'd mark them all. Sometimes this was on our property, and sometimes it was on someone else's. We, of course, considered them our bees since we found them, but neighboring landowners thought otherwise, leading to some downright difficult bargaining. We then figured it was best to sneak over in the middle of the night, cut down the section of the tree where the bees were, get the honey, and bring the whole thing home. The queen bee resided in the middle of the swarm, and required a gentle touch so as not to upset her. We would lightly shake the branch near our hive until we were certain she went into it. But sometimes, the swarm would end up on bushes, lost and confused.

We made what was called a super, short for superstructure, where the bees lived, and also where the honey was made. The structure could often be two or three levels high. Bees had to have a starter, something with which to start making honey, so our newly acquired bees, with a bit of leftover honey, began anew in one of our bee house superstructures.

After the bees collected the nectar, they stored it in honeycombs on the wooden frames in the super. The supers kept the combs with pure honey separate from the combs with the queen, eggs, baby bees, and bee bread. The screen meshing on the frames had to be big enough for worker bees to go through, but not big enough for the queen to slip in-between, otherwise newborn bees would end up in the honeycomb.

If we thought one frame was overcrowded, we would move the queen to an empty frame. We did so, by covering ourselves with mosquito bar (a fine mesh or netting), and then with a bellow, we would blow smoke on the bees to calm them down until the queen came out. Then we would pick her up gently and put her at the entrance to the new hive with a new starter comb.

*Bee Superstructure, hanging frames, and bellow smoker*

A lot of the bees would follow her and move right in. With the foundation comb right there, they could start up business again. In the comb left behind, the drone bees would sometimes bring up a new queen. Drone male bees were unlike the female worker bees because they did not have stingers and did not gather nectar. Their only job was to mate with an unfertilized queen. Then the worker bees, by enlarging the cell and by feeding the baby virgin bee certain things, could make her into a queen, a real Cinderella Story.

Sometimes, our house bees would raise an extra queen on their own; probably because of overpopulation. Then part of the colony, with the new queen, would swarm up in the air and swiftly take off for a new home. We would bang on tin pans to make noises in an attempt to settle them, but if we were too late off they would go and land in a hollow tree or somewhere else in the woods. I guess it was like having an extra woman in the house, only one can be the boss, the others would be chased off or voluntarily leave.

Bees were very precious, and so we wanted to keep as many as we could, but one time there were so many bees, we didn't know where to put them. All of the structures were full, so we tried using a cardboard structure as a beehive, but that didn't work, they just flew away. Bees don't like cardboard, I guess.

Once in a while we would get to eat a special treat called bee bread, which was the pollen the bees gathered and packed into empty comb cells, sealing the nectar with beeswax. In good hives, the mesh screen would keep the queen and her babies from the bee bread and the pure honey, but sometimes even with a good structure, you ran the risk of biting into a live baby bee when you ate the bee bread. It was a dangerous treat.

There were other risks, too. I remember one night we were trying to eat honey and my little cousin, Lois Chapman, kept poking her stick into one of our hives, chanting, "Put some honey on my stick!"

A disturbed bee came out of the hive, flew angrily in her direction, and stung her. She ran off crying, "Bitch-a, bitch-a bee-a!"

# Siloam's Sorghum Mill

Siloam Darnell ran the only sorghum mill in the county, and we took all our sorghum sugar canes there to be ground into syrup. Sorghum sugar plants had tall broad leaves resembling corn, but the crop was best known for sweet sorghum syrup. Siloam would come around to inspect the sorghum fields for ripeness, and unless they were as ripe as he thought they ought to be, he wouldn't take them. Once Siloam gave the go-ahead, we would prepare the sorghum plant for the mill by stripping the long leaves around the stalks, either by hand or with a flat paddle. Those leaves made good hay, and the seed heads on top of the plant made for good livestock feed. We would then cut the cane close to the ground, so as to render as much cane juice as possible. At the mill, the canes would be fed in between rollers, where a long pole was attached to the harness of a horse that walked round and round the mill to crush the plants into a liquid.

Siloam charged a toll for grinding the stalks, usually taking a gallon of sorghum juice for every four gallons produced, and you would have to furnish your own barrels. But we, the Eppersons and Sellers, didn't have to pay the toll because there was, in one particular spot on Grandmother's farm, a certain kind of clay that Siloam liked to mix with his syrup. This wasn't gritty clay but unusually smooth, and Siloam got his entire supply of clay from that pit on our farm. For every five gallons of cane juice he would mix in about a quart of that red clay. I don't know what that added, besides dirt, but Siloam's sorghum was known as the best in that part of the country.

There could have been another reason for its fame though – his son, Zara Darnell. The Darnell family had good bible names; Annas, Enos, and Zara. Zara was the youngest and little off mentally, but not so far off that he couldn't keep the boiling syrup moving around the sorghum vat. That vat was a pan about eight to ten feet long and eighteen inches wide and underneath it was a hot fire pit where a great deal of wood was burned. Zara's job was to push the syrup with a sort of wide wooden hoe, round and round the vat, so that it would be constantly moving and heated evenly over the fires, which were hotter in some spots than others.

It took about five gallons of cane juice with that quart of clay to make three gallons of sorghum. Zara was either very conscientious about his job, or he had no control over his bladder, because he never took time out to go to the outhouse or even a nearby bush. He simply relieved himself into the vat and kept right on pushing the syrup around.

*Sorghum mill, sorghum vat*

It took an hour or two to boil it down to the ideal consistency. But once the juice had boiled down, the whole vat would be lifted up, the sorghum poured out into a barrel, sides scraped out for good measure, and filled again with more juice to start the process all over again, where Zara had another chance to flavor it. I don't know which of these three possibilities accounted for the reputation of Siloam's sorghum; the ripeness of the cane, the addition of the clay, or Zara's personal contribution, but it sure was good.

During the sorghum heating process, a green foamy scum would appear. It was skimmed off to the side, and what was left was the amber colored syrup. That amber rich syrup had to cool before it was poured into jugs. Too long a wait for a young and eager Orval. That first foam, which was nearly raw, was sweet but not as sweet as it would be later, and the foam was full of bubbles. We were free to help ourselves to it. So we ate to our heart's content or our stomach's capacity.

I remember one time, I ate all that I could of the foam, and on my way home, I began to foam at both ends; at the mouth and elsewhere. I found a pan of cornbread, which I ate, and ate, and ate, desperately trying to soak up the sorghum foam in my gut, and to get the flavor out of my mouth. As uncomfortable as that was, it never curbed my sweet tooth. One of my favorite suppers was sorghum and bacon grease, spread over cornbread. However, now I eat it in installments.

# Fishing on the Farm

I remember going fishing with my mother while my father was plowing the fields, or something. Solitary time fishing with her was the single most pleasurable experience that I had as a child, and it instilled the love of fishing that I carried throughout my life. Indian Creek and other nearby streams were full of fish: sun perch, chub, crappie, suckers, bass, catfish, punkin seed, also eel and turtle.

We would go down to the bottom lands, and dig up great big red worms. They were very long and we could see clear through them. Some had eggs inside that were over a half-inch long, and so transparent that we could see the baby worms growing inside. After we collected several, we would take them and go down fishing. There was an old pond close to where we lived that had a lot of moss growing in it; just thick with the stuff. Fish liked to live around that moss because it provided protection and plenty to eat. Mother took me there to teach me how to fish, but instead of the big red worms, she would give me a cork as bait for the end of my homemade fishing pole.

One time when I cast my rod into the pond, something grabbed it, and took it quickly under the water. Excited, I tried to drag it back to me, but in the process, broke the thin pole right in half. It must have been a bass or something bigger than a measly punkin seed fish that frequently swam in the pond. He got away, but **I** caught the fishing fever.

My father also fished. He used to make trotlines, using the little perch fish that he caught as bait. Trotlines were an Ozark fishing tradition, long before bass boats and fancy rods. We called it trotline because when a fish would get ahold of it, it would jerk up and down like a horse trotting.

It was made with a heavy fishing line and baited hooks attached at intervals about three or four feet apart. He would stretch the line across a creek, and fasten it to a tree or rock on either side. When we'd come down early the next morning to check on it, if the line were weaving back and forth close to the shore, we knew we had something on it, but if it were quiet, the bait was probably eaten, and the fish long gone. Then we'd try our luck at something more promising like crawfish, catfish, eel, or turtles. The crawfish, or crawdads, that we caught could be eaten just like a tiny lobster. After boiling the crawfish, you'd tear off the tails and eat them, but we mainly used them as fish bait, along with worms.

I remember I tried my hand at cultivating pearls once. There were plenty of freshwater mussels in the streams near us, and I would take a nail and knock a little hole in the shell of the mussel, irritating it so it would secrete the nacre, which produced the pearl. The process worked the same way for oyster pearls in saltwater.

But I guess I was too anxious to get those freshwater pearls. In the course of a couple weeks, I would go back and look for a pearl inside the mussel, only to come up empty. I later learned that a pearl takes much longer than that that to grow.

# Animal Traps

There was plenty of wild game around the farm - rabbit, squirrel, possum, quail, pheasant. My uncles and I used to set traps to catch them. The traps we set for skunk, possum and raccoon were big steel contraptions; the kind that violently snapped down on its victim. The traps had a long, bent, iron handles that you would press down with your foot to open. The trigger was in the center of the jaws, and the weight of the animal would set it off. We laid the traps where we knew animals ventured and lightly buried it in the dirt with a few leaves covering it; too many leaves would trigger the trap. We also had to be careful not to get our fingers too close when we set it, or it would snap, breaking a digit or two.

When an animal came along they would run over it, and their weight would snap the claws shut. Sometimes, as extra incentive, we would hang a piece of meat from a limb above the trap, and in order for the animal to reach the meat, it would have to stand on its hind legs, maybe hop around a bit, and land on the trap. The trap would quickly spring open, snatch a foot or more, and that would be that.

*Figure 4 bird trap, animal trap, box rabbit trap.*

We also set little box traps for rabbits, and in that way, they were not killed or injured, just trapped. We would build a box, maybe a couple feet long, with a sliding door at one end where the animal would enter. The sliding door would be held up with a little pin. Inside the box, at the far end, we set the bait (a carrot or something), and that bait was fastened to the pin. When the rabbit went in to eat the bait, it would pull the pin out from the trap door, and slam it shut behind him.

Sometimes a dog would chase a rabbit into a hole in the ground. We would get a hoe and start digging. If there weren't too many roots to interfere, we'd pull out a rabbit. Other times, our dog would tree a rabbit in a log or a hollow tree. To get it out there, we would get a long stick and fashion a fork on the end (like a pitch fork), stick it into the hole, twirl it about bit until it grabbed the rabbit's hair, then with one final twist, we'd pull the rabbit out. It was cruel because sometimes the skin and hair would come off the rabbit, and we would have to go back in and try it again.

We used to trap birds with homemade cages. We called the cages "figure four bird traps." The figure four was fashioned by sticks balancing on each other, and holding up the cage in the process. The horizontal part of the figure four was placed clear to the back of the cage and peppered with bird seeds around it. The vertical part of the figure four balanced two sticks at the top of the cage. The weight of the cage was entirely supported by these sticks. When a bird would wander in the cage to eat the seeds inside, the motion of its body and wings would disturb the sticks and cause the entire contraption to tumble down on top of it. We caught a lot of live quail that way.

Sometimes we would find a possum in a hollow log. But most of the time we'd find it just hanging from a limb by its tail, and grinning its toothy smile at us. An old boar possum could be pretty tough though. One time, one of our dogs treed one and stuck his nose into the tree. When he backed out, the possum was still hanging on his nose. Boy, did that dog holler! We had to hit the possum on its head to get him to release its hold on the dog.

Often we would find a possum with a pocketful of little ones. You could hardly pull a baby lose from its mother's teat, it was attached so tightly. At night, a mother possum would carry half a dozen or so little joeys on her tail, arching her back, while she balanced on the narrow branches.

We ate a lot of the animals that we trapped in the nearby woods. Rabbit was especially good eatin'. You'd fry it up the same way you'd fry a chicken. The hind legs had more meat that anywhere else (there was not much meat on the ribs). I remember we had a neighbor

*Possum*

once, a fellow named Krause, who liked to eat a mixture of rabbit and squirrel brains. But I never tried it.

We didn't eat coon, either, although the meat looked good when skinned. Raccoons were clean animals, cleaner than a hog or chicken, so it would have been okay to eat, but we just never ate them. Plus, we didn't catch many, maybe one or two a year in our traps, and when we did, we would sell the pelts.

We never ate skunk either, but some people did, or possum, for that matter, they were too fat and greasy. Colored folk liked possum with sweet potatoes; the fat would grease up the sweet potatoes nicely. (In the early 20th century, the term "colored" was commonly used for "person of color.")

Rattlesnakes were plenty in our parts, and some folks like to eat rattlesnake steaks, said to be light and tender after it was skinned, gutted, and washed. It was also sold canned at the general store, but I never ate any snake.

The same went for eels and gar. I never ate those either. Garfish were extremely bony and greasy, and eel had a firm texture, high fat content, and a full distinct flavor. Neither sounded appetizing to me.

There were plenty of wild vermin that lived in our fields, and during the harvest season each year, we would find out just how many. When cutting the fields, the binder would start at the farthest point of our property, next to the fence, and go round and round in an ever-narrowing circle. By the time it got to the middle of the field, there would be a menagerie of critters (rabbit, possum, skunk, rat, snake) all congregated in the center. The animals were afraid to run in the now barren fields for fear of hawks, but if they stayed in the tall wheat fields, the sickle would eventually cut them down. So they huddled in the center until the binder stopped, at which time, we would run in there hooting and hollering, each taking a section to shoo them closer to the center. It was a lot of fun cornering these critters with sticks, clubs, hoes, or whatever we had handy. Most of what we killed that way, we didn't eat.

There were not many wild turkeys that found their way to our farm, nor did we have much luck with tame ones. Turkeys could fly, but if we put a two-foot fence around them, they wouldn't fly over it. They weren't that smart. On the occasion we did have a turkey, we would turn it loose in a field and pretty soon there were no more grasshoppers. Turkeys would eat weeds, stalks, leaves, grasshoppers, wasted grain, everything, and anything. By eating the rough vegetation, they would clean up the arable surface for the next season, and also fertilize the ground. They were like feathered goats. But in order to keep any bird disease from spreading, we wouldn't allow turkeys on the same tract of land, two years in a row.

Grasshoppers were numerous where we lived, also, fleas and ticks. If we left any rakes, forks, or shovels, standing in the fields, by the time we returned, the once smooth handles would be rough and gnawed, because the grasshoppers would chew on them to get to the salt or grease that came from our sweaty hands. They could chew the salt off the handles within an hour or so, and we learned to bring our farm tools in during lunch. That need for salt, could also account for why bees hung around manure piles, they weren't always after pollen.

I was told that the local Indians liked grasshopper soup. They would dig a deep trench, then as a group, march through the fields to scare the grasshoppers ahead of them, into the trench. When it filled, they would jump in and stomp around to smash the hopping critters. Then, they would dry out the grasshoppers, and use them for soup. It was good protein nourishment, but I never ate grasshoppers or grasshopper soup.

# Trust in God and Keep Your Powder Dry

The Sellers boys had rifles and old muzzle loading muskets. That type was shown in the old western movies where a frontiersman would carry two cow horns around his neck, one filled with powder and one with shot. Both horns were covered with cloth, and then with a cap, to keep the contents dry. If your gunpowder got wet, it would not fire. It was critical that the powder stayed dry. We used the say the phrase, "Put your trust in God, and keep your powder dry," but it was a much older saying that originated from Oliver Cromwell's Ireland campaign, and was memorialized in a long poem.

### **Oliver's Advice** by Colonel Blacker

*The night is gathering gloomily, the day is closing fast -*
*The tempest flaps his raven his wings in loud and angry blast –*
*The thunder clouds are driving athwart the lurid sky -*
*But, "put your trust in God, my boys, and keep your powder dry."*

*They come, whose counsels wrapp'd the land in foul rebellious flame,*
*Their hearts unchastened by remorse, their cheeks unting'd by shame.*
*Be still, be still, indignant heart – be tearless, too, each eye,*
*And put your trust in God, my boys, and keep your powder dry.*

Loading the muzzle shotgun was quite an operation. First, you'd pour a measured amount of loose black powder (stored in a powder horn made from a cow horn), down the gun barrel. Then tamp the loose powder with a ramrod (a long rounded steel rod that was attached underneath the gun barrel). Tamping helped remove air pockets so that the powder would explode properly instead of fizzle. Then you'd stuff a small piece of cloth, called wadding, in the barrel, and tamp that on top of the black powder. After that, you'd put a few small pellets or a single minié ball (a small ball, the size of the barrel fashioned to stabilized the spin when fired), and tamp that down. The final step was adding a wadding cloth on top of the pellets or minié ball, and tamping it down, one last time. It was time consuming, but you could also make the cartridges ahead, and store them in a dry pouch.

Wadding used between the powder and the shot prevented pellets from dropping into the powder, and to hold it all in place when you pulled the trigger. A cap was used to start the spark (like any cap gun), and that spark would ignite the gunpowder, and shoot the pellets or minié ball out of the barrel with a bang.

To load the rifle with a premade cartridge, you would bite the top of the paper cartridge off with your teeth, pour the black powder contents into the nose of the barrel, then ram the loose powder down. The phrase, "bite the bullet," came from this process; biting the premade bullet to load the rifle. But it also came to mean clenching a bullet in your teeth to cope with battlefield amputation without anesthesia during the Civil War. Antibiotics were not discovered yet, so the only way to prevent gangrene was to amputate the affected limb. The minié ball was particularly brutal because it was made out of lead, which was soft, and flattened upon impact, it didn't just break bones, it shattered them, and the exit wound was several times the size of the entrance.

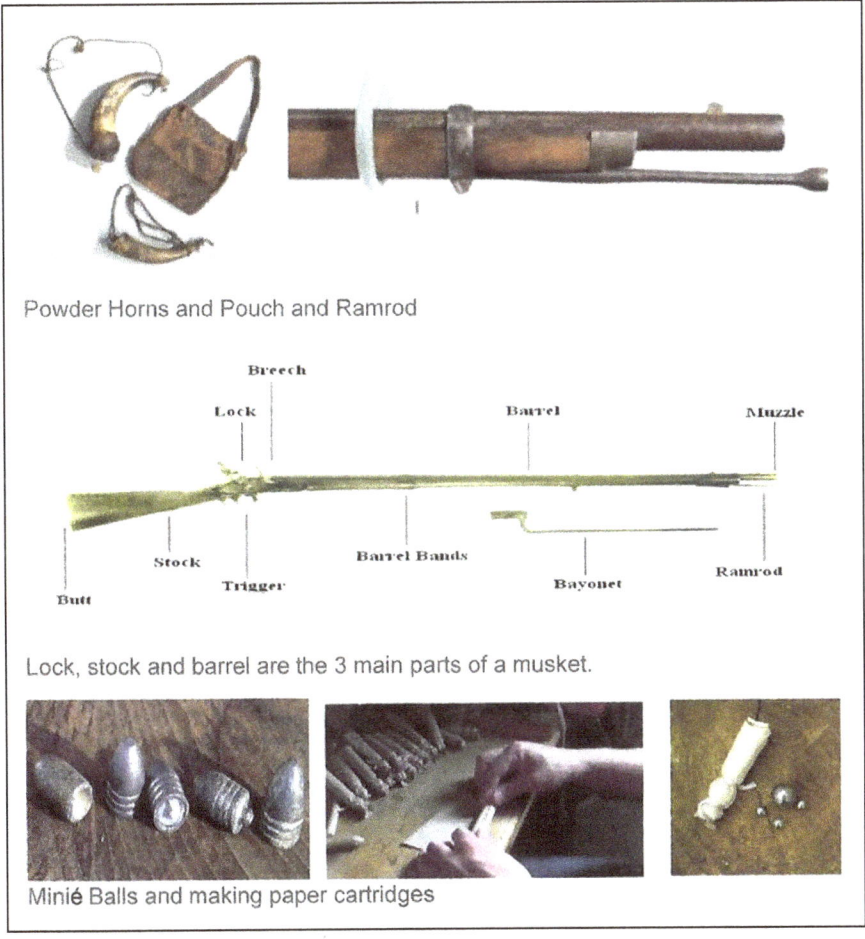

While my uncles used the old muskets, my father used the newer type shotguns, the kind that used shells you could buy at the general store, and his shotguns were always within arm's reach throughout the house. Back then, there was no banks nearby, and so the

Roark brothers, who owned the general store in town, were the closest thing. My father would have them hold on to his cash, and when he needed anything, his account would be adjusted. They didn't pay him any interest, it was just a convenience, and it was safer than having cash at a rural farm deep in southwest Missouri.

I remember one time a fellow paid my father two or three-hundred dollars for some livestock. It was too late in the day to go into town, so that night he put braces on the windows, propped chairs against the doors, and slept with a double-barreled shotgun and an old ten-gauge shotgun next to his bed so as to keep the cash safe until he could deposit it the next morning.

I was never taught to fire a weapon, and it was strange to me that my father never showed me how, although I had free use of the shotguns. What I remember the most was the kick of the gun after it was fired. It would knock me clear over. I hunted squirrel with a shotgun, not a rifle, because I was such a poor shot, and needed to be closer to the target. I was pretty good when I aimed a shotgun at a stationary target, like a squirrel sitting on a limb, even though the force of the recoil shook me for a bit afterwards, but a moving target was something else entirely.

Squirrels would run from Patterson Creek to the cornfield, crawl up the stalks, and ruin the ears, several rows at a time. I would go down to the field, see a squirrel scamper down a row, take aim and shoot. Sure enough, I would miss. Nobody had taught me to shoot ahead of the moving target, so I didn't know how to lead the squirrel. I had to learn the hard way.

My ignorance of firearms as a young boy didn't end there. Because my uncles used the old muzzle-loading muskets, there was always some loose black gunpowder around. I almost lost an eye once when Uncle Lawt and I decided to make a firecracker with it.

Lawt was the uncle nearest in age to me, and we were good companions, although there was still nine years' difference between us. Maybe he should have known better because I was only seven years old at the time, and he was sixteen when it happened. Anyway, we put some of the loose gunpowder in paper, rolled it up, twisted both ends with twine, and set a wick to it. We lit the wick and waited. And waited. And waited. Nothing happened. So we decided to take a look.

Just as we put our faces to it, the powder blasted. I was blinded for a while, and when I could see again, I spotted Lawt running across the field to the stream, so I ran after him. We splashed our faces with water, but we were both scorched. My eyebrows and lashes were burned off.

That was the year we moved back to Missouri from Adair, Oklahoma. We had moved into the Van Place, and I had just started school. I had only been in school for seven days when the accident happened, and that blast finished my schooling for the year. I was nearly eight years old before I started school again.

# Bloodhounds

While we were at the Van Place, some kinsfolk from Texas sent us a couple of bloodhound pups, a male and a female. Dad made collars attached to a stick between them so they would learn to run together. They loved to go hunting, one would pull the other and vice versa, but when they reached a tree or a bush, they would forget they were attached to each other, and get tangled and thrown about. It was a mess.

*Bloodhounds*

One night, Lawt and I took the hounds out hunting. It had to have been in the middle of the night when everyone was asleep, but Lawt was adventurous, and I was his sidekick. During the hunt, one of the dogs treed a possum up in a nice hollow mull tree, so Lawt reached in and grabbed the critter by its tail, even though it was playing possum. Satisfied, we then we started for home. We went up one hill, and down another into a valley, and before we knew it, we were lost. We kept on going, though, until we heard the sound of running water and thought for sure it must be Indian Creek, so we climbed down to it. It didn't look familiar at all, but we followed it anyway. This was during the darkest part of the night when all things look unnatural. I was young and tired, but we kept on going, for hours, until we came upon a field we did recognize, and by the light of dawn we made our way home. Lawt carried that possum the whole time. I don't recall being scared, even though we walked all night. I guess I figured Lawt would take care of me.

During that time, we had some neighbor kids named Walton, who used to go down the lane by our house to fish on Indian Creek. Our bloodhounds hated those Walton kids. They would come back from hunting, smell the trail of Walton kids, and start after them. Our hounds had a remarkable sense of smell. Twelve hours after a passerby, they could pick up the trail, and really go to town, so it was easy for them to follow the fresh track of those kids. Once spotted, our hounds would take after them, and chase them up a tree, where those kids screamed and cried the whole time. Hearing the commotion, we'd call the dogs off and help the Walton kids down. My father finally had to shoot the hound dogs because they were too much trouble.

# Holy Terrors

When Grandfather Sellers died, he left Grandmother with a lot of children to provide for. At one time, there were four generations living under one roof; grandchildren (including me), my mother (Emily Sellers Epperson) and some of her siblings, her mother (Emaline Sherer Sellers), and Emaline's mother, (great-grandmother Elizabeth Buzzard Sherer). Grandmother did the best she could but with no father to discipline her sons, they soon developed into holy terrors. She became very strict and untrusting. When she found my uncles playing cards, she would toss them in the fireplace, and she would hide her money in a billfold hidden deep within her dress, so no one could get at it. It took several years to convince Grandmother to do as my father did and keep money at the Roark brothers' general store.

My uncles, however, deserved the mistrust and were holy terrors in the community. I remember once while living at Van Place (mouse house), I was awakened by rumbling in the nearby brushes. It was Uncle Lon, thirteen years older than me, probably in his early twenties, and I was maybe eight years old.

"What are you doing here?" I asked.

"I just broke out of jail," Lon replied.

He had run all the way from Pineville, about a ten-mile clip, dodging anyone he came upon. He kept out of sight for a few days after that. I suppose the sheriff was looking for him, but he probably didn't try too hard, especially when dealing with the Sellers boys. Although no one was ever killed, they caused a lot of commotion, black eyes and free-for-alls. What Lon would start, the other three felt obliged to finish, although I am sure they each initiated a few brawls on their own.

Later on, the four constructed a moonshine still on Grandmother's farm, deep in the woods near the river and a big spring. Grandmother may have known about it but simply didn't have time to go hunt it up. Jim was the chief bootlegger, cooking up the moonshine, but he let the other Seller boys peddle it.

Grandmother was not the only one who disapproved of the still. Uncle Lon's fiancé, Blanch, a fiery red-head, was just as strait-laced as Grandmother about such things, and she suspected something was up. She warned Lon that she wouldn't put up with any monkey business like that, and as it turned out, that was no idle threat. Her red hair could have told him as much. I don't know what it was that tipped her off, but one day she followed them with a 38 caliber revolver to the moonshine still. Sure enough, she cornered them at their place of business.

"Stand back, boys," she said, "I'm going to blow this thing up, and if anyone gets in the way, he'll get it, too."

Either Uncle Lon didn't believe her, or he was just slow getting out of the way because along with the still, she plugged him in the leg. I remember him sitting around the house all bandaged up for weeks. He must not have held it against her, nor she him, because they went on to get married, and they stayed married, although who knows how much commotion lied behind the simple inscription on their tombstone: Sellers, Blanch-1970 / Lon-1963.

Years later, they took over Home Place on Indian Creek and remodeled it, so that it looked completely different. It was sold to strangers after her death. They had no children, and the last time I saw Blanch she was about 80 years old, and her hair was as red, if not redder, than when she was younger, thanks to modern chemistry.

That moonshine still, to my knowledge, was never rebuilt.

*Destroying white lightning*

# PART III
# MIDDLE YEARS

❦

*MY SIBLINGS*

*MY EDUCATION*

*I LEFT HOME AT FIFTEEN*

*TRAIN-HOPPING AND THE FROG HUNT*

*FISHING FOR CHICKENS*

*WEEKENDS IN ANDERSON*

*SELLERS DRILLING WELL*

*FOX HUNTING AND MY FATHER LOST HIS EYE*

*A BACHELOR IN NEOSHO*

*NEOSHO BUSINESS DEALINGS*

# My Siblings

I was the only child in my family for a decade. Memories of my parents were mainly of my mother who took care of me, and who also disciplined me. When she was angry with me she would just spank me. The only true whipping I remember in my life was from my father. I guess I had been doing something along with my little cousins (I forget just what it was), but he called for me to come; he was gonna, "dress me up." I didn't understand what he had in mind, but it turned out to be a good lashing with a ragweed switch, and it stung for a long time afterwards.

My closest sibling was James Edward Epperson, born at Van Place in 1901 when I was ten years old. When baby Jim was less than a year old, Mother would go pick wild huckleberries and leave me alone to care for him. If he smeared himself, I would take him by the arms, walk down to the creek, and slosh him back and forth in the cold water to clean his bottom end.

*Orval William Epperson, age 10, with baby James Edward Epperson*

Just before I was to go into the ninth grade, my folks moved from Van Place to the house on Patterson Creek. The small creek was about two or three miles west of Anderson and ran principally west into the Territory. I remember the move because I had to carry my little brother all the way to the new house. He was a little guy, maybe three or four, but he was heavy for the several miles walk.

Graydon Love and Ina Mildred were both born at the Patterson Creek house. Love, in 1905 (soon after we moved), and Ina, several years later, in 1909. I don't know where my mother got the name, Graydon Love, but perhaps it was from a novel, because in 1905, there was one famous Graydon, the author William Murray Graydon, who published a new dime novel about Sexton Blake tracking down a missing British heir in India, only to find a savage boy raised in the jungle by wild panthers. The novel was called, "Jungle Boy," or "Sexton Blake's Adventures in India." No matter how my mother chose his name, she was not alone because in 1905, the name Graydon, broke the top 1,000 baby boy names for the first and only time in history. Love, on the other hand, remained an uncommon name. I do remember when Ina Mildred was born. I was living in Neosho by then, but I helped name her from a pretty girl I once knew at school and had a crush on named, Ina Sears.

*1912 Epperson farmhouse. Left to right: James Edward, standing, Orval William, (me) holding younger brother, Graydon Love. My mother, Emily Jane holding baby Ina Mildred, and my father, William Stanley Epperson, standing.*

*Orval Epperson (me) holding my younger siblings, while they hold farm kittens. Left to right: Graydon Love, James Edward, Ina Mildred.*

*1912 Epperson farmhouse. Orval William (me) standing tall next to my much younger siblings: Graydon Love, James Edward, and Ina Mildred.*

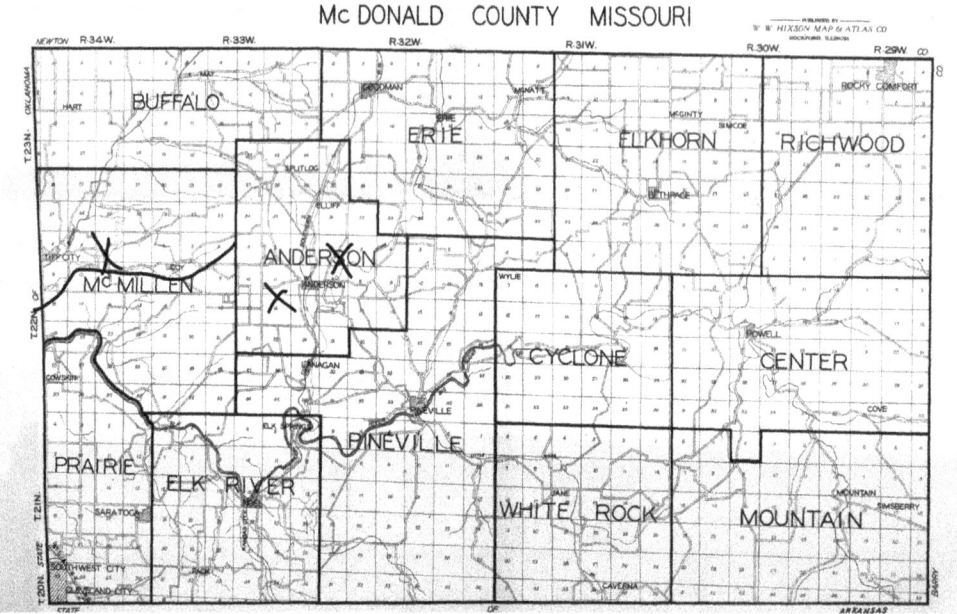

*Map of entire McDonald County giving a general idea of the farm locations (marked X). Home Place was northeast of Anderson. G.W. Epperson farm was below Anderson. William Stanley Epperson farm was near Tiff City in McMillen County, with Patterson Creek running east to west.*

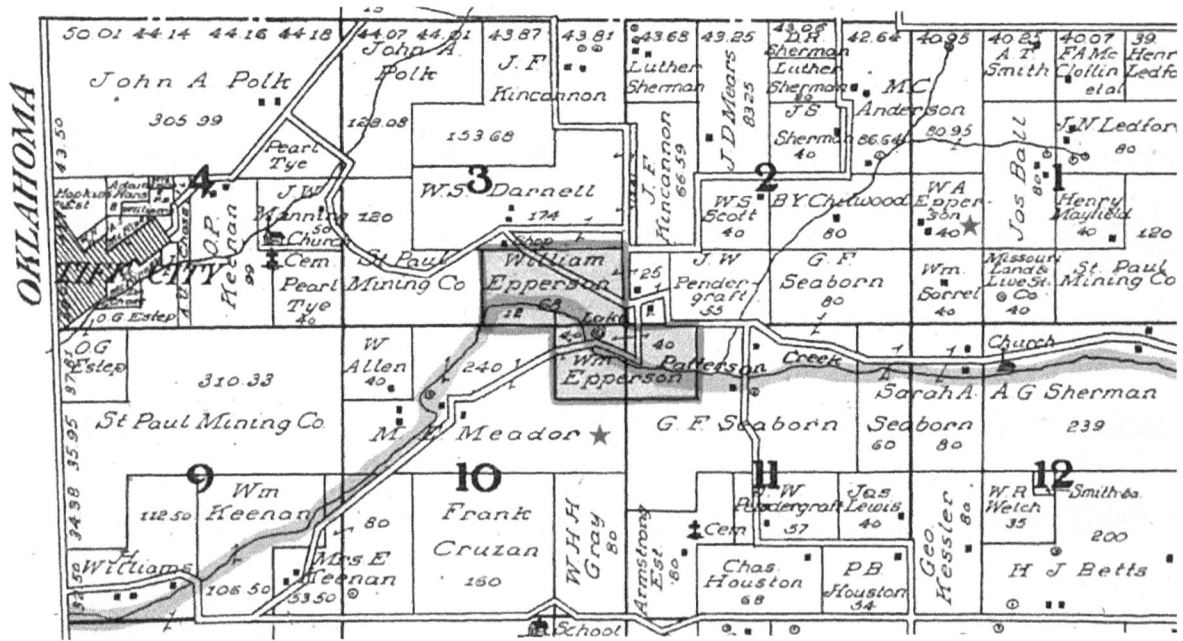

*1909 Map of Township 22N, Range 34W. William Stanley Epperson farmlands (highlighted) with Patterson Creek running east to west through property. Familiar family names (with star) appear including M.E. Meador (Martin Meador), a distant relative, and W. A. Epperson, who was a cousin to William Stanley Epperson and son of Martin Van Buren Epperson (my grandfather G.W. Epperson's older brother).*

# My Education

Nearly all of my education was at Beaver Springs. When we lived at the Van Place, I would walk a couple miles to school, the halfway point being Home Place, where I snagged an apple or two from Grandmother's Apple Hole.

There was only one school building in Beaver Springs, and all nine grades could be found there, with several classes in each room. The requirements were to finish McGuffey's Reader, Ray's Arithmetic, Buell's Geographies, Pinneo's Grammar, and Webster's Speller. Very few students advanced beyond grade school. My schooling ended just before my 16th birthday.

I still remember some of the Latin I heard in school, although I never took Latin myself. I could hear them parsing Latin in the next classroom, "amo, amas, amat," which were Latin verb conjugations for, "I love, you love, he, she or it loves."

*Young Orval William Epperson*

In that manner, I also picked up some Latin phrases such as, "gallia est divisa in partes tres," from Julius Caesar De Bello Gallico, "Gaul is divided into three parts," and a lot of Latin words like, segeta (arrow), mensa (table), piane (bread), aqua (water).

Some of the teachers were George Moss and Anna Kincannon Tandy. Anna's husband, Orrin, ran the bank in Anderson. But I vividly remember my teacher Virgil Green. Virgil lived in Neosho for a long time afterwards and ran a hardware store on the north side of the square. When Virgil was a teacher, though, he kept a rubber tube handy by his desk. It was the kind that you would see attached to an enema bottle, and he used it on the kids as a whipping stick instead of a switch. I guess one time, when he sent a student out to find a proper switch stick, he came back with a little tiny one, not nearly big enough to suit Virgil's disciplinary needs, so he switched and began using an enema tube.

One time there got to be a note-writing clique in class. I guess we were in about sixth or seventh grade. Virgil rounded up a bunch of the note-writers and rubber-tubed every single one of them. I didn't happen to be one because I didn't have enough nerve to pass notes in class to my crushes.

But Ina Sears was one of them. She was the girl I liked best. She was a pretty girl, and her brother, Arthur, and I were chums. I didn't go with Ina, but I was just sort of stuck on her. Ina wrote notes to Alfred Patterson. She and Alfred were pretty thick, at least thicker than she and I were.

Alfred's father, Bob Patterson, was one of the earliest depositors in the First Bank of Anderson, which was established by Arthur Diamond. Bob Patterson owned a farm machine outfit and was a good steady depositor in those years.

During the school year, there was a girl named Laura Burch, a tall girl with long yellow hair, who sat right in front of me. In those days, each desk had its own little inkwell. When Laura leaned back, her pigtail would dangle over my desk, just above the inkwell, tempting me to dip the ends of her hair into that black ink. The inkwell had a lid on it, so I would have to lift the lid up, to poke her hair in it. She and I would constantly argue about whether or not the ink lid was on when she flung her ponytail back, but I was the only one who ever got reprimanded.

We had a three-hole toilet there at school that was raised off the ground a bit, and Glen Elliff liked to get down and look up at the occupants. It was Glen's father, Jesse Elliff, who ran the little side-track, Elliff's Switch. Glen was a meddlesome kid a few years younger than me. One day he stuck his nose up under there to take a peek and at the same time a girl, who had loose bowels, probably from taking castor oil, just plastered him. His whole head was covered. He had to go down to Beaver soputs and wash it off.

At that time, teachers got paid good money, $30 a month. So at one time, when I was in the eighth grade, I got the notion to try to take the qualifying test for the teaching certificate examination. I was never very good at math because I couldn't figure out how to divide. Addition, subtraction and multiplication were okay, but division was hard for me. Anyway, when I got my grades back from the test, I had gotten a 20 in math. I did all right in grammar, but I guess it was ambitious on my part to think I could take the test without knowing how to divide. They told me that my grade in math precluded me from taking the test for the certificate, and so I wasn't chosen. When I came to Neosho, my ambition was to learn enough to become a school teacher, and get paid upwards of thirty dollars a month.

At the end of the school year, the teacher at Beaver Springs would treat us to some candy. I was one, of only two kids chosen (and trusted) to walk to town to get it. We would sneak out of school with her tiny coin purse, follow the railroad tracks into town, buy the little bags of candy, and sneak back into school through a back door. There were gumdrops and jelly beans in each sack, one for each child in her room. She paid for it all out of her $30 a month paycheck. It was a very generous thing to do, and it made a permanent impression on me.

When we moved to the house on Patterson Creek, it was several miles away from the Beaver Springs school, too far for me to walk, so I lived with Aunt Maud and Uncle Tom Roark that final school year. I remember that Aunt Maud was subject to some kind of spells, and Uncle Tom used to call for me in the middle of the night to help, saying that Aunt Maud had another fit. We would sit with her and rub her hands, until she came to. As far as I know, she only had the spells at night.

While living with Aunt Maud and Uncle Tom, I decided I was going to buy a pet calf all by myself. In the winter time, I would catch skunks, possums, and minks, and skin them, and sell the furs. In the spring I picked strawberries and did odd jobs, and with those earnings I had enough to buy myself a calf. I kept it at the family farm on Patterson Creek, but one day, I came home only to find that my father took my pet calf and traded it for a colt. He never even consulted me. I wasn't happy about it, but I learned to ride a horse that way, bareback mainly. My father owned a saddle but rarely let me use it.

During the school week, I stayed with Aunt Maud, but on the weekends, I would take the long walk back home to the family farm on Patterson Creek. The solo journey was not without dread, because along Patterson Creek were caves with sordid pasts, and I was afraid to go too close to them. Those caves were reputed to have been where Civil War veterans hid when bushwhackers came recruiting, and where Jesse James and the Dalton Boys hid out after their bank robbing exploits. The caves, at certain points, were only about the width of a body across, and must have run clear all the way up to the cornfields, because when it rained, you could see cornstalks coming out of the caves. The caves went down along a bluff, by a long field called Shoestring Field, a narrow strip of fertile land between the bluffs and the creek. The most menacing cave was found on that bluff. I feared that if I were forced into it, I would never find my way back out again.

One weekend I came home to find that my father had bought a phonograph so the family could enjoy music. The receiver consisted of a tin foil wrapped cylinder and a very thin membrane called a diaphragm, that attached to a needle. Sound waves were directed into the diaphragm, making it vibrate. The amplified vibrations played back the recorded sounds, and he could record his own music that way, with local musicians, whom he invited over.

One of his favorite groups was the Darnell family (the ones with Old Testament names who ran the Sorghum Mill). Siloam Darnell played the fiddle, his son, Enos, played the guitar, and his daughter, Annas, played the pump organ. His youngest son, Zara, came along, too, but as he was mentally off he

*Phonograph*

never learned to play an instrument. He would lie on the floor enjoying the music, then slowly doze off. Pretty soon, urine would start running out of his pant legs and puddle all over the floor since he had no control of his bladder.

During the recording sessions, my father would watch the cylinder, and when it was almost finished he would sign to all that the end was near, by pressing on Siloam's foot. I remember, once, the music going lickety-split, and my father was afraid they were getting too near the end of the disc, so he pressed hard on Siloam's foot, which caused such a commotion that the whole group stopped abruptly in surprise nowhere near the end of the song. In order to erase that bad ending, they just recorded on top of it. Some of the tunes included popular bluegrass songs such as, "Red Wing," or "Silver Bell."

### RED WING

*There once lived an Indian maid,*
*A shy little prairie maid,*
*Who sang all day a love song gay*
*As on the plains she'd while away the day.*

*She loved a warrior bold,*
*This shy little maid of old,*
*But brave and gay he rode one day*
*To battle far away.*

*Now the moon shines tonight on pretty Red Wing,*
*The breeze is sighing, the night bird's crying,*
*For afar 'neath his star her brave is sleeping,*
*While Red Wing's weeping her heart away.*

*She watched for him day and night;*
*She lit all the campfires bright;*
*And under the sky each night, she would lie*
*And dream about his coming by and by,*

*But when all the braves returned,*
*The heart of Red Wing yearned,*
*For far, far away, her warrior gay*
*Fell bravely in the fray.*

*Now the moon shines tonight on pretty Red Wing,*
*The breeze is sighing, the night bird's crying,*
*For afar 'neath his star her brave is sleeping,*
*While Red Wing's weeping her heart away.*

### SILVER BELL

*Beneath the light of a bright starry night*
*Sat a lonely little Indian maid.*
*No lover's sweet serenade, has ever won me.*
*As in a dream, it would seem, down a stream,*
*Gaily paddling his tiny canoe,*
*A chieftain longing to woo, sang her this song:*

*Your voice is ringing, my Silver Bell.*
*Under its spell, I've come to tell*
*You of the love I am bringing, o'er hill and dell.*
*Happy will dwell my Silver Bell.*

*For many moons, many tunes, many spoons*
*Woke the echo of the silver night.*
*As down the stream gleaming bright they float a-dreaming.*
*In his canoe, only two sat to woo*
*As they listened to the sigh of the breeze*
*That seemed to sing to the trees this sweet refrain.*

# I Left Home at Fifteeen

I left the farm home near Anderson a month before my sixteenth birthday. The school at Beaver Springs didn't go beyond the ninth grade, and Neosho had the nearest high school, so I left with $15 saved up to buy school books, and entered into the tenth grade in a town I had never lived in.

I remember a report I did for my teacher, Mrs. Daugherty, who liked it so much she had me read it out loud to the class. It was about the Civil War, and I worked out the strategy that each side had incorporated. I drew up a diagram on a big board, and while the students sat on logs and watched, I explained the tactics and troop movements on both sides.

I lived with the high school custodian, George Proctor, for $2.50 a week. He paid me ten cents an hour to sweep floors and erase the blackboards. A neighbor paid me ten cents an hour to chop wood and cut it into small logs to fit his stove. A widow paid me fifty cents a week to feed, water, and curry her horses, and clean the stables.

I remember classmates walking by while I was working. They would ask if I could go play with them, but I never could. I barely had time to go to school and work my side jobs. I had been enrolled in school for a couple months when the school principal heard that the Bank of Neosho was looking for a dependable and bright young boy to help out around the bank. They offered me $1 a day, to work six days a week, so I quit school, and began my lifelong career at the Bank of Neosho, just after my sixteenth birthday.

As I recall, it was December when I started work. In a couple of months, they raised my salary to $7 a week, still for a six-day work week. And in a year or two later, my pay was raised to $35 a month. To my happy surprise that amount was better than the $30 a month teacher salary I had longed to earn just a few years earlier.

*1906. Bank of Neosho*

I met a boy named Mont, and we became fast friends. At age seventeen, Mont and I rented an upstairs room in the private home of Mrs. Helzer, for $2.50 per week. The house was only one-and-a-half stories high, and we lived in the half-story part. Our lofted room had sloping walls with poor ventilation. It was hot and sticky in the summer and freezing cold in the winter, but as young bucks, we enjoyed our freedom. We ate whenever we wanted, wherever we wanted, and whatever we could afford. Sometimes we ate together and sometimes separately.

For breakfast, I would usually go to Runt Boyd's Hole-in-the-Wall, squeezed in between two large buildings. It was tiny (just like the owner), but that little six by twenty space housed the whole counter-service, kitchen, and about 5 round top stools. If you didn't get there in time, you didn't eat. One egg on toast and half pint of raw milk ran 15 cents. At noon, I might go to Bill's Beanery across the street from the pawn shop. Bill was famous for his chili con carne, which was mostly beans. The extra carne was when you spooned up a well-cooked cockroach. That, too, was counter-service-only. For 5 cents, I could get a small bowl of chili with exactly six crackers. A refill was another nickel, but you got nine crackers that time around.

*1909 Neosho, east side*

In the evenings, if I felt prosperous, I would squander as much as 20 cents at Steve's Specialties, down on Spring Street. Steve had been a school teacher and municipal judge for the Neosho Township. He, his wife, and two teenage daughters, ran the restaurant. There was no menu; you could order anything as long as you could list the ingredients. If it were in his cookbook, he'd use that recipe, if not, he would get a general idea on how to make it from your description, which often produced a better product. I remember when I first ordered graveyard stew, Steve was stumped. It was not in his cookbook. I suggested three slices of toast and a pint of boiling milk, seasoned with salt and pepper. Impressed with his result, he directed me to sit at the table right in front of the big plate glass window next to the sidewalk, where he served my graveyard stew in style. I tried to appear unaware of the envious stares from the passers-by as they glanced at my exotic dish.

People began ordering graveyard stew so often that the price was boosted to 25 cents to everyone except me. Mine was on the house. That was a blessing because I had splurged so often that I was often forced to skip one or more meals until I was once again in funds. But not all of my money was spent on food, some of my splurges were taking girls on buggy rides.

*July 13, 1910. Buggy rides. Orval William Epperson (me) and my date. My friend, Mont, and his girlfriend, Ruth.*

# Train-Hopping and the Frog Hunt

Mont and I were good friends as well as roommates. So, one day upon hearing one of my glowing accounts of frog hunting on Indian Creek, Mont decided he wanted to experience it for himself, so we planned to go down the next weekend. We were so excited just thinking about it that we never considered how we would get there. It was about twenty-two miles away, and neither of us had a bicycle, nor could we afford to hire a horse and buggy for the trip. So we conjured up a plan to become railroad hoboes.

The main line of the Kansas City Southern Railroad went through both towns. For the first three or so miles south of Neosho there was a steep upgrade, and the last four or so miles north of Anderson there was an equally steep upgrade, but the middle fifteen miles were practically level. In the flat lands, the train sped up, but where the land rose uphill, heavy freights slowed to about a walking speed. We figured we could easily climb aboard safely at both Neosho and Anderson without anyone noticing.

Saturday found us at the side of the tracks and when the first freight came by at a slow pace we jumped aboard, unlatched the lock, and climbed into an empty box car, which had previously been used to haul chat (fine gravel waste from limestone mining.)

We were sitting back, happy as two hoboes enjoying a free ride, when the railroad brakeman discovered us and yelled, "Get off or go up to the engine and shovel coal for the fireman."

We begged him to let us stay, and when he learned it was our first time, he granted us exclusive use of our private car for 10 cents each (highway robbery for two poor boys). Then he cautioned us to wait until the train slowed before jumping off.

We heartedly agreed but in our eagerness to get off we misjudged the speed of the train and jumped too soon. The train hadn't slowed down

*Train hopping*

enough. Furthermore, we were sorely unaware of the proper technique for jumping off a train. When we jumped, we landed with both legs locked, in one solid movement. We should have taken a more running type landing which would slow down our fall. The result of our clumsy landing included somersaults, sliding, rolling, and a general flopping about, to the bottom of the right-of-way. We were fortunate, with no major damage, except grass stains, and maybe our pride.

Once we cleared the tracks, we walked to my cousin Hubert's house. Hubert Chapman was about seven years younger than me and was the son of Aunt Mary and Uncle Jeff. That evening, we ate a wholesome meal cooked by Aunt Mary, and then the three of us (Hubert, Mont and I), hit the hay in the barn, restless for the day ahead.

The next morning after a hearty breakfast, Hubert snuck six eggs in a paper sack, six slices of bacon in waxed paper, a loaf of bread, salt, and a long-handled skillet, all tied up in a burlap bag he carried over his shoulder. We then set off on our frogging adventure.

Mont and I had a butterfly net and a burlap sack, and we waded in the waters and along the shoreline searching for big fat frogs, while Hubert stayed on the land and followed us from there. We looked for them in certain spots where there wasn't any running water, and where water lilies could grow. There, a frog could hop up on a lily pad and sun himself, or he could relax on the shore, smiling over his domain, his big white bosom exposed, as though he were all dressed up in a white tuxedo shirt.

Or sometimes we'd see just a pair of eyes sticking out of the water. We would quickly drop the butterfly net on top of him. The frog would jump and jump trying to escape, but he couldn't get out of the net. After he settled down a bit, we would reach in, pull him out, and place him in our burlap sack.

Hubert followed us along the shoreline, and as he did, he would run into fenced properties so he would toss the bag over the fence and climb over after it. There were several fenced in lands, and Hubert repeated his toss and climb, toss and climb.

Around noon, we stopped to eat. Hubert fried the bacon, and we dressed a couple pans of frog legs, which we fried up in the leftover grease. Then we opened up the sack of eggs. It was a scrambled mess and full of shells. We picked out most of the fragments, poured the mess into the skillet, and scrambled it all together. It still tasted fine, with bits of bacon, frog, and eggshells. With our stomachs content, we took a long afternoon nap.

Then, later in the day, after the heat burned off, we resumed our frog hunting. By nightfall, we used a flashlight, and shined it directly into the beady eyes of the frogs, blinding them such that we could reach down with our bare hands and pick up the stunned croakers. But if we took the spotlight off, they'd be gone.

We collected a bountiful sack of frogs and decided it was time to go home. We caught a freight train back to Neosho, finding another private car, for which we had to tip the brakeman yet another dime. By the time we got home, we were exhausted, so we decided not to clean the frogs right then. Instead, we tossed the frog bags into the kitchen sink and crawled up to our beds.

I thought we had tied the bags.

Along about four o'clock the next morning, Mont and I were awakened by a pounding on our bedroom door, from an angry landlady.

"Get down here to the kitchen, right NOW!"

So we got up. The kitchen was a sight seldom seen. Somehow, the frogs had escaped from the burlap sacks. One was clinging to the screen door, one or two were on the oven door, some were halfway up the curtain, some under the table, under the chairs, and all over the floor. Still more were clinging to the tablecloth, and one had even climbed up on the table and was just sitting there on one of Mrs. Helzer's plates, looking as surprised as anybody else.

"Clean up this kitchen, or else!" she ordered.

So we got busy corralling the frogs and went to work cleaning both the frogs, and the kitchen. We filled a big platter full of frogs and took them to our landlady as a peace offering.

That put us back on speaking terms.

The next day, before we left for work, she called to us, "Don't bother to eat downtown. You can eat here tonight."

That tickled us. When we sat down at the supper table that night, we were pleasantly surprised. There in the middle of the table was a big platter of fried frog legs, surrounded by cakes and pies, and all the makings of a celebration. We really feasted.

She had forgiven us our trespasses; at least we got delivered from evil. And we were all on good terms again.

We kept our promise to bring no more live frogs into the house, but we did bring her several dressed ones from time to time. Frogs were plentiful on Shoal Creek and around Neosho's springs. She would cook them up, and we would eat together just like a family. She enjoyed those frog legs as much as we did.

# Fishing for Chickens

The Bank of Neosho closed at noon on Saturdays, so I often went fishing with my friends for the night. Sometimes we'd fish at Buffalo Creek, which began south of Neosho, meandered toward Tiff City, connected with Patterson Creek and Elk River, and eventually dumped into Grand Lake in Oklahoma.

I remember one time Virgil Smith and I took Eddy Shimer fishing on Buffalo Creek. Eddy was Kenneth Matters' cousin and was a "city boy" from Florida. We took Virgil's old horse and a one-seated hack after work one Saturday afternoon and headed for the Breaks of Buffalo. I drove the little wagon while Eddy and Virgil sat in the back on the hay, which was used to feed the horse throughout the trip. We packed a frying pan, blanket, our fish-hooks, lines, and poles - everything needed for a fishing trip.

The road went right by Bob Woods' house where his flock of chickens wandered freely all around the road. It wasn't a very fast conveyance, and Eddy would amuse himself by throwing out a fish-hook with a grain of corn on it and drag it along. A chicken would peck at anything that moved, and one old chicken decided to grab that corn and hook and swallowed it whole. I guess after that you could call it a corn-fed chicken.

Anyway, at that point Eddy dragged in his line and hook with the chicken on it. We meant to rescue it, but upon further examination, we decided to take it with us for dinner. When we got down to the Buffalo, we killed it and used its entrails as bait to catch crawdads. We had planned to have fish for dinner, but we ended up with a skillet full of chicken instead. After we fried the chicken, we burned the feathers in the flames, so there would be no telltale evidence of our wrongdoings.

The Buffalo ran in a steady stream part of the year, but at other times, when the creek was partly dry, there were potholes of water, four or five feet deep, around tree stumps. Fish could hide there, crawdads, too. The water seeped underground from one pothole to another pothole, and there would be a gravel bar between the holes.

That was where we camped. We moved the hack between two potholes on the gravel bar. Then we unhitched the horse and tied him to the back wheel of the hack, where he could leisurely eat the hay, and an ear or two of corn. We set our lines, baited with the entrails and crawdads in the two little potholes, and settled down to sleep.

Virgil and I slept on the gravel bar on a quilt, but Eddy, being a city boy, didn't want to sleep on the ground, even though the river pebbles were not uncomfortable. So he slept on the hack using hay as a blanket. Sometime during the night, Virgil and I heard an unearthly scream. It seemed that the horse had taken a chunk of Eddy's hair along with the hay. With Eddy being a towhead, it was an understandable mistake for the horse to confuse straw colored hair with hay, but no doubt it was painful.

As funny as that was to Virgil and me, we had our own problems. The crawfish would crawl from one pothole to the next searching for food, and they took the shortest distance between the potholes which was, of course, right where we slept. They crawled right over us, over our hair, our face, anywhere you can imagine, and their claws were cold, jarring us awake when they touched our skin. Virgil even got one tangled in his hair that did not want to leave.

We left bright and early the next morning, having caught no fish, and as for city-boy Eddy, well, for some reason he never wanted to fish with us again. Also, I never told Bob Woods about his chicken, even though I have fished with him for over 30 years. Somehow the conversation just never came up.

# Weekends in Anderson

Weekends I would try my best to get home to visit my family. Often, I would catch a ride with J.J. Burns and his sister. They were related to the Darnell family (from the Sorghum Mill), and they had also gone to school in Neosho.

During our drives to Anderson, they confirmed what was generally believed, that some of the Darnell and Burns family members were peculiar, and it was probably due to frequent intermarriage. Close relatives sometimes married in those days, and the Darnells and Burns were no exception. The culture of intermarriage was common throughout southwest Missouri, and two of their family members were affected by it. Zara Darnell (the slow one) and his uncle, Bill Burns, had about the same mental capacity. But they weren't the only families that intermarried. The parents of Hallie and Poka Gibson, for instance, were cousins. Hallie (short for Hallelujah) grew to be 6'6" tall, and Poka (short for Pokahontas) had a mouth that dragged over to one side of her face.

But one member of the Burns family was unaffected, and in fact, became somewhat famous. Dennis Burns, brother of Zara's mother, was a baseball player for the Philadelphia Athletics in 1923/1924. He was a right-handed pitcher and also an alumni of University of Missouri.

| Biographical Data | | | |
|---|---|---|---|
| Birth Name: | Dennis Burns | High School: | Undetermined |
| Nickname: | None | College: | University of Missouri |
| Born On: | 05-24-1898 (Gemini) | Bats: Right | Throws: Right |
| Born In: | Tiff City, Missouri | Height: 5-10 | Weight: 180 |
| Died On: | 05-21-1969 (100 Oldest Living) | First Game: | 09-19-1923 (Age 25) |
| Died In: | Tulsa, Oklahoma | Last Game: | 09-26-1924 |
| Cemetery: | Rest Haven Cemetery, Sperry, Oklahoma | Draft: | Not Applicable |

*Dennis Burns (May 24, 1898 – May 21, 1969) was a professional baseball player. He was a right-handed pitcher over parts of two seasons (1923–24) with the Philadelphia Athletics. For his career, he compiled an 8-9 record, with a 4.62 earned run average, and 34 strikeouts in 181 innings pitched.*

I was happy to spend weekends visiting my family because I was so much older than my siblings. It gave me a chance to get to know them, and on those trips home, I would also visit Home Place where my grandmother and uncles lived. Although there was plenty of work to be done on the farm, my four uncles: Dan, Jim, Lon and Lawt, liked to take time off for fun. They were close in age, all being born within nine years, and they formed a formidable clan in southwest Missouri. They liked to play cards in the stuffy barn loft, away from Grandmother's judgmental eyes, and I learned to play Pitch from them up there. They wouldn't play for money amongst themselves, but it was a different story when they went into town.

At the end of my weekend visits, while waiting for the train to arrive, I often spent time watching my uncles and a dozen or so other men play cards over at the drug store. Penny ante, poker, stud, 21, Pitch. Everyone would ante up and feed the kitty, although the stakes were never high because no one had much money. My uncles drank so much moonshine throughout the day, they would have noticeable indentations on the bridges of their noses, from drinking out of fruit jars.

Of all the remaining Sellers boys, Dan was now the oldest. Silas had died at 25, and Willy had died as child. Dan was also the strongest, weighing 200 pounds. He was built like an ox and always carried a pair of brass knuckles. Lon was the least strong. However, in spite of this, or because of this, he was the fighting-est, especially when he had a little corn in him. Perhaps, he knew that he could count on Dan to rescue him, and he was usually right. Lon would start something and leave it up to Dan to finish.

The boys never quarreled among themselves, and always behaved in front of Grandmother, but it was a "one for all and all for one," the "one" usually being Lon, when it came to outsiders and even some locals in Anderson.

The four had their bluff called on a few occasions, where they had to admit their wrongdoings. Uncle Lawt was put in the jug once, I recall. Lon was a frequent guest of the local jail. When the Grand Jury was in session in that part of Missouri, everything came to a grinding standstill, and the four of them would hide out for a while, obedient as Christians.

*1911 Orval Epperson and siblings Graydon (with cat on his shoulder) and Ina Mildred.*

# Sellers Drilling Well

Grandmother Sellers died in 1907, and the proceeds of the farm were divided among her surviving children. Her four sons bought the farm and divided it into four equal sections. They were not known to be money-wise and tried various schemes throughout their lives to make a buck. Dan and Lon, had either saved enough or earned enough to clear all their debts, but Jim and Lawt let their bills accumulate and were nearly down-and-out when they died.

*Grave marker for Emaline Sellers and Nathaniel S. Sellers*

But early on, the Sellers brothers decided to go into the drilling business. They bought a well drill and moved it from farm to farm throughout southwest Missouri. They were familiar with it because there was a well drill on Home Place.

The derrick drill crane had a long, heavy, iron arm which hoisted a drill-bit at the end. The drill-bit was made from a very hard metal composite, like steel, which would not flatten out when it bore into the rocks, as iron would. To form the bit, the iron deposit would be heated at a very high temperature, then quickly doused in water to harden fast, then lifted to the end of the drill string. Once in place, the heavy drill bit would be dropped into the hole, and the weight of it would pulverize the earthen rock. This was called percussion drilling.

Percussion drilling consisted of continually dropping the heavy weight into the wellbore to chip away at the rock. Every so often, they would need to stop the drill, take out the crushed rock, bail out the water, and drag the larger rocks up with a big metal bucket. Sometimes they would

*Derrick crane in field*

have to go down a long way to remove the large rocks blocking the path of the drill. The process was extremely physical, dangerous, and time consuming.

    If I remember correctly, I loaned them $1,000, and my mother loaned them another $1,000 (that she inherited from her share of the farm), to start the business. At some point they borrowed from Shartel Mortgage to pay us back, and later borrowed additional monies from George Tatum in Anderson. I was never sure why the business didn't make much money.

# Fox Hunting and My Father Lost His Eye

One of the principle pleasures of the menfolk during those days was fox hunting. The most amusing thing about it was that nobody ever caught a fox, nor even really tried. It was just an excuse for them to get out in the open air, and drink a little moonshine.

My father lost an eye on one of those fox hunting trips.

We would travel deep into the Ozarks, looking for those elusive animals, and sometimes we had to cross over someone's property and sneak through their fence. We would walk long distances until we'd come upon a barbed wire fence, where we would look for a weak link to climb through. One man would hold the two sides of the barbed wire apart while the next man crawled through.

Well, it was dark, and either the fence was in disrepair or the man in charged pulled too hard because it broke as we pulled the fence apart, and the staples holding the wire flew off the post and struck my father directly in the eye, shattering his pupil.

He was only thirty-years-old at the time, and it blinded him in that eye for the rest of his life, but that never stopped him from hunting.

After one of those hunts, someone took a photo of me with my baby sister, Ina Mildred, and my trusty hunting dog, Buck. I likened myself to the bible character named, Nimrod, who according to the Book of Genesis and the Book of Chronicles was the son of Cush, son of Ham, son of Noah. The bible stated the he was, "A mighty hunter before the Lord… and became mighty on the earth." I also

*August 22, 1911, Orval William Epperson, the Nimrod, and sister Ina Mildred, and Buck the Dog. After the Hunt, on my vacation in Anderson, Missouri. Observe the Hat.*

liked the straw hat that I was wearing. It reminded me of my youth in Adair, waving my straw hat to shoo off wandering cattle.

While on the hunt, we never fired a gun, so "fox hunting" may even have been a misnomer. Once out in the woods, the men simply sat around the old fence post pile on Schambaugh's Hill in the crystalized air, swapping stories, while the dogs sniffed around, searching for the long gone fox trail. We would hear the dogs bark in the distance and recognize each hound's clear and mellow sound, carried by the wind. Upon hearing the hound's bay, the conversation would pause, then one of the men would announce, "That old Tig."

A few minutes later, as another bark echoed off the hills, someone would add, "That's Bowser."

Then pretty soon, here would come the fox, right by us, as if we weren't even there. We could see him in the firelight. It looked like that ole sly fox was having a good time, teasing our dogs. They were well behind him.

Eventually, along about midnight, then men would call their tired dogs back with a long blow from a cow horn. The hollowed out horn made a deep resonant sound that lasted a good long while and signaled to all that it was time to head home.

Why did we do it? Oh, I guess just for the fun of hearing the dogs, telling stories, and sitting around. I think the hounds enjoyed the chase, too.

# A Bachelor in Neosho

My bachelor years were happy. Neosho became my home, and I met numerous friends and joined many groups where we spent weekends together on picnics and float trips. Our shenanigans included swamping overloaded canoes, climbing tall trees, posing near railroad tracks, and dressing up for silly staged photos.

I grew from a boy to a man in Neosho. I learned to act like a man, dress like a man, and as I searched for what God had in store for me, I worshipped like a man. I became involved in the First Congregational Church in Neosho, where I found my voice. I spoke about various missions and ways the church could help. On one particular evening, I spoke about a Christian ministry called Industrial Missions, which was a way to teach Christian values in the workplace.

The *Neosho Daily Democrat*, May 24, 1913, reported in the *Services at the Church* section, "First Congregational Church - The pastor most earnestly urges all members of the church to be present at this service. Christian Endeavor at 7 o'clock. **Orval Epperson** will speak on Industrial Missions. S.A. Willard, Pastor."

*Picnic Party 1914. I am the fellow on the sinking end, with my foot in the air.*

My social life had vastly improved as well, and I was invited to many house parties. News of these private affairs were broadcast as far as Joplin. The *Joplin News Herald*, October 11, 1914 reported, "Misses Ruth Simmons, Donnie Simmons, Montie Simmons, Amy Johns and Opal Johns entertained at dinner last Sunday at the home of Misses Simmons of 216 North Connor avenue for Messrs. Lloyd Wilson, **Orval Epperson**, Aaron Choates, Gene McGowen and Lewis Tretbar of Neosho, Mo."

I was a trustworthy steward at the Bank of Neosho, where I was selected to count the votes for a contest that the *Neosho Times* held to expand their readership. On November 26, 1914, it was reported, "First Prize Won by Mrs. Frank Austin, a Ford automobile or $500 in cash and Miss Pearl Lanear the second prize, a $400 Ellington Piano, in the Neosho Times subscription contest that closed this Friday…. **The judges that counted the votes were Orval Epperson**, W.E. Sims, W.H. Duff and J.M. Harmon.

*Top left: Railroad track posing. I am 3rd from the right, wearing seaman sennit straw hat.*
*Bottom left: Railroad track posing. I am 2nd from the right, wearing a straw hat and petting a dog.*
*Right: Staged photo on a fake train prop with two friends on either side of me.*

*Outing with friends. Orval William Epperson (me) in the center of the photo, sitting on the ground, caught mid-laugh hugging my friend.*
*With my friends in our work suits. I am in the middle with my arms around my two mates, while the ladies look on.*

*Standing in the tree amongst lovely ladies, I am wearing only a men's one-piece wool bathing suit, trying my best at modesty by crossing my arms.*

# Neosho Business Dealings

I had been at the Bank of Neosho for about five years when I was newly promoted to Bank Director at the age of twenty-one. Mr. Wills had hired me as a young, inexperienced boy and apprenticed me into a responsible adult. He trusted me with the wellbeing of the bank and its assets. In fact, while I was away at war, he even held my position for me until I returned.

As I came into my own, I met other bankers and was privy to a lot of stories about Neosho business dealings that spun around the town square. One story of shrewd business acumen was about a man named E.I. Garner, who had earned his money from sowbellies (salted pork) and was also on the Election Board. The story was told to me by Louis Kelly, the bank cashier for the Neosho Saving Bank. Louis was a minority stockholder in Neosho Savings Bank and wouldn't have even been to the bank board meeting, except that he ran the day-to-day operations.

*1912 Bank of Neosho staff, left to right W.G. 'Willy' Wills, Cashier and Principal Operator, Vance Davis, Lester Mahan and O.W. Epperson, Neosho Bank Director at age 21.*

Emory Garner intended to become a major player on the Neosho Savings Bank board, and so at the next board meeting, there was a vote. Each board member could cast one vote for every $100 invested. Up to that time, there was a gentlemen's agreement that each man would divide his vote equally so that the same board members stayed in power. But Garner, who had I believe $10,000 invested, voted all 100 votes on himself. So that was how he came to be elected to the bank board. It was all perfectly legal. No flies on him. Just savvy business sense. He remained the director of the Building and Loan Association of the bank until the day he died.

It was also around that time, that a group of businessmen decided to go into the granary business, and so we formed a corporation. O.W. Epperson, was President, C. E. Davis was secretary and bookkeeper, and C. M. Robeson represented the First National Bank with stocks in the company. We had accounts at both the Bank of Neosho and First National Bank. Dave Stout and a number of others were stockholders.

At the time, there was a good market for corn meal down in Louisiana and we had access to our own mill. So, we shipped corn from Iowa to Neosho, ground it into meal, and the shipped it off south. We took advantage of the periodic stops that freight trains took to switch crews and refuel, and because Neosho was a normal stop for the trains, we benefitted from the short amount of time they were there.

Railroads had different rates for long haul versus short haul. The rate from Iowa to Neosho was so much, and the rate from Neosho to Louisiana was so much, but the rate from Iowa directly to Louisiana was discounted. Usually the long haul rates were cheaper than short haul because of the directness of the route and the time needed to load and unload. But since Neosho was on the route, we could easily switch out the cars that had corn from Iowa on them with the cars that had processed corn meal. For every carload we got out of Iowa, we would use that billing to get the long haul rate to Louisiana. Things were lively and booming, and we were doing an expanding land-office business, until bad luck set in.

A mysterious fire had started in the granary at the most inopportune time, when there were bins overflowing with corn. We worked fast to save whatever we could. Some freight cars on the track that night were full of the processed corn meal, and a switch engine moved some cars around to spare those, but the granary got wet from the fire hoses, and the corn stored there was beyond redemption. So, we had to sell that corn for hog feed. To fulfill our outstanding corn meal contracts, we then had to buy meal elsewhere. We had some insurance but not nearly close to reimbursing us what was lost. We never recovered from that fire, and we liquidated at 10 cents on the dollar.

We also never found out who, or how, or why the fire started. It was speculated that it was arson, but a lot of people had stock in our company, so I didn't think it was a Klan job. The Ku Klux Klan were known to intimidate, in the cover of darkness, those who did not belong or believe in their ideology.

It was probably more related to the U.S. entering into WWI. The United States had mobilized the entire population to produce soldiers, food supplies, and ammunition necessary to win the war. Many German Americans opposed American involvement and there were rumors of German plans to sabotage our war effort. In fact, German agents were found to have set fire to ammunition plants on the East Coast. So, it was not a stretch to think they could have burned our warehouse, stored with corn that was potentially destined for military bases in Louisiana.

But, I did not believe that all Germans were bad and thought many were treated unfairly. For instance, American Germans were required to carry federal registration cards at all times, German street names were changed, and in fact, the German American Bank in St. Louis had to change its name in order to stay in business. My close German friends, the Lutz family, were as good a people as you would want to meet, but because of their German descent were put under enormous strains. They were unfairly judged and lost many friends during that time.

# PART IV
# THERESE DEBROSSE

*I FELL IN LOVE*

*THERESE DEBROSSE*

*THERESE'S FIRST HOLY COMMUNION*

*SISTERS, BLANCHE AND GRACE DEBROSSE*

*THERESE'S EDUCATION AND TYPHOID*

*THERESE'S DOUBLE COUSIN*

# I Fell in Love

I met a girl named Therese. She was staying in the rooming house right across the street from Mrs. Helzer's, where I lived with Mont, and you could bet that I noticed her. I would see her come out the front door and walk down the street with her nose held high in the air. I would try to time it so that I would leave my place at about the same time she left, so that I could happen to run into her. We began to date a little, although we both dated others as well.

*Therese Gertrude DeBrosse*

Therese loved to dance, but I didn't dance well. There used to be Square Dances over at McGinty's, given by the Knights and Ladies of Security. It was a social club combined with insurance, and by paying dues, you got so much life insurance and were also entitled to attend the dances. It was similar to Odd Fellows (Independent Order of Odd Fellows - I.O.O.F.), which was one of the largest fraternal and benevolent orders, although Odd Fellows was a secret society with its own system of rites and passwords that changed every so often.

We would go to these dances with about two or three dozen people in attendance, but also folks would have smaller parties at their homes. I remember attending parties given by the generous German Lutz family.

At one of these events, Therese was having a gay time dancing with all the fellows, and I decided I wanted to go home. She said I could go ahead if I wanted to, she was going to stay and dance.

So I did. And she did.

It was some while after that before we started going together again.

During that time, I learned more about Therese. I found that she moved to Neosho in 1915, as a stenographer and worked in what was called a steno pool, usually single women who took dictation with shorthand to be later transcribed. It was a low paying job, but there weren't many opportunities for women past administrative positions, and entire floors with rows of desks were filled with ladies listening to various dictations and typing away. Therese was happy to have the skill and believed that her degree in stenography was the ticket to her first job. She was also a firm believer that "a girl should be prepared."

Although Therese was reserved, she had no problem making friends. She rode horses, went to dinner parties, and even brought girlfriends home to visit her family. The *Monett Times* was there to report, "April 2, 1915, Miss Margaret Callas and Miss Therese DeBrosse, stenographers at Neosho visited in Monett Sunday."

*1918. Therese DeBrosse posing alone near blooming tree. August 18, 1918. Therese DeBrosse horseback riding. She wrote on the back of the photo, "Off for a drive or something like one. Have on my new hat and dress, although they do not show up well."*

Therese worked at William P. Stark Nursery, located at the northern edge of Neosho in the Mutual Wagon Factory building. Mr. Stark was a prominent businessman in Neosho. He had purchased 700 acres of land between Newtonia and the little hamlet of Chester, to establish a nursery for fruit trees, changed the name of Chester to Stark City, and launched the William P. Stark Nurseries. The business shipped fruit trees, ornamental trees, rose bushes, grape vines, bulbs, shrubs, and strawberries to every state in the union. The company promoted two fruit trees that they developed, the Delicious apple and the J.H. Hale peach. The J.H. Hale peach, touted as superior to the Elberta peach, was exclusive to William P. Stark Nurseries. The company also published an annual illustrated catalog that listed many varieties of fruits and vegetables for the gardener with planting instruction and glowing testimonials from satisfied customers with horticultural experts cited.

Therese was asked to become a model for the Neosho Nurseries Company. In 1919, she was photographed peeling an apple next to "WHAT THEY SAY," testimonials in the catalog, one from as far as Yokohama, Japan.

> A thoroughly good tree or bush is worth whatever you have to pay for it; the first bushel or the first quart of fruit will pay for it. A poor or undependable plant is worthless at any price. P.S. Lovejoy, in Country Gentlemen, Sept. 27, 1919.

> The trees received from you were number one in every particular and have made satisfactory growth this season. The DELICIOUS trees that I could not obtain from you were purchased from another large nursery company, but were not nearly so good trees as yours and I wish now that I had waited another year and purchased them from you. H.A. Rice, Grand Isle County, Vt., Sept. 10, 1919.

> I am in receipt of your letter of the 25th of January last, informing me of the dispatch of trees, etc. I ordered last December and this day have received the three parcels of plants which I am glad to say are all in splendid condition. - H. Lewis, Yokohama, Japan, March 12, 1919.

> I recommended your stock very highly and always take pleasure in doing so. The state representative and the County Agent both say that the trees that I got from you, 1000 J.H. Hales, and 500 apple trees, have made the best growth they have ever see in a young orchard. - L.C. Beirne, Ky., May 2, 1919.

*1919 William P. Stark Nursery Illustrated Catalog. Therese DeBrosse models cutting an apple.*

# Therese Gertrude DeBrosse

Therese Gertrude DeBrosse was born on Friday, April 21, 1893, in the small town of Monett, Missouri, deep in Ozarks between Joplin and Springfield. Monett was a newly created railroad town established 13 years before she was born by the St. Louis and San Francisco railway. The small railroad stop began in 1880, the same year her parents were married.

Her father, Frances Seraphin Eloi (he later shortened it to Eli) DeBrosse was from a French family in Shelby County, Ohio. He was the fifth child out of eleven to Denis and Marguerite (Hummel) DeBrosse and was named after his older brother, Francis Xavier Eloi, who died at 8 months of age, a year to the day before Eli's birth.

Eli's father, Denis, had immigrated with his family to America in 1828, from a small village in France called Vernois-le-Fol. He took the mighty Mississippi up from New Orleans in a steamboat and

*Young Therese Gertrude DeBrosse*

then canal boat through the newly dug Erie canal. Once there, Denis's father, Jean-Jacques DeBrosse, a bred-in-the-bone Catholic built the first log cabin church called St. Walbert. But while in France, Denis was recognized as a brilliant student by the local curé and became highly literate. In fact, he was instrumental in securing a false passport for his older brother who was still conscripted in Napoleon's army. While in Shelby, he was a beloved schoolmaster and renowned violinist. At age 33, Denis married 15-year-old Marguerite Hummel and later moved to McDonald County, Missouri, with his family, including Eli.

Therese's mother, Margaret LaVelle, was the seventh child out of ten to Patrick and Mary (Conrey) LaVelle, and she was one-hundred percent Irish Catholic. Patrick and Mary, both from County Mayo in the Belmullet peninsula, immigrated to America separately by way of coffin ships to escape the ravages of the potato famine. Mary Conrey, at the age of sixteen, and her older brother John Conrey, fled Ireland in 1847 on the ship called Montezuma. For weeks they endured unhygienic misery and filth in the dark, noisy, smelly, stuffy bunk dormitories where there was little to no privacy and limited access to open air.

Once in America, Patrick LaVelle and Mary Conrey wed, and they, along with her father, Patrick Conrey, and sons, moved to Schuylkill County, Pennsylvania to work in the coal mines. Twenty-years later, after the premature death of their son, John LaVelle, they moved to Monett following the railroad expansion and hopes of plentiful lands and fresh air. It was in Monett where their daughter, Margaret LaVelle, met and married Eli DeBrosse. In fact, three LaVelles married three DeBrosse children in Monett.

Therese was the seventh and youngest child to Eli and Margaret (LaVelle) DeBrosse, and all but two of her siblings died during their childhood.

Mary May–lived 10 days (1882-1882)

Gertrude–lived 9 years (1884-1893)

Blanche Mary–lived 86 years (1886-1972)

Margaret–lived 2 years (1887-1889)

Joseph Patrick–lived 3 years (1888-1891)

Grace Rosalind–lived 81 years (1889-1970) (Conflicting records have her birth year as 1892 and even 1896 but Grace was at least two years older than Therese.)

Therese Gertrude–lived 98 years (1893-1991) (Conflicting records have her birth year as 1894 and others. Throughout Therese's life she changed her age on historical records for reasons unknown.)

*Eli and Margaret (LaVelle) DeBrosse*

Her oldest sibling, Mary May, was born the first day of May 1882 (perhaps that's why her middle name was May). She died ten days later, but was able to be baptized when she was six days old.

The next sibling was Gertrude, who lived for nearly a decade, the longest of the children who died. She died young at the age of nine, the same year that Therese was born.

Blanche Mary was the third child and survived to adulthood. She was to be the oldest sibling that Therese knew.

Margaret, the fourth child, died at age two, which was four years before Therese was born.

Therese's only brother and fifth born, Joseph Patrick, died when he was only three-years old, two years before Therese was born.

Grace Rosalind, the sixth child, survived to adulthood. She was the closest sibling in age to Therese, four years older, but only one year ahead in school, and they were very close.

Finally, the seventh child and baby of the family, Therese Gertrude, was born in 1893. She was born the same year as the 1893 Chicago World's Fair (World's Columbian Exposition), and the Panic of 1893, (New York Stock Exchange crash that started a four-year economic depression). Therese's middle name was Gertrude and although she never met her older sister, she knew that she was named after her.

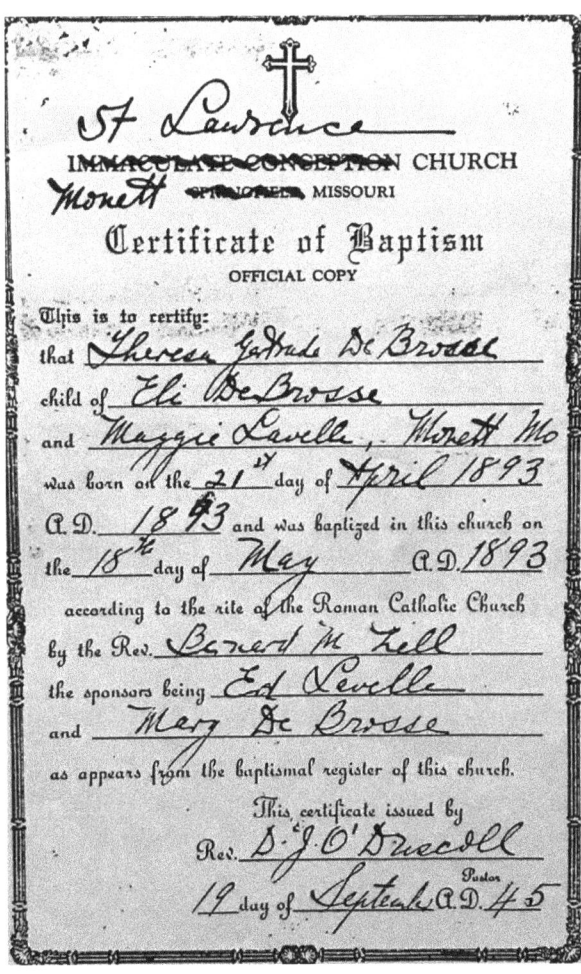

*May 18, 1893 Certificate of Baptism at St. Lawrence in Monett, Missouri for Therese Gertrude DeBrosse, born April 21, 1893. Her Catholic Sponsors were Ed LaVelle and Mary DeBrosse who were both her mother's siblings. Ed LaVelle was her mother's younger brother who eventually moved to California. Maryann was her mother's older sister who married Louis DeBrosse, Eli's younger brother.*

1900 United States Federal Census, State of Missouri, County of Lawrence, Township of Peirce. Patrick LaVelle, head of household, age 74, born March 1826, widowed, from Ireland, parents from Ireland, immigrated in 1847, living here 53 years, not naturalized, occupation: Miner lead zinc onsetter, did not attend school, but can read, write, and speak English, and rents a dwelling. All his children could read, write, and speak English and his sons were day laborers. Son, Michel, age 40, single, born Jan. 1860 in Ireland, immigrated in 1863, living here for 37 years. Son, Edward, age 32, single, born Feb. 1868, in Pennsylvania. Daughter Bido, age 30, single, born May 1870 in Pennsylvania. Daughter Mary A. DeBrosse, age 42, widowed (her husband, Louis DeBrosse was born in Ohio), born April 1858 in Ireland, immigrated in 1863, living here 37 years. Her children were all born in Missouri: John, age 19, born Feb. 1881. Mary, age 18, born April 1882, Louise, age 16, born Mar. 1884. Daughter Maggie DeBrosse, age 36, married for 20 years with 7 births and only 3 living, born July 1863 in Ireland, immigrated in 1863, living here 37 years. Her husband, Eloi DeBrosse, age 42, born May 1858 in Ohio, day laborer unemployed for 12 months. Their children were born in Missouri: Mary (Blanche), age 14, born Jan. 1886, Bridget (Grace), age 7, born Oct. 1892, Addie (Therese), age 6, born April 1894. There is a discrepancy on this census and other historical records for birth years of Grace (1889) and Therese (1893).

Childhood deaths were not unusual during that time. In fact, parents could usually count on a third of their children not surviving. If a child died, the name of the beloved deceased was often used again. Therese knew there were other siblings who died young, ones she never met, but she rarely spoke of them. She also never really knew the year she was born, perhaps her parents never kept track of that, but she spent her entire life not really knowing her exact age, or if she did, she never shared it.

Therese's parents were poor. By 1900, her family lived on the outskirts of Monett, in a tenant building #40, next to a cemetery. There, her grandfather Patrick LaVelle, rented an apartment where her aunts, uncles, cousins, and siblings resided; 13 in all. Her grandfather worked as a miner, a lead zinc onsetter who worked at the bottom of the pit loading the cages with rocks. The building was overflowing with people. The 1900 census had J. Orick in one apartment, W.S. Zenner (who housed four separate families in his apartment), and L. Withers (who housed 10 people). These low cost apartments were adjacent to the John Conrey estate, who was the brother-in-law to Patrick LaVelle, and

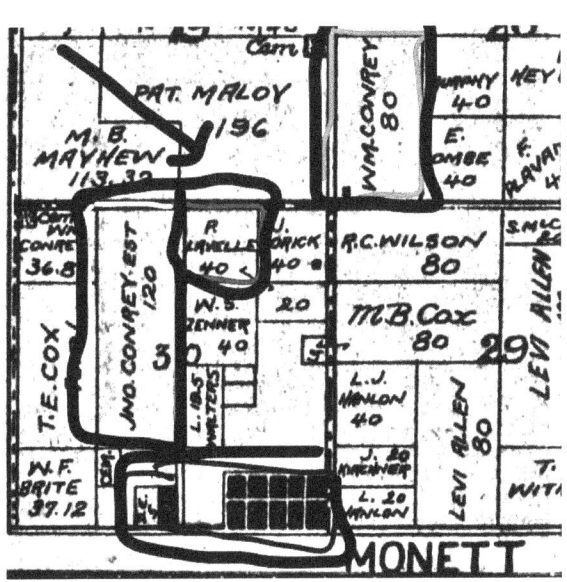
*1900 Monett Map*

older brother to his wife, Mary (Conrey) LaVelle, who had died a decade earlier. Also nearby was the home of John Conrey's son and Therese's first cousin once removed, William Conrey.

While in Monett, Therese's father, Eli became an air inspector for the railroad which paid 25 cents an hour and required long working days, seven days a week. He was then promoted to head machinist and roundhouse boss, but there was still little money. They never owned a home and moved every year or so from house to house. As roundhouse boss, Eli oversaw the operations of the locomotives. The roundhouse was the heartbeat of the railroad, where locomotives were serviced in open air bays in a building shaped like a semi-circle. He was well-liked and was known to entertain his workers by playing the harmonica or something called a jewsharp.

Later, Eli would be caught up in the Great Railroad Strike of 1922, which occurred because of wage cuts. The railroad companies brought in strikebreakers to fill the jobs and broke the strike with an agreed 5 cent pay cut. Eli lost his job, and with no money, they eventually moved to Neosho and lived with us.

## TOWNSHIP 26 NORTH, RANGE 27 WEST, OF THE FIFTH PRINCIPAL MERIDIAN,
### INCLUDING PARTS OF
# PEIRCE, SPRING RIVER AND FREISTATT TOWNSHIPS.

SCALE, 1½ INCHES 1 MILE.

*1900 Pierce, Spring River and Freistatt Townships. P. LaVelle, building #40 (arrow) was where Therese DeBrosse's Grandfather Patrick LaVelle rented an apartment. The occupants were: Patrick LaVelle, his single sons: Michel and Edward, single daughter Bridget (known as Bido), widowed daughter Maryann (LaVelle) DeBrosse and her children: John, Mary, and Louise. Also living there was married daughter Margaret (LaVelle) DeBrosse and her husband Eli DeBrosse and their children: Blanche, Grace, Therese. Next door was the estate of John Conrey #120, brother to deceased Grandmother Mary (Conrey) LaVelle. Above was the home of WM Conrey #80, son of John Conrey, first cousin to Margaret (LaVelle) DeBrosse. A cemetery was nearby (circled at bottom of map), and perhaps where Therese's siblings were buried.*

# Therese's First Holy Communion

Therese's faith grew strong during her childhood. She once wrote about a mystical event she experienced while receiving her First Holy Communion at St. Lawrence Catholic Church, on September 10, 1905, at the age of twelve.

Therese wrote that the morning of her First Communion, just before she left for the ceremony, she fought with her older sister. She doesn't say which one. Afterwards, she was so contrite that she wanted to go to confession before receiving the Holy Eucharist, but because of the argument she was running late. She arrived just as the priest was ascending the steps to the altar. Therese, distraught, looked toward the red sanctuary light that hung from the arched ceiling. There she "beheld with her own eyes, the vision of Our Saviour, Himself, holding up the Host and looking toward me."

Therese went on to say that from then on, she never entered a Catholic Church without concentrating on the red sanctuary light in the hopes that the vision would return. It

*September 10, 1905 Therese Gertrude DeBrosse, First Holy Communion, age 12.*

never did, and she wondered if it were because she was never again worthy to look upon such beauty. She kept her secret close to her heart and told very few of her transcendental experience. A typed note detailing her encounter was found in the little study off the kitchen, and she said that in times of dread or danger, she would light the candle that she carried during her First Communion procession, and her First Communion prayer book was always her daily rouser.

## THE VISION

Many, many years ago, forty-four to be exact, I saw a vision. The occasion was my First Holy Communion day, September 10, 1905. The night before, I, with dozens of other children, had gone to confession in preparation. The next morning, for no reason at all, I got into an argument or quarrel with my older sister, and all the way to church I repented and hoped it would be possible for me to go to confession all over again and tell the priest of what I considered a sin.

I arrived at the church just as the procession of white flowing veils and wreaths of beautiful flowers was floating by and boys with Sunday best suits. I was greatly disturbed, knowing that I should immediately join the procession – but all the time trying to see if it would be possible to drop out of the line just long enough to talk to the priest in the confessional again. This desired consolation was not to be – for as I looked down the aisle, I already saw the priest ascending the steps to the altar.

All through the Mass, I repented and was so excruciatingly sorry that I had not been able to confess all over again. The Lord must have been pleased with this contrition (perhaps He didn't consider this too big a sin, after all, and in any event was pleased with my sorrow), for He, Himself, was to be my consolation, not only in a spiritual way, but in a material way, for in looking ahead into the red light that hung from the arched ceiling, I beheld with my own eyes, the Vision of our Saviour, Himself, holding up the Host and looking toward me.

I can't describe the feeling of exultation at that moment, nor the beauty of His Face, but it was a very similar to this picture enclosed – only much more ethereal, and the halo above his head was clearly outlined, and the garment white, and He was holding the Host between the thumb and forefinger, as the priest does.

My first thought, upon seeing this, was, "I wonder if all the other children have seen Him, too? And what do they think?" So after taking another long look at the Vision, I gazed across the aisle to detect the reaction of others, at which time, I'm convinced, from the look on their faces, that they had seen nothing at all. I returned, to gaze with rapture, upon my Vision-only to find that It was no longer there. But the red sanctuary light burned on seemingly unaware of what happened.

Even then, at that tender age, the regretful thought came to me, that I did wrong in leaving Him for others and not staying and talking with

Him while He was there. As times goes on, there has been times when I would wonder if that REALLY did happen. If it were a figment of the imagination, or was it really true?

This all took place in the time of Pope Pius X, and since reading about his life and his great hope of establishing frequent and even daily Communion, I wonder…...THE VISION. Could it have meant Daily Communion? Maybe, "Give us this day our daily bread," does mean more than just physical food.

In any event instead of growing away from this Vision and erasing it from my mind, it has persisted all these years and seems even clearer as time goes on. I never enter a Catholic Church without concentrating on the red sanctuary light and hoping the Vision will come again-- just to make me more certain, but it never has, and I think I know why. I have never again been worthy to look upon so much beauty. I've wandered as I did- but still I've always been brought back to try again through the memory of this Beautiful Face in the light.

I've kept the secret all these years. Many times I've been tempted to reveal it but always the fear would come-no one could possibly understand or believe it, so why tell it? It was too sacred to be talked about anyway. Then again I'd doubt if it were right to keep it. Maybe it would help someone. It is for this reason that I am revealing the secret treasure of my heart for the glory of His Sacred Heart.

When invoking the Holy Spirit in times of dread or danger, I light the candle I carried in my First Communion procession, and of course my First Communion prayer book is my daily rouser.

Therese DeBrosse Epperson 1949

*Therese DeBrosse First Holy Communion*

# Sisters, Blanche and Grace DeBrosse

Therese's oldest sister, Blanche, who was seven years older, worked at the millinery in Monett where she made and sold hats. Blanche first worked for Mrs. White, and then for Jacques Millinery. In 1911, while Therese was in high school, Blanche married William Smithmier, a railroad machinist from a well-known railroad family in town. Blanche, ahead of her time, continued to sell hats, and on March 22, 1912, she was mentioned in the *Monett Times*, "Mrs. Will Smithmier and Miss Gene Price are assisting in Mrs. Jacque's millinery store."

As the Smithmier family grew, Blanche and Will, along with their children; William, Lawrence, Blanche, Henry, Florence, Louis, moved to Springfield, Missouri and finally to Kansas City, Missouri, where they remained.

Therese's other sister, Grace, was closer in age, and they were best friends throughout their lives. Therese, who was just one grade below Grace, was demure, while her sister was more outgoing and starred in many high school plays. Grace's senior high school quote was an example of her colorful personality. "To be agreeable is not necessary to be amusing." But they were both considered town darlings and were mentioned frequently in the *Monett Times* newspaper, during a time when local and regional papers followed the comings and goings of its townsfolk.

Both sisters attended Missouri State Normal School in Springfield, Missouri, Therese in business and Grace in education. In 1915, Grace earned a regent certification (30 credit hours) to teach at any Missouri Public School. She returned to Monett and taught at the local high school where she once attended, becoming a beloved educator.

Although older than Therese, Grace was the last DeBrosse girl to be married, and it made front page news in the *Monett Times*. Therese had, just the year before, surprised everyone in town, including her parents, by eloping. So the townsfolk pulled out the stops for their popular school teacher, who on November 24, 1920, wed Joseph Hartmeier, a self-employed plumber from Elk City, Arkansas.

*Monett Times,* November 26, 1920

Miss Grace DeBrosse, a popular teacher in Monett Junior High was married to Joseph Hartmeier of Elk City, Okla. at 6:30 o'clock Wednesday morning, November 24. The ceremony was performed at St. Lawrence Catholic Church, the Reverend Father McNamee officiating.

Louis Hartmeier, of Ft. Smith, Ark., was best man and Miss Adeline DeBrosse was bridesmaid.... The chorus from St. Joseph School choir sang. The ceremony was witnessed by the faculty of Monett public schools.... The bride is the daughter of Mr. and Mrs. Eli DeBrosse of this place. She spent most of her life here. Since her graduation from Monett high school, she has been employed in the city schools, being one of our best grade teachers. Out of town guests at the wedding were Mr. and Mrs. Will Smithmier of Springfield, Mr. and Mrs. O.W. Epperson of Neosho.

They moved to Ft. Smith, Arkansas and had three children: Therese Marie, Joseph Robert (Joe Bob), and Margaret (Margie). Many years later, and for many years, Grace and her children would visit Therese in Neosho, sometimes showing up in the middle of the night without notice, and the cousins became very close. When they were older, Therese Marie and Margie, were both asked to be bridesmaids in the weddings of our daughters, Joan and Tirzah, and Joseph Robert Hartmeier, affectionately called, Joe Bob, a boisterous character, was asked to sing.

# Therese's Education and Typhoid

During Therese's high school years, she was a shy and modest student, quite the opposite from her older sister. During her junior and senior years of high school, the Monett High School Yearbook regarded her as, "and with a glow of your dark eyes cometh a grace of long ago," and "a mild, meek maiden with deep soulful eyes."

*Young Therese DeBrosse*

*1911 Therese DeBrosse, Junior at Monett High School.*

*1912 Therese DeBrosse, Senior at Monett High School.*

On February 14, 1914, Therese left to attended the Normal Business School to learn the Gregg method of shorthand. The *Monett Times* announced, "Miss Theresa DeBrosse has gone to Springfield where she will attend business college."

The Gregg method was a popular form of shorthand writing used while taking dictation. Like cursive longhand, it was completely based on elliptical figures and lines that bisected them. As a phonetic writing system it recorded the sounds of the speaker, not the English spelling, and all silent letters were omitted. Phrasing was another mechanism for increasing speed. For example, "I have not been able" was written, "avnba," and it looked like a precursor to social media acronyms.

# Part IV. Therese Debrosse

*Therese DeBrosse's shorthand. It has not been translated.*

The first summer when Therese came home, Monett was experiencing a typhoid outbreak, and she became one of its victims. The *Monett Times*, June 26, 1914, reported her visit, "Miss Therese DeBrosse has returned to Springfield after a three weeks visit with her parents, Mr. and Mrs. Eli DeBrosse." Two weeks later, she was back in Monett very ill from the waterborne disease and the *Monett Times*, July 10, 1914, then reported, "Therese DeBrosse is threatened with typhoid fever."

Typhoid fever became nationally known from 1907 to 1915, due to an outbreak from an Irish immigrant named Mary Mallon, better known as Typhoid Mary. She was a domestic cook who worked in the private homes of the wealthy in New York and Long Island. She was the first person identified as an asymptomatic carrier, who infected 51 people (three of whom died). Once discovered, she was forcibly isolated and eventually died while quarantined.

Typhoid fever, a bacterial disease caused by Salmonella typhi, had symptoms ranging from mild to serious, and usually developed one to three weeks after exposure to the bacteria. Symptoms included headache, nausea, constipation or diarrhea, loss of appetite, and fever, which could lead to intestinal bleeding and perforation, delirium, sepsis, inflammation of the heart, meningitis, kidney infection and pneumonia. But a rash was the most valuable single sign of typhoid, along with fever and chills, to diagnose the disease. The mortality in women was greater than men, and the low muttering delirium with tremors meant a close fight for life. In 1914, there was no cure for the disease, instead, hydrotherapy with cold water was found to be life-saving in reducing the patient's temperature. Vaccination against typhoid was still in its infancy.

The source of Monett's water supply had been the culprit. When the town was formed in 1887, a shaft was sunk into a subterranean stream at a depth of 18 feet with an inexhaustible supply of water. After a steam pump was put in, it seemed to be enough to guarantee all the water required for the people in the town. Twenty-seven years later, Monett, bustling with hundreds of men in railroad jobs, along with their families, had unexplained typhoid outbreaks. Unaware of how typhoid was transmitted, folks believed it was seasonal and caused by the flies that multiplied during the summer months, so they advised caution with the proper disposal of sewage. But the source of the typhoid was actually contaminated water, and the outbreaks were directly proportionate to the inefficient drainage of the water supply. The disease flourished more in the countryside than in the town because in the country, the privy vault was often in close proximity to the well.

As a small town, Monett was ill-equipped for an epidemic. The town had six doctors, five dentists and one hospital. The hospital accepted medical and surgical cases but not cases of contagious disease, so those suffering from typhoid, like Therese, were kept at home.

Monett had an ice plant that was near the railroad, and it saved the town during the 1914 typhoid outbreak because it was the only well deep enough to furnish safe drinking water. The problem was not completely solved until 1916, when multiple typhoid epidemics caused by contaminated water forced the city to drill a series of deeper wells. It would be another five years until Monett endorsed the anti-typhoid vaccine, stating it could be practically eliminated. The vaccine was painless, given three injections at ten day intervals, and lasted for up to three years.

But in 1914, Therese fought the disease for months. One of the strange phenomena of typhoid was hair loss. Therese lost all of her hair. When it finally grew back, it grew back slowly, and was darker and curlier, and for the rest of her life she went to great lengths to take care of it. She captured rain water in buckets, and used that water to wash her hair. She would never lose her hair again, and even as it turned grey, it was soft, beautiful and curly.

Once cured of the disease, Therese returned to Springfield to finish her education and was reported by the *Monett Times* to have come home to visit her folks again on January 8, 1915, "Miss Therese DeBrosse has come home from Springfield to spend a few days with her parents."

After graduating, she worked a short time for the Shartel Mortgage Company in Neosho, before finally settling on a job as stenographer for the Stark Nursery. The *Monett Times*, always keeping up with the DeBrosse girls, reported on February 17, 1915, "Miss Therese DeBrosse has accepted a position as a stenographer with the Stark Bros. Nursery at Neosho."

*1909. Therese, with big curly hair and bow facing the camera & Grace, with arms crossed, both riding in buggy in front of Mrs. White's house (Blanche's employer).*

*Therese's sisters. Blanche, on left wearing hat and Grace.*

*1912 Monett train stop. Grace on left, Therese on right. On their way to attend Missouri State Normal School, Springfield, Missouri.*

*1961 DeBrosse sisters. Left to right: Blanche, Therese, Grace.*

# Therese's Double Cousin

Therese had a cousin who was a priest, Fr. John LaVelle. She referred to him as her double-cousin because he was a cousin from the LaVelle side as well as from the DeBrosse side. Fr. John's mother was Flora Julienne DeBrosse, the older sister of Eli, and his father, Martin LaVelle, was her mother's older brother.

The two cousins were close, and when he was ordained a priest, she kept the Ordination Memorial card. On June 7, 1916, the Reverend Daniel L. Healy was inspired to write a poem for the occasion. He was the very Fr. Healy who baptized Therese and also wrote the moving elegiac for her grandmother Mary (Conrey) LaVelle.

It was an appended anapestic quatrain expressive of congratulatory soul effusion, which meant a spiritual poem (soul effusion) with four lines (quatrains) each with separate themes that were in anapestic tetrameter (four lines, each foot with two unstressed syllables, followed by a stressed syllable). This style was sometimes referred to as a reverse dactyl, and shared the rapid, driving pace of the dactyl.

*June 7, 1916. Fr. John LaVelle Ordination sacerdotal with poem*

Years later, Fr. John worked with the Missions of St. Vincent de Paul in Jiangsu, China, Perryville, Missouri, and finally in Los Angeles. He was also the superior of the Vincentian House of Studies in Washington, D.C. during the 1940s.

Therese decided that she needed to tell someone about her childhood mysticism and so in a letter dated 1949, she wrote to Fr. John.

> And now last but not least, John, I enclose the story I've carried around with me since September 10, 1905. It almost frightens me to be writing about it, for it is the first time I've seen it on paper, and you are the first one to whom I have divulged it. Do you think if it were imagination at that time that I would still be thinking about it and carefully concentrating into the Sanctuary light in every church I enter? Does this make sense to you? Do you approve of the way it is written? It's not polished up, as I am not a writer – but then would a vision like this have to be dressed up to become significant? If you think this should be made known after all these years, who would be most likely to be interested in printing it? Or should it first be sent to the Bishop of this diocese, Bishop O'Hara, for his remarks? He is a great devotee of the later Pope Pius X, during whose reign this happened and who was also an advocate of frequent and daily Communion. So–does all that means anything?
>
> It's so nice to have you to talk to for in that way I do not have to display my ignorance to outsiders or do anything rash that would be misinterpreted.
>
> I am enclosing the nearest photo I have of Jesus that is similar to my Vision, but of course as I remember there was much more of a halo above the head and more of the upper parts shown with white garment flowing. The outstanding and memorable part, though, was that Christ himself was holding the Host between the same fingers and in the same manner as priests do.

# PART V
# WORLD WAR I

*I JOINED THE ARMY*

*MY WAR JOURNAL*

*POSTCARD BACK HOME*

*COUVERTPUIS, FRANCE*

*MEMOIRS OF FRANCE AND THE 88TH DIVISION*

*AMERICAN EXPEDITIONARY FORCES UNIVERSITY*

*TIME TO GO HOME*

# I Joined the Army

I registered for military service at the age of 25, and was enlisted on May 27, 1918, nearly two years later. When the time came to leave, about 80 of us from Newton and McDonald Counties marched around the town square and down to the Kansas City Southern Railroad that was to take us to Camp Dodge, Iowa.

*Orval William Epperson WWI Enlistment Record, May 27, 1918*

Therese marched right along with us and even got on the train as a far as Joplin, Missouri. She was the only girl to do that. She was wearing my diamond ring then. But, as I recall, things were still up in the air between us. I was sure about us, but I wasn't egotistic enough to think that I was the only duck in the puddle.

She might have wanted to grab Glen or True Morse (brothers of her best friend, Helen), or even Rector Mace. Or someone else she liked better. I didn't want to stop any prospects she might decide on. And, a lot of things could happen while I was at war. I could be disabled, and then she would be burdened with a cripple.

Therese said she was sure about us, and wearing the ring meant she was going to wait.

She had always thought that I traded in my Hamilton watch to get her that ring, but I think I paid for the ring outright, and traded my Hamilton watch for her new little Swiss watch. At any rate, I was making $75 a month at the bank, and thought I could afford a ring.

Therese also recalled that she returned alone to Neosho from Joplin on the Vickers Jitney, instead of the train. A jitney was a privately owned vehicle used for bus service at set prices, usually five cents. The word, jitney, was slang for a nickel.

When we reported to Camp Dodge, they ran us into a turnstile that had four exits. As the turnstile spun each soldier exited into a different area. The first soldier exited through door one, the second through door two, the third through door three, and so on. Round and round we'd go. The Newton and McDonald County boys all thought we would remain together, but as it turned out, only a fourth were put in the same outfit. That was done so that if there were a lot of causalities in a Company, they wouldn't all be from one part of the country.

*Jitney*

But one of my friends was assigned to my group. His name was John Proctor, from around Diamond and Tipton, Missouri, and I spent a lot of time with him in France. He was a wagoner and drove the horse-drawn wagons that carried artillery and heavy loaded machine guns. (In later wars, army trucks replaced horse-drawn wagons, and tanks replaced horses.)

The warship convoy that took us to France, was called the S.S. Kashmir. In my war memorabilia, I kept the service card, which I carried on my person at all times, that identified my sleeping quarters and where I ate (Section 2 Upper and Mess No. 5). I also kept my spent train tickets that were used for military transport.

*Orval William Epperson's SS Kashmir service card and used train tickets.*

On arrival in France, the Division was instructed to turn in all its field ranges, overcoats, and any other provisions except one blanket per man. Means of cooking had to be improvised with the extensive use of camp kettles and water cans, or from French stoves in our assigned billets. All troops were billeted in small towns, and training was carried out in the recently cutover grain fields and on unused pasture lands.

On September 20, 1918, a wide-spread epidemic of influenza set in, and in eight days, there were 1,370 cases in one regiment alone. This epidemic increased until October 14, 1918, on which date there were eight deaths. All told, there were 6,815 cases of influenza and 1,041 cases of pneumonia reported, from which 11 deaths resulted.

To reach the sector, the infantry and engineers of the Division were forced to make long marches, sometimes 16 miles a day, on congested roads, pulling with them their heavily loaded machine gun carts, and combat and field wagons. The average weight pulled per man was around 250 pounds. Furthermore, we were forced to go without essentials because all available transportation and supplies were being used to the maximum in the Argonne drive.

I was stationed with the Battalion Headquarters Company, which was situated just behind the lines. It was closer to the front than most and was certainly closer than the Division Headquarters in Belfort, France, but it was not as close to the front lines as the Company Headquarters, which included four companies, A, B, C, D, plus a medical detachment. Those posts were located in dugouts in the woods, and the aid station would evacuate wounded to the field hospital at Bellemagny, all except gassed patients, who were sent to the triage at Retzwiller.

Companies would alternate between being active in the front line to moving back to safety in reserves, which required additional marching to rearrange the forces. As one company moved up to the front, another would move back. They would change every few days or so, alternating between active and reserve. Close to the battle, and further away from the battle line.

Companies were to be ready with only two hours' notice to relieve other units, and I, as Corporal, under the Supply Sergeant (I might have been called the Supply Corporal) would requisition two days' ration for each soldier, and personal equipment for officers. I would gather and organize the correspondence and requisitions, and the Sergeant would appropriate the supplies. I was the messenger between the battalion headquarters and the companies on the front line. My business was to go back and forth between them, collecting reports from each company's supply clerks (rations, sick lists, ammunition spent, requisitions, etc.), and I did so on a bicycle. When riding to the companies at the front line, I had to be very careful not to get shot. Once I arrived there, I began the long walk through the trenches to find the Sergeant in charge.

*WWI trenches dug deep below the surface to protect soldiers from gunfire and artillery attacks.*

In the daytime riding my bike wasn't too bad. I could maneuver between potholes, deep mud tracks, ditches, and mine craters, but at night it was more difficult, not just because it was dark but because the roads became stickier from the rains. Mud would cake up on my tires making it slow going. There would be six to eight inches of the sticky sludge on the so-called paved roads, making it nearly impossible to peddle the bike, and if there was a downpour, it became even more intolerable.

Most of my travel occurred at night in order maintain secrecy, but some nights it was so dark that I could hardly see, and I privately hoped for distant night raids which would light up the sky every so often allowing me to check my path. On other nights, I used the outline of the trees that lined the road to navigate. The trees, set on either side of the road, were tall and slender and high enough that they didn't hang over the road and in my way. On a good night, I could see the sky above me, and by the light of the moon, I would use the shadows of the trees to stay on course. But on the darkest of nights, when there was no moon, it was slow going because I could never use the light on my bicycle. No, that would make me a prime shooting target.

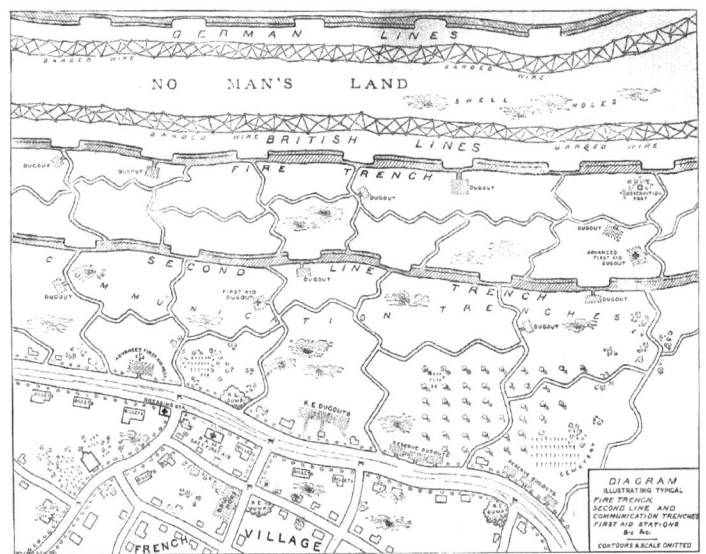
*Trench warfare and No Man's Land*

Once I left the company on the front line, I would bring back the reports, and consolidate them for the Sergeant, who would then get the supplies from the division headquarters at the railhead. Everything behind the front line was called support, and railheads were the nearest point to the front from which men and supplies travelled by train. Once they left the railheads, they were taken to the battle line by horse, or on foot.

In between the front lines of the Allied Powers (USA, France, Britain), and the front lines of the enemy Central Powers (Germany, Austria, Hungary), was call the Quiet Zone, or No Man's Land. But very nearby, German Stormstruppen troops, assigned to the duty of roving (between the Vosges and the Swiss Border), made several raids, accompanied by gas projector attacks, and intense artillery bombardments.

The entire front line where we fought was 11.8 miles long, and the width in some areas of the Quiet Zone could be as narrow as 300 meters. That area was unoccupied, and it was strewn with dead trees, belts of barb wire, and muddy dirt. But, if you were so inclined, the walk across would only take about 10 minutes. Both sides respected the area, but you couldn't really count on it being quiet because whenever the guns would shoot at the planes overhead, the fragments of shells fell everywhere, and there was constant shelling. Also, you could never tell when someone (on either side) would get antsy and start shooting.

I remember when we were near the Belfort Section, on the border of Switzerland, and no further than a few football fields away from the Germans, we were so close that we could carry on a conversation with them. One night one of the guys in our company was at the entrance of his dugout trench, and unaware that a German on the other side let loose a volley of fire. It was a direct hit. All we ever found of him was a foot and a shoe.

I was near the front line when a rumor started that an Armistice was going to be declared. On November 11, 1918, we had stashed our surplus materials (barracks bags and personal effects), and began to replace the men on the front line. We heard that the Armistice had been signed and would go into effect at 11 o'clock that morning, but we were already issued our orders and on our way. We began firing across the Quiet Zone, at an aggressive pace and had to keep shooting in order to prevent the Germans from coming across. They shot back. As it got closer to 11 o'clock, the shooting became even more fierce. Everyone seemed to be trying to shoot as much as they could, but at 11 o'clock everything went quiet. Dead quiet. Slowly, far in the distance, you could hear a chirp of a bird, and then another, and another. It was as if nature was replacing the sound of bullets. The Armistice began on the eleventh hour of the eleventh day of the eleventh month.

The war was over.

By the end of the war, there were 27 battle deaths, 63 wounded, and 9 prisoners (2 officers and seven men) from the 88th Division Infantry and Machine Gun Battalion. A war poem, written by a Canadian doctor who had lost a friend in battle, came to symbolize WWI.

## IN FLANDERS FIELDS

*In Flanders' Fields the Poppies blow*
*Between the crosses, row on row,*
*That mark our place: and in the sky*
*The larks, still bravely singing fly*
*Scarce heard amid the guns below.*

*We are the dead. Short days ago.*
*We lived, felt dawn, saw sunset glow,*
*Loved and were loved, and now we lie*
*In Flanders fields.*

*Take up our quarrel with the foe;*
*To you from failings hands we throw*
*The torch; be yours to hold it high,*
*If ye break faith with us who die*
*We shall not sleep, though poppies grow*
*In Flanders Fields.*

# My War Journal

As Supply Corporal, I was used to keeping records, so it was easy for me to write a daily War Journal. My documentation was detailed, and years later it was found to correspond exactly with the historical records of the 88th Division.

*Orval Wm. Epperson. Corp. Hq. Co., 1st Sq. 308 S. Hamilton St. Neosho, MO.*

## ORVAL EPPERSON'S RECORD OF EVENTS OF THE 338th MACHINE GUN BATTALION

### AUGUST

The 338th Machine Gun Battalion left **Camp Dodge, Iowa**, 10:00a.m. August 4, 1918 and arrived at **Camp Upton, Long Island, New York** at 8:20p.m., August 7, 1918.

Organization left **Camp Upton, New York** 10:00a.m. August 15, 1918 and embarked on P & O SS, (H.M.S.) "**Kashmir**" at Cunard Line Pier at 3:45p.m. the same date. Left Pier at 6:00p.m. August 15th. Anchored during the night and left the harbor at 1:00p.m. August 16, 1918 and started on the voyage.

Arrived at **Liverpool, England** at 4:00a.m. August 28, 1918 and docked at 8:00a.m. Disembarked at 4:00p.m. on same date and marched to train.

Entrained and left **Liverpool** at 6:00p.m. and arrived at **Winchester, England** at 4:30a.m. August 29, 1918, then marched to English Rest Camp at **Camp Morn Hill**.

Headquarters being near Luxe, Companies "A" and "B", in Luxe, "C", in Couthenans and "D" in a suburb of Couthenans.

### OCTOBER

The 338th Machine Gun Battalion left their billets at 7:50 P.M. October 5th, 1918 and assembled at Luxe, France. Left there at 8:00 P.M. and marched 18 kilometers to Sessoncourt, arriving at 3:00 A.M. October 6th, 1918. Companies "B" and "D" left Sessoncourt at 8:00 P.M. October 8th, 1918, and marched 14 kilometers up to the front lines. Company "B" took up positions near Baoken and Company "D" near Buethwiller, both in Alsace and on what had been a part of Germany before the war, relieving French troops who were holding it up to that time. October 12th, 1918 about 8:00, the enemy shelled the sector with great violence and caused a few casualties. Companies "A" and "C" left Sessoncourt, France at 9:00 A.M., October 20th, 1918 and relieved Companies "B" and "D" respectively. Companies "B" and "D" left their positions and returned to Sessoncourt, starting at 3:30 P.M. and arriving at 12:25 P.M. the same October 23rd, 1918. Companies "B", "D", Headquarters and Medical Detachment left Sessoncourt, France at 6:00 A.M. October 30th, 1918 and marched 15 kilometers to Lepuix y, France arriving at 9:30 A.M. October 31st, 1918.

### NOVEMBER

Companies "A" and "C" were relieved by the French October 31st, 1918 and left their positions the same date. Marched to Lepuix y, France, arriving at 11:30 A.M. November 1st, 1918. Left Lepuix y, at 9:00 P.M. November, 6th, 1918 and with Headquarters and Medical boarded the train at Belfort at 10:00 A.M. November 7th, 1918. Companies "B" and "D" left Lepuix y at 3:30 A.M. November 7th, 1918 and boarded the train at Belfort at 2:00 P.M. November, 7th, 1918. The entire battalion arrived at Menil la Tour or rather a railroad near there at 7:30 A.M. November 8th, 1918. Detrained and marched 8 kilometers to Bouvron, France, arriving at 11:30 A.M. November 8th, 1918. Prepared to depart November 10th to participate in the drive on the front nearby but before they could start the emergency had crisis had passed and they were not sent forward. Armistice was signed effective November 11th at 11:00 A.M. and promptly on the minute all firing ceased and everybody breathed a sigh of relief.

*Orval Epperson Record of Events of the 338th Machine Gun Battalion War Journal*

Entrained and left **Winchester, England** at 12:05p.m. August 31, 1918 and arrived at **South Hampton, England** at 1:15p.m. the same date.

Embarked on ship "**Maid of Orleans**" at 5:30p.m. and left **South Hampton** at 7:00p.m. August 31, 1918.

**SEPTEMBER**

The 338th Machine Gun Battalion arrived at **Cherbourg, France** at 1:00a.m. September 1, 1918. Debarked at 7:00a.m. and marched to Rest Camp 1 arriving there at 11:30a.m.

Marched back to **Cherbourg** and entrained at 1:00p.m. September 2, 1918, started on the journey at 2:15p.m. the same date and arrived at **Marigny-le-Cahouët** at 12:30p.m., September 4, 1918.

Left **Marigny-le-Cahouët** at 12:30p.m. September 17, 1918 and marched to **Les Laumes**, France arriving at 5:30p.m. same date.

Left **Les Laumes** by train at 3:50a.m. September 18, 1918 and arrived at **Héricourt, France** at 4:30p.m. the same date.

Marched to **Luzé, France** arriving at 5:30p.m. the same date. Billeted and spending the remaining of the month in the vicinity.

The Headquarters being near **Luzé**.

Companies A and B in **Luzé**.

Company C in **Couthenans**, and Company D in a suburb of **Couthenans**.

**OCTOBER**

The 338th Machine Gun Battalion left their billets at 7:30p.m. October 5, 1918 and assembled at **Luzé, France**.

Left there at 8:00p.m. and marched 18 kilometers to **Bessoncourt** arriving at 3:55a.m. October 6, 1918.

Company B and D left **Bessoncourt** at 6:00p.m. October 6, 1918 and marched 14 kilometers up to the **Front Lines**.

Company B took up positions near **Hecken**. And Company D near **Buethwiller**. both in **Alsace** and on what had been a part of Germany before the war, relieving French troops who were holding it up to that time, October 12, 1918.

About 8:00, the enemy shelled the sector with great violence and caused a few casualties.

Companies A and C left **Bessoncourt, France** at 9:30a.m., October 20, 1918 and relieved Companies B and D, respectively.

Companies B and D left their positions and returned to **Bessoncourt**, starting at 3:30a.m. and arriving at 12:20p.m., October 23, 1918.

Companies A, B, Headquarters and Medical Detachment left **Bessoncourt, France** at 6:00p.m., October 30, 1918, and marched 18 kilometers **to Lepuix Oy, France** arriving at 9:30a.m., October 31, 1918.

**NOVEMBER**

Companies A and C were relieved by the French, October 31, 1918, and left their positions the same date.

Marched to Lepuix Oy, France arriving at 11:30a.m., November 1, 1918.

Left Lepuix Oy at 9:00p.m. November 6, 1918 and with Headquarters and Medical boarded the train at Belfort at 10:00a.m., November 7, 1918.

Companies B and D left Lepuix Oy at 8:30a.m., November 7, 1918 and boarded the train at Belfort at 2:00p.m., November 7, 1918.

The entire Battalion arrived at Ménil-la-Tour or rather a railhead near there at 7:30a.m., November 8, 1918.

Detrained and marched 8 kilometers to Bouvron, France arriving at 11:30a.m., November 8, 1918.

Prepared to depart November 10th to participate in the drive on the Front nearby, but before they could start the emergency crisis had passed and they were not sent forward. Armistice was signed effective November 11th at 11:00a.m. and promptly on the minute ALL FIRING CEASED and everyone breathed a sigh of relief.

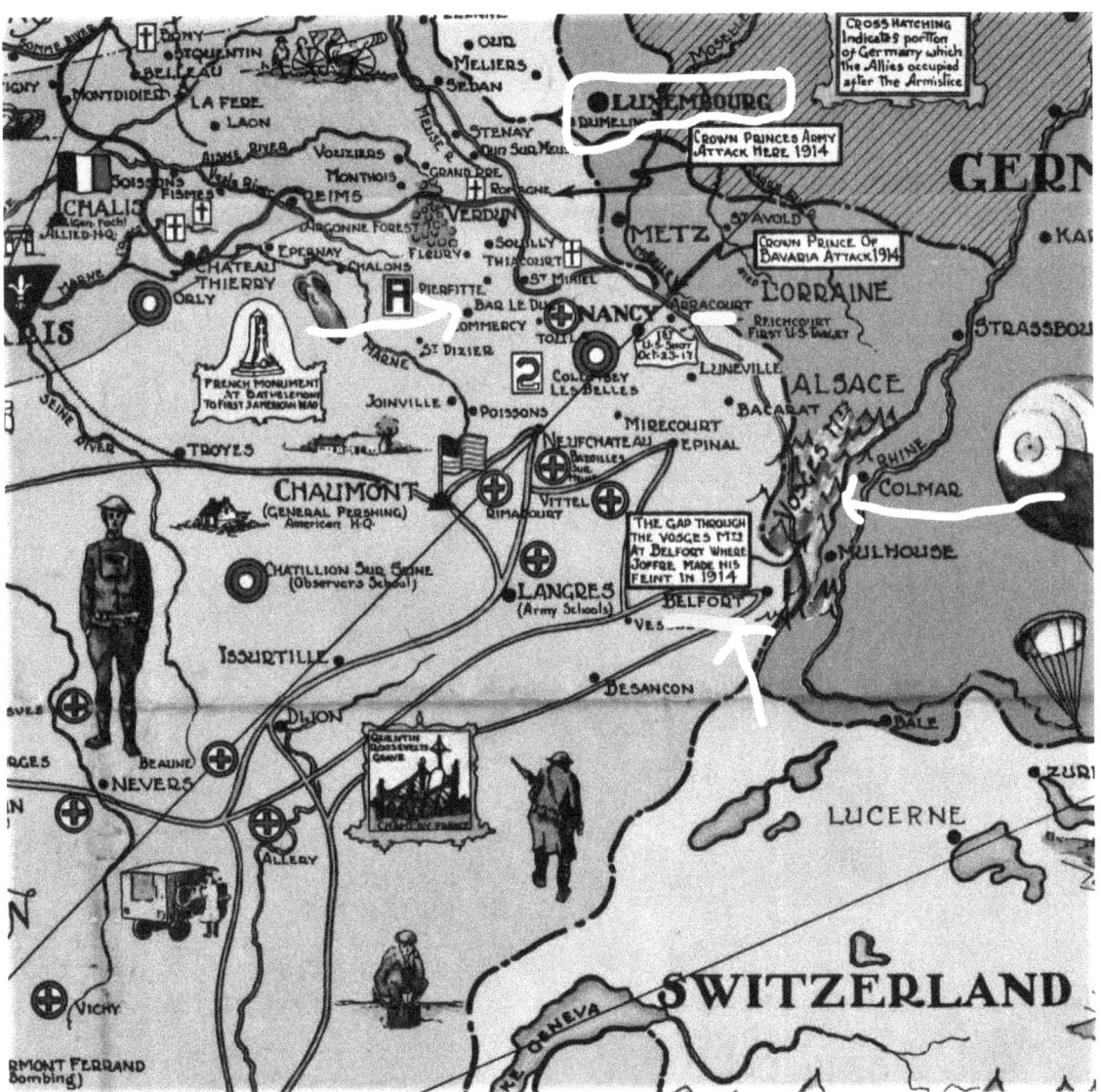

*WWI Map of France with marked areas where I traveled. Arrows point to Bar le Duc, Belfort, and the Vosges mountains, and Luxembourg is circled. From October–November 1918 we were in the Vosges mountains stationed in Lepuix, France. The Division Headquarters was in Belfort, France (underlined with arrow) south of Lepuix. I traveled often between these towns as a Supply Corporal. December 1918–February 1919 we were stationed in Bar-le-Duc and regions including Ligny-en-Barrois and Couvertpuis. Then in February 1919 to Luxembourg. The remainder of my time, March–May 1919, was spent in Beaune in the far south of France (not on the map) and was where I attended A.E.F. University.*

# Postcards Back Home

I wrote postcards back home to my family, my boss at the Bank of Neosho, and of course, to Therese. Every letter or post card was mailed by soldier mail and read by regional officers in the U.S. Army before it was approved with a stamp, "passed as censored." Censorship was an indispensable war weapon. Its main purpose was to avoid mention of operational details that might prove valuable to the enemy. Forbidden information included references to locations, numbers of troops, criticism of superiors, and even the weather (which might have indicated the state of the trenches). But, letters were an important way to maintain morale, not just in keeping families informed of the wellbeing of their loved ones, but also to help sustain popular support for the war effort at home.

I had told Mr. Wills at the Bank of Neosho, that I would keep in touch and send him foreign currency. I wrote a postcard dated August 8, 1918, while at Camp Upton in New York, "Sure are some skyscrapers in NY City. Haven't been uptown yet but expect to go tomorrow or the next day. If I do, may visit bank of Cam. Had some trip across country. Scenery great. Epp."

In a letter I wrote on February 21, 1919, I enclosed one franc, dated 1914, and a prized French cancelled check that was nearly 60 years old at the time. I knew that the Paris check, dated 1863, would thrill Mr. Wills as much as it did me even though I could not read it. And the personal checks that I wrote while in France made it all the way back to the small town Bank of Neosho.

```
On Active Service with the AMERICAN EXPEDITIONARY FORCES
Couvertpuis, France A.P.O. 795. February 21, 1919
Dear Mr. Wills,
I returned last night from the journey up to Luxembourg where I saw the
football game between the 88th and the 5th divisions. Th+e score was 5 to
0 in favor of the 5th. It was a good game anyway even if we did not beat
them.
While there I went into the bank at the place, which by the way seems
to be a branch of a French bank but its name is Elsassische Bank
Gesellachaft. They told me when I wrote out the check to just leave
the payee space blank and they would stamp it with their stamp but on
the slip they gave me it is marked as the Societie General Alsacienne
```

De Banque and on the letter of credit they just entered it as the Societie Generale, and something else that I could not read. It was in the town of Bach. I am sending you herewith a 1-franc bill that is current in the state of Luxembourg also a coin of that country and one from Germany. I thought you might be interested in them.

You may keep the coins, but I would like to have the other things, i.e. the one-franc bill and the duplicate of the Decompte des Effets (whatever that is) as well as the old draft that I picked up in our garret when we first arrived in France, at Marigny le Cohouet. You will notice that it is an old timer, dated in 1863. I want to keep it as a souvenir of that town. While in each, I sent you a postcard. One of the 5th division officers was kind enough to censor it for me.

It is quite a town they have large iron smelters and carry the ore several miles from the mines to the smelters by means of aerial tramway. (I guess this is what they call them.) It is simply a string of big buckets on a long cable or series of cables (sort of endless chain) and it is quite a sight to see all that line of buckets moving along the skyline as far as one can see in either direction. That might be used at mining at Spurgeon where the shaft is very far from the mill. Well, I do not know much to write so will close for this time.

Sincerely yours, Orval

*1918. One franc, dated 1914, sent to Mr. Wills at Bank of Neosho.*

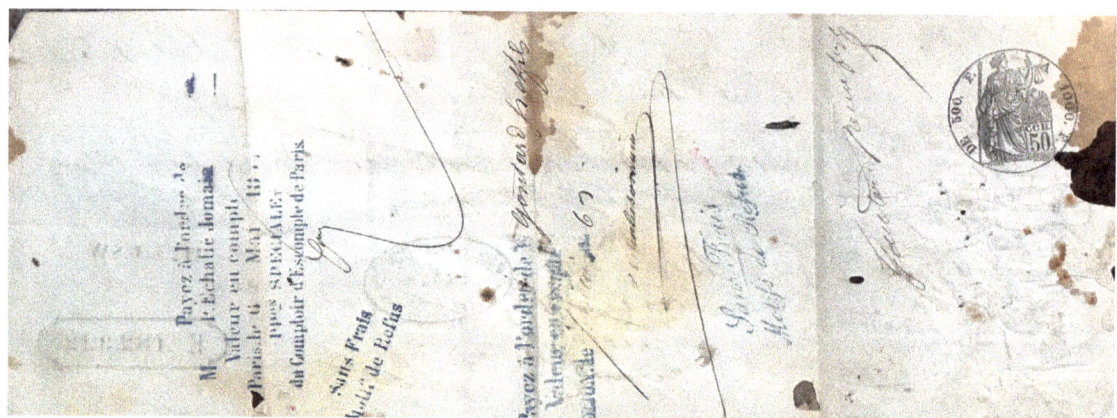

*French cancelled money order, dated April 2, 1863, for the sum of 608.70 francs, from Jorden de P. Echalie Jomain payable to the order of the Paris discount counter. Discovered in 1918 by Orval Epperson in Marigny le Cohouet, France (now over 170 years old)*

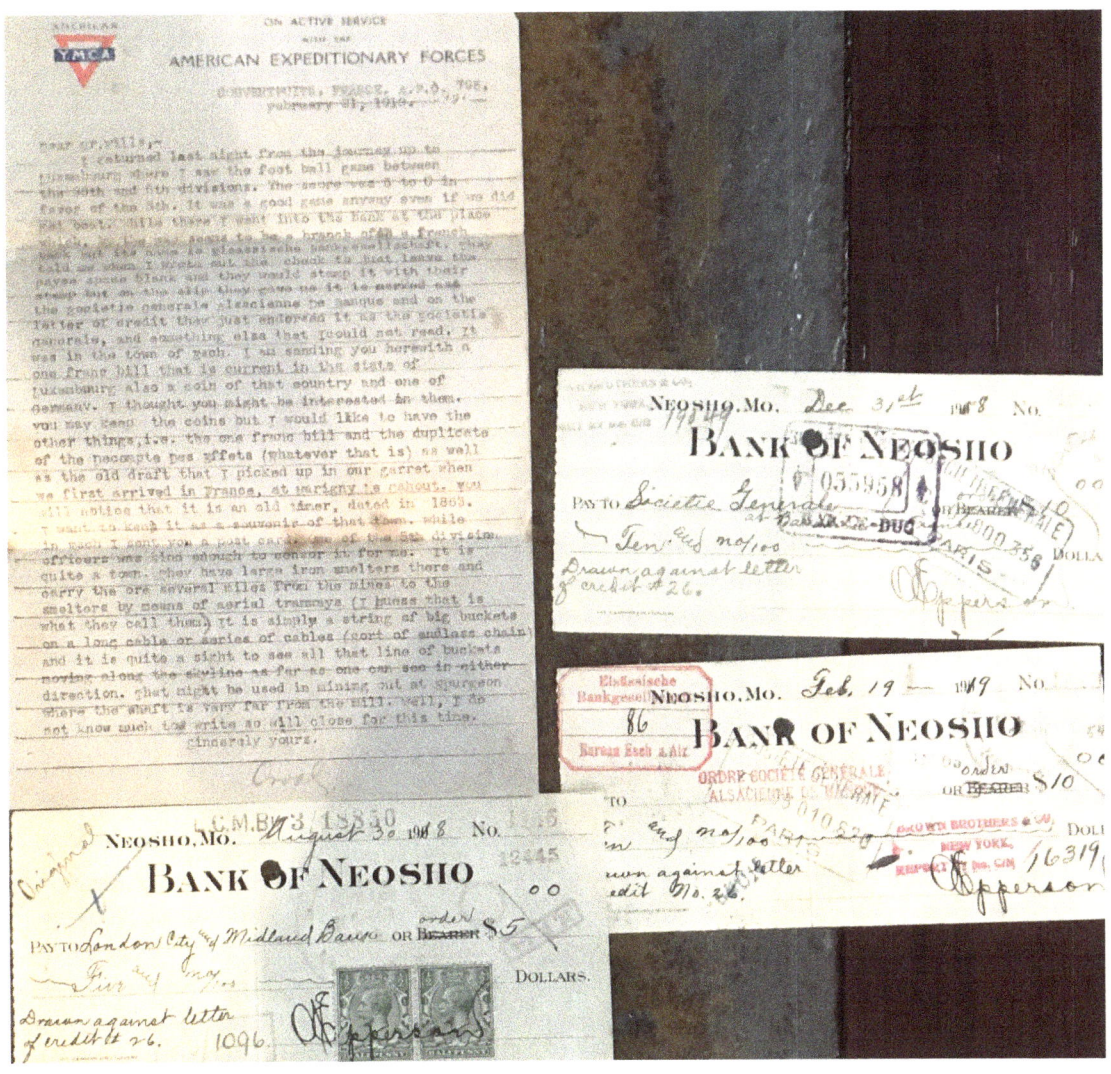

*February 21, 1919. Letter from Orval W. Epperson to Mr. Wills at Bank of Neosho and canceled checks written by Orval while stationed in France during WWI. One dated, August 30, 1918 from London City and Midland Bank for $5. Another dated December 31, 1918 from Societe Generale for $10, and another dated February 19, 1919 from Odre Society General for $10.*

When I wrote to Therese, I addressed her by many nicknames ranging from "Trix," and "Dearest Kittie," to "The Girl I left behind," or "One I hope to see soon," or "One I am coming back to." I signed my letters as Epp, Orval, and O.E.

During October and November 1918, I sent postcards after we crossed over the Vosges, a range of low mountains in eastern France bordering Germany. The valley was beautiful to behold with cows roaming the grassy pastures, but the mountain range was challenging to cross, and I said as much in one of my postcards, from Le Drumont, a small farm village at the summit of the Vosges mountains at an altitude of nearly a mile. "Another scene which gives you an idea of the country. It is alright for seeing but not so nice for marching. Epp."

I sent several postcards to Therese from **Lepuix, France** set in Les Vosges mountain region. It would have been an idyllic little town tucked in the valley, if it weren't so close to the front line. I lived there for several weeks and our offices were about 50 feet from the church, whose unwelcomed bells rang loud and incessantly, day and night. On occasion, I traveled to the division headquarters in **Belfort**, nearly 200 miles south, for correspondence and requisitions.

From December 1918 through February 1919, I was stationed in **Bar-le-Duc**, in the region of Lorraine in northeastern France. The town was known to be artistic and full of architectural history, but to us, it was the beginning of the Voie Sacrée (Sacred Way), the road that ended at the Verdun battlefield.

Our troop then moved to **Ligny-en-Barrois**, an arrondissement of Bar-le-Duc, about 10 miles south that followed the canal that linked the rivers, Rhine and Marne. I had marked an X on the very store from where I purchased the postcard, named Imprimerie Papeterie. The storefront was under the Fournitures de Bureaux and just behind the bronze statue of General Barrios, Earl of the Empire in 1774. One evening a Lieutenant, Captain, and two privates, and I drove the thirty-mile route to **Couvertpuis,** where we took in a real supper that lasted late into the evening and returned content to our billets with only a candle for a headlight.

Late January to late February 1919, I was stationed in Couvertpuis, and I sent Therese a pressed flower love letter written in French. I was also able to write a long letter as we rode to **Esch-Alzette, Luxembourg** where I gave her a rudimentary description of war-torn France and Germany. We thought we would have to assist the Army of Occupation (troops assigned to serve Germany after the war), and traveled in crowded convoy trucks over what used to be the front and into enemy territory. When we arrived to the ruins of Luxembourg, we slept on the floors of desolate and vacant buildings, with only wood shavings for comfort. The city had been occupied by the Germans during the war, and some areas were off limits because of the widespread sexually transmitted diseases found there. I managed to cash a check at a bank and sent some German and Belgium coins to Mr. Wills at the bank, and to my mother. Upon leaving Luxembourg, the locals pitied us when they found out that some of us were destined for Germany.

In March 1919, postwar France had limited supplies, so I used what I could and wrote, "Must write cards. All I get. I need more envelopes. Red Cross had given all theirs away today. Am writing a rather extended letter and mail it as soon as I can get an envelope. Our organization proceedings are moving smoothly, and we are moving well. Moved three times yesterday. Each one has a certain bunk assigned him, and until he finds it, he keeps moving. Think I have located mine at last. Will write more later. Epp."

The last group of postcards were sent on April 20, 1919. It was Easter Sunday, I was alone, and had a weekend pass, so I wandered the streets of **Lyons, France**, where I found evidence of the DeBrosse family name. I wasn't sure of Therese's heritage, but I found it interesting that the names were so similar.

*October and November 1918. Les Vosges, Lepuix-Gy, Vue Generale. The building marked X was our offices and 50 feet from there was the local church where the bells bothered us continually. I was billeted in a house (circled) which was a short walk to the military offices.*

*November 1918. I often passed by the large Belfort lion on my way to Division headquarters in Belfort, which stood 36 feet tall and 72 feet across, made entirely of red sandstone, and symbolized the heroic French resistance. It was built in 1880 by Frederic Bartholdi, the artist who sculptured the Statue of Liberty.*

*December 31, 1918. Ligny-en-Barrois (Meuse) – Place Nationale et Marie. To the Girl I left behind me. Purchased this card at the place marked X, Imprimerie Papeterie. Took a real supper in the town of Couvertpuis. Two privates, myself, a captain, and a 1st Lieutenant occupied a table exclusively and I enjoyed myself quite a bit. Came back with only a candle for a headlight.*

*January 28, 1919. Pressed flowered letter stamped 'passed as censored' with a French love letter. Tout passe avec le temps, Le Temps passe Lui Meme. Mais mon Amour pour vous. Sera toujours le meme (Delille). Miss Therese DeBrosse. "Me," Epp. Avec les Meilleurs Voeux, Et Souhaits pour une, Bonne et heureuse Annee (rough translation: everything passes with time, but my love for you will always be the same)..*

*April 20, 1919. Easter Sunday. Lyon– Vue Generale su la Saone. Let's take a ride down the river. Doesn't the stream look inviting? The Saone is quite a nice river. There is a Debrousse Hospital. Notice the similarity of name? Did your folks come from this part of France? I did not have opportunity to learn much about this institution. I saw it on Easter morning about one o'clock a.m. Rather early wasn't it? Am now on board the train to go back to Beaune. Spent a weekend pass to Lyon. Was sure I'll go back all the time. Saw a lot of scenery today. Wish you could have taken in the sights here with me. Orval.*

Couvertpuis, France. A.P.O. 795 A.E.F. February 22, 1919

Dearest Kiddie –

I just thought I had better write you today to let you know I arrived safely at the same old burg after my trip to the land of Luxembourg. I had quite a trip over some hotly contested territory that had originally been the front. I will give you a general outline of the route taken so you will be able to trace it on the map I sent you some time ago.

We left Couvertpuis about seven o'clock Tuesday morning and went by way of Traverey and Hevillers to Menucourt where we joined the convoy or train of trucks from all over the divisional area. There were 17 of the Liberty and Packard trucks and quite a few little Fords for the officers to ride in. We did not have much room in our trucks either, for there were 27 and part of the time 28 of us in the back part, besides the three in the front seat including the driver and assistant. We then went by way of Ligny and up the big hill there which by the way is more than two miles of steady climb and pretty steep most of the way, too. We then went through Commercy and on in a north easterly direction to the shot up territory in the vicinity of the Limey and Flirey, passing through both towns hence east to Pont-a-Mousson, which by the way means 'Bridge of the Mousson.' And there crossed the aforesaid river and proceeded north near the river through the suburbs of Metz and other towns on the road to Esch, Luxembourg.

Arrived there about eleven o'clock at night and by the time we were herded through the streets to our sleeping quarters, we were ready to go to sleep. They put a lot of excelsior (soft shavings) on the floor of a vacant building and I was crowded in one corner of a place just long enough for me and about a foot and a half wide. I slept fairly well, however, we got up rather early next morning and began stirring around town.

The Insignia of the 88th was seen all over town. NO! I will have to take that back. There were several streets that had the sign on each corner 'Off Limits,' and to take it doubly sure had guards stationed at various intervals to see that no soldier passed up or down those streets. The town had formally been open all over, but the medical authorities finally objected because there were certain diseases that were being spread by reasons of the visits made there by the boys so they had to forbid them to visit their fair frauleins. Since then, I hear that the damsels just transferred the scene of their activities to another street or streets.

I just bummed around during the morning and bought a few postcards and sent some home. One of the 5th division lieutenants was kind enough to censor them, and I mailed them in the A.P.P. 745. However, my address remains the same (795). While in that town, I also went into the bank there and cashed my check for $10.00. That makes three different countries in which I have cashed my personal checks on the Bank of Neosho. One in England, one in France and one in Luxembourg. Don't suppose I will cash anymore unless I visit some other country as I just cash them to have them as souvenirs when I get back and just to see if I could do it. I also got some queer money in change when I would buy anything. Among other things were Belgian and German coins besides Luxembourg currency. I sent W.G.W a few of them and also some to mamma and if I have room in this envelope, I will send you a bunch of them, too. That was about all I brought back in the way of souvenirs, I could have bought some iron crosses and helmets but did not.

We had quite a bit of fun along the road in addition to seeing the towns or rather heaps of ruins in the shot up territory. When we would go through a town, we made an imposing spectacle, and when it looked like our division might be moving, they would ask where we were going and we would say Germany, and they would look with pity on us just to show us how sorry they were for us. If we had been going to stay I expect we would have appreciated their sympathy, too. I don't think there will be any of us drafted men in the army of occupation if they can get enough of the regular army men to do it.

Well, will write again later when I get some spare time.

Lovingly yours,

Orval

# Couvertpuis, France

Months after the war ended, any hope for an early return home slowly diminished. We were ordered to salvage the aftereffects of the war and duties were divided between the troops. The Division was tasked with removing from the battle area all traces of four years of bitter war. We were billeted in the small village of Couvertpuis. The name meant "covered wells," and the town got its drinking water from those wells. But not all of our company made it to Couvertpuis. The American Camp at Allerey, a small village nearby was where an immense hospital-camp was set up to care for the wounded-sick that arrived by the hundreds, fresh off the train from the front. Those who were injured went there, those who were not joined us at Couvertpuis.

*Postcard of Couvertpuis (Meuse) Le Pont. My sleeping quarters marked X. Some barn loft, too! Some of the boys have straw and hay under them ten feet deep.*

The townspeople had to put up the soldiers in their homes. Running up the side of each front door was a billet list with so many officers and so many men assigned to that particular residence. Houses were made of solid stone and roofed over with clay tiles, all joined to each other and all faced out onto the street. All the residents from Couvertpuis lived right there in town and each house had a little tract of land outside of town, instead of attached to the house. Just beyond the street was a little crocked stream, and all the houses followed the bend of that stream.

We didn't happen to have any officers in our billet, but there were about eight men, including a friend from home, John Proctor, from Diamond, Missouri. We were billeted in the home of Shotgun Liz, as she came to be known. She lived with her husband who was disabled and they were quite a pair. Her mother-in-law also lived with them, and her brother lived right next door with just an entryway separating the two homes and a solid wall the length of the houses that opened to their shared backyard where livestock was kept. The house was arranged with the living room, dining room, and kitchen all combined.

They had a long iron rod hanging from the chimney where they hung their pots and another pole stretched across the ceiling where they strung their bread like doughnuts. They would bake only once a week, or maybe even less than that, and hang the bread on the pole. When you wanted some bread to eat, you would just slice a piece off. It would get pretty dry, but we ate it just the same. They also hung their meat there, supposedly away from mice and rats. They didn't have an oven, but rather a big, open fireplace where they used faggots (little bundles of brush) instead of logs. They had a little bellow to blow the wind, and a little three-legged tripod they used for cooking. Nearby was bacon rind on a stick that was used to grease the pans.

They had a horse, and a sort of a wagon they would hitch it to, and rode that out to their fields. Land was so valuable that there were no fences. They just knew where their property began and ended and cultivated right up to the line. Together, the townspeople grew wheat, and the menfolk, as a group, would go out to cut it, bind it in sheaves, and bring it back to town in their little wagons.

Shot Gun Liz had a little coffee pot of a threshing machine, which she used to thresh their wheat. Liz and her mother-in-law would manually turn the crank to operate the machine, while her husband fed the grain in. Her brother would have a bucket or something there to catch the wheat as it threshed. Then they would tie the straw in little bundles and toss those aside. It seemed like the women did all the hard work. They had the labor intensive job of grinding the wheat, while the men did the light work of just collecting it.

They didn't eat a lot of meat, but when it came time to butcher, they did things differently. Now, down on the farm in Anderson, when we'd get a hog up there, we would hit it in the head with an axe, take a knife, and bleed it out, so the blood wouldn't be all shot through the meat. We didn't keep the blood; it would just be wasted. But over in France, they didn't do that. Instead of knocking it in the head, they would get it down on the floor, and tie its legs down, then jab a knife in its jugular vein to drain the blood, which was then used for blood sausage. They also used the hog's intestines as casing for sausage, like wienies.

Before we left Couvertpuis, we wanted to take something to remind us of our time there, so we all chipped in and bought a Kodak camera, and took a lot of pictures. When we got ready to leave, one man was supposed to sell the camera, and use the proceeds to send us the pictures. But he didn't, and I never saw any of the pictures, or I would have had a lot more memories of Couvertpuis. There is only one known photo of the group, taken on February 28, 1919, and I sat front and center holding the frying pan.

*February 28, 1919, Couvertpuis, France. Orval Epperson, holding frying pan, front and center. Left to right and numbered: Honee, Harmon, Jermstad, Eugwall, Schmitz, Miller, Busner, Hartwig, Rawlins, Epperson, Peterson, Spart, Green, Strom, Buzzard, Cearz, Ichmalll.*

# Memoirs of France and 88th Division

There is a book published years ago called *Memoirs of France and the Eighty-Eighth Division*, by Edgar J. Dwight Larson, and I submitted a short story that was printed in the book.

**Adventures of Couvertpuis**

After the Armistice was signed and the 338th Machine Gun Battalion was snugly billeted in the little town of Couvertpuis, in the Province of Meuse, it seemed the chief ambition of the Headquarters bunch was to dodge as many details as possible and spend their leisure moments in the neighboring town of Morley, where no Americans were quartered and there were no "off limit" signs to mar their pleasure. Part of the Headquarters Co. was billeted in a combination house and barn belonging to Mr. and Mrs. Henri Rochere. The latter was nicknamed by the boys "Shot Gun Liz" much to her chagrin. In fact, this name was so distasteful to her that at the mere mention of it she would pick up her broom and pursue the offender.

Our sleeping quarters were in a loft which was reached by a ladder and also by the odors from the cows, pigs, horses, and the ever present manure pile. To get to this ladder, it was necessary to go through the front room. The inhabitants of this loft, besides the rats and cooties, were Corp. Orval William Epperson (in charge), Private Ernest M. (Gun Boat) Smith, Private Loren (Affidavit) Buck, Private Andrew G. Anderson, Private George States, Wagoner Axel Jermstad, Wagoner Thomas (Red) Nagle and Wagoner John Proctor.

One night after taps had sounded, our attention was attracted to noises downstairs. This proved to be Wagoner Jermstad returning from an afternoon and evening at Morley where he was with a fair mademoiselle who very graciously smiled on him as she poured him his 'encore cognac" and took his francs.

The Rocheres had killed a hog that day and hung it just inside the front door, and as he was groping his way toward the ladder, leading to the loft, he grasped the suspended hog in his arms, which at every advanced step pushed him backwards. Jerry, feeling that he was making no progress in reaching his sleeping quarters, began to call aloud: "Erikson, Erikson, someone is trying to knock me down!"

Jerry had dallied in the café until it had closed, and he now wondered if that had not been too long. He finally mounted the ladder to the loft without any assistance and after lighting a candle, prepared to get into bed, removing his hat, coat, and shirt. His other wearing apparel consisted of boots, trousers, etc. were left on. He had no sooner reached the bed that he decided he was sick and asked "Gun Boat" Smith to take him to the Infirmary. His requests being ignored started down the ladder, sans hat, coat or shirt. Smith, who had been feigning sleep, seeing his rifle disappear, yelled for him to come back and wait until morning when the ambulance would come for him.

Jermstad complied and crawled into bed and soon began begging Smith to come and see what was on his feet, something that was in bed with him. The "something" proved to be his boots, which he had forgotten to remove. Later he was disturbed by the mournful wailings of a cat somewhere in the darkness, and crawled out of bed, taking Smith's shoe in one hand and a lighted candle in the other and started out in pursuit of the offender. The "Cat" which proved to be Corporal Epperson, immediately ceased his whining until Jerry was snugly tucked in his bed again.

It may be interesting to relate here how a few of our Headquarters' boys earned the titles they bore.

One wintry night when the thermometer stood about 2 below by the centigrade, our reputed champion checkers player, Private Ernest M. Smith, his favorite cigar tucked at the usual angle of 45 degrees from the right corner of his mouth, his cap pulled over his left ear to balance his head, sallied forth with intention of extending his conquests in his much loved game. The darkness of the night, further intensified by the fact that he had just come from the house brilliantly lighted by two tallow candles, blinded him to such an extent that his footsteps strayed from the narrow road and before he realized it he was plunging headlong into a creek, which flowed between banks about 5 feet high, and was only a few feet from the road at this point.

Ordinarily a "cootie" could swim it with ease, but recent rains had transformed it into a stream of considerable depth. When he came up sputtering he was minus both cap and cigar. The former was recovered the next day with the aid of a pole, but the cigar was not found. No doubt if the villagers had known that beneath that foot of mud lay one cigar that had been barely lighted they would probably be endeavoring yet to find it. He scrambled up the bank and hurriedly retraced his steps, his only thought being to get warm and dry. His ardor for checkers was cooled for the time. As his wardrobe consisted of what he was wearing at the time of his plunge the only thing left for him to do was to go to bed and have his clothes put by the fireside to dry. His chief regret was that this plunge had not occurred earlier in the week as he had already taken the weekly bath which was compulsory. It was not to his liking to take two baths in one week. From this date, he was named, "Gun Boat" Smith.

Private Loren Buck was assistant to the billeting officer. A certain Frenchman missed about 8 feet of gutter pipe from his building and suspicioning some American was using it for a stovepipe put in a claim against the United States for the loss of it. Buck was given the task of getting affidavits to either establish or reject this claim. He loyally performed this work by hiding out each morning after mess, his refuge being at the fireside of "Shot Gun Liz" mother-in-law, where he and Corporal Epperson would "parler" with her and incidentally persuade her to fry "duo oeufs"; and by paying "cinq francs" and supplying "graisse" and "sucre", induce her to furnish the balance of the ingredients to make "gaufres."

She would squat in the center of the hearth with batter on one side and bacon rind with which to grease the waffle iron on the other. During these morning socials, Minnie, the cat, and Henri, the dog, would sit at opposite ends of the fireplace and wistfully await an opportunity to partake of the dainties. If the old lady's back was turned, Minnie would avail herself of the chance to lick the surplus grease from the bacon rind while Henri would lap a few mouthfuls of the batter. She would yell, "Allez, Allez," which meant "Go on, Scat." Nevertheless, we ate them with as much relish as if they had been cooked in the most sanitary kitchen. After spending a week thus, Buck's ruse was found out with the result that he was sent to school at St. Joire as punishment, but the nickname "Affidavit Buck" stuck.

O.W. EPPERSON, NEOSHO MISSOURI

338th MACHINE GUN BATTALION

HEADQUARTERS 338TH, Machine Gun Battalion:

Epperson, Orval W., Corp., Anderson, Mo.

Jermstad, Axel, Wag., Aneta, N D.

Nagle, Thomas A., Wag. McCausland, Iowa.

Proctor, John A., Wag., Joplin, Mo.

Anderson, Andrew G., Pvt., 210 15rd St., Duluth, Minn.

Buck, Loren, Pvt., 3205 Elliot St., Minneapolis.

Smith, Ernest M., Pvt., Atchison, Kan.

States, George E., Pvt., Topeka, Kan.

# American Expeditionary Forces University

In February of 1919, the army started the American Expeditionary Forces University (A.E.F. University) in Beaune, France, where it remained in operation until June of that year, had 9,500 students, and over 600 professors. The university was on the site of a former military hospital that had been hastily built in just four months.

Anybody that wanted to go to school could apply, but very few were selected. Out of the 800 or so men in the 338th Battalion, I was one of only four chosen to attend. On the application you had to tell why you wanted to go to the University and what classes you wanted to take, such as architecture, accounting, commercial law, business organization. I gave them my background, that I had been with the Bank of Neosho for so long, and I was a Director of the Bank, and that I was also President of Thurmond-Davis Grain Company, which I had started with Bill Thurmond and C.E. Davis, and so on. Once I received notice of my acceptance, I left all my buddies behind at Couvertpuis, and was shipped to Beaune, France, where I took classes in Commercial Law, Business mathematics, and the like.

There was a mess hall at the University and it was set up similar to the army, where one entire Company went through the line before the next Company could eat. Well, just as I entered the long line to the mess hall, there was Bryan Davis, son of C.E. Davis, my business partner, standing in the line. He didn't even know that I was in the army. He was from the 89th Division and I was from the 88th Division, and we got reacquainted and spent the next few months recounting our adventures.

My time at the A.E.F. University was the first time I was able to sit down and read a newspaper, *The Stars and Stripes*. I kept one as a memento. It was dated Friday, April 25, 1919, and recounted the day of Armistice, "Yanks advancing east of Meuse on eve of Armistice. Powerful attacks stopped only by cessation of hostilities. Close union with the French." Two months after this paper was written, I was on a ship heading home.

*April 25, 1919. Stars and Stripes Official Newspaper of the A.E.F.*

# Time to Go Home

When it came time to go home, I was supposed to rejoin my company stationed in Couvertpuis. We had heard that the 88th Division was due to leave soon and waited for our orders, and waited, and waited, until finally we got word to join them at the coast of France at Saint-Nazaire.

Saint-Nazaire was one of the most important harbors for France and western Europe. It was full of Americans and was known to be the gateway for jazz music into Europe. Between 1917 and 1919, almost 198,000 troops, and a daily average of 4,000 tons of material transited through Saint-Nazaire.

A bunch of us went down there, reported to our Company, where an old sergeant informed us, "Well, we already have our sailing list made out. We can't fit you in. You'll have to get back the best way you can."

Each fellow was given his travel orders with his name, address, etc., and we could present it to any Company and get fed wherever we were, and if we wanted to travel on a train or boxcar, we could present our orders and ride for free. It was enjoyable to travel and eat for free in a newly liberated country, so we debated on what to do.

Bryan Davis and I thought, well, we've got travel orders and can be fed anywhere with our service records, so why don't we stay a bit longer to see the sights of Europe? But then we got to thinking, we didn't know how long this would last, and we were kind of homesick anyway, so we passed on the opportunity to explore.

A bunch of us from the University got together and elected a leader and organized ourselves as a Casual Company, attaching to the 313th Engineers. We came home on the ship called U.S.S. Madawaska, which left St. Nazaire, France, May 25, 1919, and arrived two weeks later in Hoboken, New Jersey, on June 6, 1919. From there we were based at Camp Mills in Long Island, New York, for a couple weeks until we were released from the military on June 18, 1919.

Before we left France, however, we had to go through a delouser, to remove any lice that took up residence on our persons. We went into a barracks, took off our clothes, and a fellow with a fire hydrant type hose sprayed a strong soapy solution under our arms, groin, head, everywhere. That was called delousing. We, then, went into a shower room and tried our best to wash the strong odor out of our hair and eyes. Afterwards, we walked to the other side of the barracks where we were issued a fresh set off clothing, except for shoes.

Once we were aboard the ship we would take shirt readings every morning, in case a new crop of nits and things hatched on our clothes. That meant taking off our clothes, and examining every seam in our shirts and pants to see if there were any lice hiding. We would sit on the deck of the ship and read the seams on our shirts. If we found any nits, we would crack them with our fingers.

When we got to New York, we were sent down to yet another delouser, and in addition to stripping down again, everything in our barrack's bag was pulled out, even our wool overcoat and wool shirts, and run through a steam compressor. We would sit there and swap war tales while our clothes were cooking. That high pressure steam killed any residual eggs or nits, but when I got my overcoat back, the wrinkles were permanently set in and I was never able to iron them out. I also brought home a reserve ration of the hardtack biscuit that was given to us while we lived in the trenches, and on the package I typed, "Reserve Ration. Carried in 1918 by O.W. Epperson. Still keeping it in reserves for the next war."

*Reserve rations. Carried in 1918 by O.W. Epperson. Still keeping it in reserves for the next war.*

*June 18, 1919. Honorable Discharge Paper from United States Army. To all whom it may concern, this is to certify that ORVAL W. EPPERSON, 13229296, Cpl. Unassigned last assig 338 M.G.B. The United States Army, as a Testimonial of Honest and Faithful Service, is hereby HONORABLY DISCHARGED from the military service of the United States by reason of: Expiration of the time of service, Per S0168 HQ C.Z. Seq. 6-17-14. Said ORVAL W. EPPERSON was born in Anderson, in the state of Missouri when enlisted he was 26 ½ years old and by the occupation of Banker. He had grey eyes, brown hair, ruddy complexion and was 5 feet 10 inches in height. Given under my hand at Camp Zachary Taylor KY this 18 day of June, one-thousand-nine-hundred-and nineteen. Arthur J. Taylor, Major FA, USA Commanding.*

# PART VI
# THE MARRIED YEARS

*THERESE VISITS MY FOLKS AT HOME*

*THERESE DEBROSSE AND ORVAL EPPERSON MARRY*

*344 SOUTH HAMILTON DEEDS*

*MARRIED LIFE AND CHILDREN*

*OUR SON BILLY*

*CORRESPONDENCE WITH ROMERE MARTIN*

*GRANDFATHER GEORGE WASHINGTON EPPERSON*

*MY SIBLINGS AND PARENTS LATER IN LIFE*

*OUR CHILDREN AND GRANDCHILDREN AND GOLDEN WEDDING ANNIVERSARY*

*MY INVESTMENTS*

*ORVAL THE FISHERMAN*

# Therese Visits My Folks at Home

Before I left for France, I went to see Therese while she visited her family in Monett, and in that way, I met her folks. I had to work on Saturday, and was anxious to see her again so I rode a bicycle there on Sunday, a distance of over 25 miles. The local newspaper reported on my visit to Monett, but perhaps not wanting to acknowledge the courtship of one of their town darlings, the Society Page kept us far apart. That weekend, May 13, 1918, the *Monett Times*, reported on different columns, "Miss Therese DeBrosse of Neosho visited her parents here Sunday," and at the very end of the page, "O.W. Epperson of Neosho visited friends here Sunday."

While I was in France, Therese would visit my family at the Epperson farm, near Anderson, and it thrilled my mother. She took photos of my beautiful Therese at every opportunity; while she sat on a bridge, or tossed feed to the chickens, or even as she spent time with my much younger siblings. My brother Jim, was ten years younger than I, Graydon Love was fourteen years younger, and my baby sister, Ina, was eighteen years younger.

*1918. Therese DeBrosse at Epperson Farm with Ina (age 9) holding farm dog, and Jim (age 16) holding a cow with Ina.*

*September 1, 1918. Therese DeBrosse at Epperson farm tossing feed to chickens, and on wooden bridge near creek.*

Years later, when the Bank of Neosho asked Therese to write a short biography on me, she recalled visits to the farm and stories about my early life.

The subject of 'This is Your Life' was born on a farm about a mile east of Anderson on October 13, 1891. He lived on a farm near Siloam Springs a few years, and when he was five years old, he moved to a farm near Adair, Oklahoma. From there his parents moved by covered wagon, back to another farm east of Anderson, where Orval began his formal education. He walked a mile and a half each way to the nearest school at Old Beaver Springs Park and was able to start in the second grade because his primary learning had been acquired from newspapers that covered the walls of the one-room house where he lived in Oklahoma. As a boy, he loved to fish and would walk barefoot down to the creek bank. It was also his job to keep mice out of the flour barrel.

In September 1907, he enrolled as a sophomore at Neosho High School, which was located on the hill where the CRC building now stands. He stayed at the home of the school's janitor, George Proctor, and helped him before and after school for his board and room, which amounted to $2.50 a week. In order to make some spending money, he worked for neighbors on either sides of where he lived. He fed and curried Mrs. Hawkins' horse for 50 cents a week and split wood for Mr. Smith on Saturdays for 10 cents an hour.

In December of that same year, Willie Wills, cashier of the bank, asked the Superintendent of the Schools, W.E. Veerkamp, to find a student who would like to learn the banking business. Orval's teachers, among them Mrs. Ray Daugherty, recommended Orval for the job, which he enthusiastically accepted at a salary of six dollars a week.

His working hours were ONLY from 7:00a.m. in the morning to 8:00p.m. at night or until the work was finished. His duties included chasing dust with an old feather duster, which only stirred it up. In winter, the old coal stove constantly put out soot and ashes, which settled on everything, and in summer unpaved streets provided plenty of dust through the open windows and doors. Orval posted the individual ledger with pen and ink, without any adding machine to prove it, and wrote remittances.

In his eagerness to learn more about other bank operations, one day he was looking through the general ledger kept by the assistant cashier. When the assistant cashier discovered him, he told him in no uncertain terms to keep his nose in his own books ONLY. His reason was disclosed a few months later when the bank examiner found the assistant cashier was short several thousand dollars in his accounts.

Orval then assumed the duties of the assistant cashier but without the title until he became twenty-one-years-old. When he reached 21, he was permitted to buy 10 shares of stock to be paid for on the installment plan and was made assistant cashier at a salary of $50 a month. His next advancement was being selected to the board of directors and being made secretary of the board. In the meantime, he had taken a correspondence course in commercial law and negotiable instruments. From early on in his banking days, he would save unique and outdated currency, either in coin or paper. He especially collected two-dollar bills, civil war currency and collectable coins.

At the time Orval was called to the military service in 1918, he was making $100 a month. He served overseas in the 338th Machine Gun Battalion and after the Armistice. While waiting to come home, he studied higher accounting, business organization and commercial law at the A.E.F University in Beaune, France. To pass the time, he would play the card game, Pinochle, a game he still enjoys.

The military gave him money to buy new shoes because his toes were sticking out from the hundreds of miles that he walked. With the money, he bought a new hat instead, and has worn a hat ever since. He was discharged in June 1919.

# Therese DeBrosse and Orval Epperson Marry

*Therese Gertrude DeBrosse*

The summer I returned from war, Therese and I were married, on July 4, 1919. She had the sweetest giggle, and when she was with her sisters, it was contagious, and became known as the DeBrosse giggles. I was desperate to hear her sweet voice again.

I had sent Therese a telegram to tell her I was on my way home. I left St. Nazaire, France, on May 25, 1919, and arrived in the States two weeks later. Therese had been staying with her folks in Monett for her vacation the week before I arrived. After being released from Camp Mills, I made my way home by train, and arrived on the first of July. That was a Tuesday, and by Friday of that week, we were married. I rented a little buggy and we road it to Stilwell, Oklahoma, where we secretly married at the County Courthouse. Afterwards, we had a short weekend honeymoon in Siloam Springs, Arkansas.

Our Oklahoma marriage license stated that I was from Westville, Oklahoma, in Adair County, and Therese was from Springfield, Missouri, in Green County. It wasn't a bold lie. We both lived in those towns at one point in our lives. And, of course, we thought that would buy us some time before we would have to tell our family and friends. We didn't have anyone standing for us and neither did the couple before us, so I became the witness to the marriage of Claude Brogden and Opal Walker and the witnesses for our marriage were Charles Williams and Ruby Lee, all strangers. We would have kept it a secret longer if it weren't for a fellow Neosho businessman traveling to Stilwell, Oklahoma nearly one week later, who saw the name, Orval Epperson, in the marriage license section of the *Standard-Sentinel Newspaper, Official Organ of Adair County, Oklahoma*, Thursday, July 10, 1919, "Orval W. Epperson, 27 Westville. Miss Thelma [sic] G. DeBrosse, Springfield, Mo." Once the news was out, the entire southwest Missouri was abuzz, and every local paper covered it.

*Neosho Daily Democrat*, August 14, 1919

> Epperson–DeBrosse. News of the marriage of Orval W. Epperson, Assistant Cashier of the Bank of Neosho, and Miss Therese de Brosse [sic] which took place July 4 became public only a few days ago.
>
> Friends of the young couple expected the event soon after Mr. Epperson's return from army service, and they were greatly surprised when they learned that the event had taken place as they expected, but that they were not let into the secret. They were married at Stilwell, Oklahoma, on the 4th of July and returned to Neosho on the 5th.
>
> The bride's home was at Monett, but she has been employed as a stenographer in Neosho for several years, first with the Shartel Mortgage Co., and lately with the Neosho Nurseries Co.
>
> Mr. Epperson's parents live in McDonald county, but he has been in Neosho as assistant cashier of the Bank of Neosho for a number of years. He was with the A.E.F. in France for over a year and returned about six weeks ago to resume his old position with the bank.
>
> Mr. and Mrs. Epperson are not keeping house now but have purchased the W. B. Keller home at 408 South Hamilton St., already furnished, and will occupy same within a short time.

*Joplin News Herald*, August 17, 1919

> Kept Wedding Secret. NEOSHO, MO. – The fact that Orval W. Epperson, assistant cashier of the Bank of Neosho, and Miss Therese DeBrosse were married at Stilwell, Ok., on July 4 has just been learned by their many friends in this city, a Neosho man having stumbled on the news while on business in Stilwell.
>
> Their wedding was expected by their friends soon after the arrival of Mr. Epperson, the first of July from a year's service with the A.E.F., but even their intimate friends had no knowledge that the ceremony took place so soon after his return.
>
> Mr. Epperson has been employed at the Bank of Neosho for ten years, coming here from McDonald County, where his parents still reside.

His bride comes from Monett but has been here the past few years as stenographer for the Shartel Mortgage Company and the Neosho Nurseries Company.

They will reside at 408 Hamilton street, which they purchased.

*Monett Times,* August 22, 1919

EPPERSON- DEBROSSE.

News of the marriage of Mr. Orval W. Epperson, cashier of the Bank of Neosho and Miss Therese G. DeBrosse, which took place July 4th became public only a few days ago.

Friends of the young couple expected this event soon after Mr. Epperson's return from army service and they were greatly surprised when they learned that the event had taken place as they expected, but that they were not let in on the secret.

The bride is the youngest daughter of Mr. and Mrs. Eli DeBrosse of this city and has grown to womanhood here. She has been employed as a stenographer in Neosho for several years, first with the Shartel Mortgage Co. and lately with the Neosho Nurseries Co.

Mr. Epperson's parents live in McDonald County but he has been with the Bank of Neosho for the past 11 years.

He was with the A.E.F. in France for over a year and returned about six weeks ago to resume his old position with the bank.

Mr. and Mrs. Epperson have purchased the home of the Vice President of the Bank of Neosho, Mr. W.B. Keller, and will occupy the same within a short time.

*Oklahoma, County Marriage Records July 4, 1919*

*MARRIAGE LICENSE*

*State of Oklahoma, Adair County. In County Court to any person authorized to Perform and Solemnize the Marriage Ceremony, Greeting: You are hereby authorized to join in marriage Mr. Orval W. Epperson of Westville, County of Adair, State of Oklahoma, aged 27 years and Miss Therese G. DeBrosse of Springfield, County of Greene, State of Missouri, aged 22 years.*

*And of this License you will make due return to my office within 30 days from this date.*

*Witness my land and office seal, this 4th day of July A.D. 1919.*

*R.D. Holland, County Clerk*
*By Lora T. Browning, Deputy*
*Recorded this 5th day of July, 1919 R. D Holland*

*CERTIFICATE OF MARRIAGE*

*State of Oklahoma, Adair County*

*I, O.D. Snell, Minister of the Gospel, Stilwell M.E. Church South of Stilwell in Adair County State of Oklahoma do hereby certify that I joined in marriage the persons named in and authorized by this License to be married, on the 4th day of July A.D. 1919 at Stilwell in Adair County, State of Oklahoma, in the presence of Bessie Snell of Stilwell, Okla. and Orval W. Epperson, of Neosho, Mo.*

*O.D. Snell, Minister of the Gospel*
*Returned and recorded on this 5th day of July 1919. R.D. Holland, County Clerk*

# 344 South Hamilton Deeds

*344 South Hamilton*

We had been living at 408 Hamilton Street, just one house away from our dream home at 344 Hamilton. We both admired the large estate and fancied one day living there. It was a stylish Queen Anne Victorian home in the English Baroque architecture that was revived and popularized from 1880 through 1910.

Our dreams came true in 1921, after it went on the market. It was originally built by Dr. Henry Mixer, a surgeon from Ohio in 1890s, and he lived there with his wife, Mary Mixer, their daughter Mary P. Briggs, son-in-law Franz Briggs, who ran the hardware store. It was the first home built in the Hamilton Terrace district. The other four homes were built from a single builder, at the turn-of-the-century, in 1905.

In March 1921, I purchased it for $9,000 with two loans; one for $2,000 from J.H. Kraft, and the larger amount of $4,000 from my employer, Mr. Wills, at the Bank of Neosho. Our small family moved into the large, sprawling estate where we spent the rest of our lives.

There were three Deeds for 344 South Hamilton, the original deed written in 1896, my purchase in 1921, and the addition of our daughters in 1977.

The first Quit-Claim Deed for 344 Hamilton, dated, June 20, 1896, was for one dollar, and was between John T. McElhany and his wife Mary V. McElhany, and M.P. Mixer (grantor of Benjamin Eiseman assignee), in the Recorder Office of Newton County, Missouri. It might be worth noting that John T. McElhany was the leading business merchant and the largest real estate owner in Newton County in the early 1890's, and as such was perhaps the most influential citizen in the area. However, he met with financial reverses in the business depression of 1896, his store went into receivership, and his extensive real estate holdings were taken over and sold. That was perhaps how M.P. Mixer was able to purchase the land on which 344 would be built.

> All that tract in the city of Neosho, consisting of the larger and southern part of what is commonly called fractional lot five (5) in said city bounded beginning on one-hundred-sixty-five feet (165) south of the south east corner of block number ten (10) of said city on Hamilton Street and returning south to McKinney Street (otherwise known as Stanton Avenue) on the north of Abbott's Addition, thence west to Lafayette Street, then north with Lafayette Street to within one hundred and sixty-five feet (165) of the southwest corner of said block number ten (10) then east to point of beginning.

I became the second owner, 25 years later, for the price of $9,000. The indenture was made on the 9th day of March, 1921, between Mary P. Mixer, a widow of Green County, Missouri, and O.W. Epperson, of Newton County, Missouri.

> The sum of Nine Thousand Dollars. All that part of fractional lot five (5) in the town, now city, of Neosho proper, bounded and described as follows:
>
> Beginning 165 feet south of the southeast corner of block ten (10) of said Neosho proper on Hamilton street, thence, on the west line of Hamilton street, to McKinney street, thence west on the north line of Stanton avenue commonly called McKinney street to Lafayette street, thence north on the east line of Lafayette street to a point 165 feet south of the southwest corner of block ten (10) of said Neosho proper, thence cast to the place of beginning.
>
> This deed is made subject to two incumbrancers. viz: One in favor of J.H. Kraft for $2000 recorded in the office of the recorder of deeds in mortgage record book 39 at page 418; and also one in favor of W.G. Wills for $4000 recorded in said recorder's office in mortgage record book 51 at page 617, both of which said incumbrancers said grantee assumes and agrees to pay as part of the consideration hereof.

Then 56 years later, the deed was changed to add the daughters, as joint owners with Therese.

> This Quit-Claim Deed made on the 28th day of October 1977 by and between Therese Epperson, a single person, of the County of Newton, State of Missouri, party of the first part, and Therese Epperson, a single person, Joan E. Giles and Tirzah E. Federer, as joint tenants and not as tenants in common in consideration of the sum of one dollar and other good and valuable consideration to her paid by said parties of the second part.

*Quit-Claim Deed 1921 and Survey and Plat of Fractional Lot 5*

# Married Life and Children

*Mr. and Mrs. O.W. Epperson*

We hadn't been married for long when we decided to line my old army buddy, John Proctor from Diamond, with Therese's best friend, Helen Morse, who was a teacher. We had them over for supper one evening. Therese wanted to make sure everything was ready when they came, so she started hours and hours ahead, boiling the corn so that the cob would be tender. Not being an experienced cook, she didn't realize it was only the kernels that cooked.

Well, those corn cobs never did get tender. And neither did John and Helen. He probably didn't think that evening was much of a recommendation for marriage.

Years later, Helen married someone else, but he was a drunk and a no-account. Helen had her share of hard luck. She taught country school for a while, and he may have kept house when he was sober, but they eventually divorced, and he died not long after.

My mother-in-law, Margaret DeBrosse, and Therese's sister, Grace, came to visit once during our early married years. I volunteered to cook dinner and told them we were having squirrel. But I had been out fishing that day, and caught a great big turtle, so, I cooked that instead.

I took a hatchet and chopped the shell open, and each leg came out by itself. The belly was not edible because it was just a hard plate, but I removed the neck, and chopped it crossways. The rest of the turtle meat was cut up into big chunks and cooked in a nice gravy. I recalled that Therese helped me cook the turtle, but she has since vehemently denied it. At any rate, it was really delicious. Margaret and Grace enjoyed it, too. They even remarked how they had never tasted squirrel before.

Afterwards, I invited them out to the incinerator to see my collection of squirrel skins, and there sitting on top of the incinerator barrel was the big turtle shell, cracked, and broken into pieces, with fresh innards exposed.

They began to get a little pale around the gills, and excused themselves. "We wouldn't have eaten it, had we known what it was beforehand!"

Needless to say, it was awhile before they returned for another visit.

On April 23, 1920, just after Therese's birthday (later confirmed as age twenty-seven), my very pregnant wife and I sacramentally married in the small rectory of St. Canera's church. The short ceremony was performed by Pastor Reverend P. J. Donohue, and witnessed by Therese's parents; Mr. and Mrs. Eloi DeBrosse.

Our firstborn child, Joan Rosalind, was born on Saturday, May 22, 1920. The *Monett Times* reported on May 29, 1920, "Mr. and Mrs. O.W. Epperson of Neosho announce the birth of a daughter on Saturday, May 22. Mrs. Epperson was formally Miss Therese DeBrosse of this city."

*Therese, Orval, and baby Joan Epperson*

The ever curious *Neosho Daily Democrat* continued to report on us. Ever since our sensationalized marriage, the public wanted more on the Eppersons, and it drove Therese crazy. Just two months after moving into our home at 344 Hamilton, a fire broke out. Perhaps Therese was an uneasy cook getting used to her new kitchen, or perhaps she was preoccupied with her nearly one-year-old daughter, Joan, but in any case, on May 20, 1921, it was reported,

> The fire alarm sounded about 8 a.m. today and the fire wagon made a quick run to the home of O.W. Epperson at 344 South Hamilton street. The fire, however, was not a serious one, and the firemen did not have to use their apparatus. An oil stove got out of control and was flaming freely, but no damage was done beyond covering parts of the room with soot.

As our family grew, so did my position at the Bank of Neosho. After the unexpected death of my friend and mentor, Mr. Wills, I was promoted to cashier, a month shy of our son's birth, and on November 11, 1921, the *Monett Times* reported, "O.W. Epperson Elected Cashier. At a meeting of the board of directors of the Bank of Neosho held November 2, O.W. Epperson was elected cashier to fill the vacancy caused by the death of W.G. Wills former cashier. Mr. Epperson has been with the bank for fourteen years. Mr. Epperson married Miss Therese DeBrosse of Monett and is well known here."

*May 24, 1926. Bank of Neosho, behind the counters. Orval Epperson in front with mustache.*

On Thursday, December 15, 1921, our son Orval Wilford Epperson was born, and we called him Billy. It was front page news in the *Neosho Daily Democrat*, "The Bank of Neosho has a new depositor today – a fine baby son who was born at 2:45 a.m. to Mr. and Mrs. Orval Epperson at their home at 344 South Hamilton Street. The new arrival has been named Orval Wilford."

Soon after Billy was born, Therese's parents left Monett and moved in with us. In 1922, Eli, as roundhouse boss, had participated in the Railroad Shopman's Strike for more pay. The strike was doomed, and Eli lost his job at the age of sixty-seven. Margaret and Eli were helpful to us around the house with cooking and gardening, and soon, as a babysitter for our third child.

Tirzah Madelon was born December 20, 1926. We chose the unique name after a character in the silent movie, *Ben Hur*, that had just been released. In the movie, Tirzah was the young sister of Ben Hur, who along with her mother, had contracted leprosy and was eventually cured by Jesus.

Her birth was reported by the *Neosho Daily News* on Tuesday, December 21, 1926, "Born, on Monday, December 20, to Mr. and Mrs. O.W. Epperson, a daughter who has been named Tirzah Madelon."

Our children were a joy; curious, kind, smart, and talented. Therese was an excellent mother and teacher who found ingenious ways to educate their growing minds. She contacted libraries in the bigger towns to send books each month for them to read and spark their imagination. Therese came from a very musical family. Her father Eli played the harmonica, and her grandfather Denis was a known violinist and composer of church hymns in Shelby, Ohio. She intended to continue that tradition and secured piano lessons for Joan, violin lessons for Billy and Tirzah, and voice lessons for Tirzah.

When the children were young, I would take them on long walks following the railroad tracks out of town through woods and fields, crossing streams that ran to the old Zimmerman mill. During those hikes I would show them the land that I knew well, and the animals, bugs, and all manner of critters that lived together there. We would roll old tree trunks to find caterpillars or worms or look at the bark on trees to see where animals had sharpened themselves. If we saw any wildlife, I would name them Ricky raccoon, or Jimmy Skunk, or Reddy Fox, or Grandfather frog. But their favorite stories were of Tweedles and Twaddles, two rabbits who had wonderful adventures in the woodland forest.

If we came across a stream, we would take off our shoes and wade in the cool waters. Sometimes we planned ahead and packed our long wool tanks for a proper swim. Neighborhood kids, mainly Marbles and Tavins, knew of these walks and would join in. On the way home I would tell them stories of the old days when Indians roamed the lands and the time when I was visited by a phantom Indian in the middle of the night. On that night, as a young boy, I was awakened by the soft footsteps of a moccasined Indian whose silhouette framed the farmhouse door. All was silent, the shadow unmoving, only the moon casting a dim light on the warrior's face, and then just as silently, he vanished.

*November 3, 1925, Joan, age 5 years and 5 months, 28 days. Billy Epperson 'Orval Wilford' age 3 years, 11 months, and 5 days.*

*1930-1931. Tirzah Epperson, age 4 or 5*

Our home had a large plot of land, and in one section I fixed a gunnysack to a large elm tree so the children could swing. In another corner, I established a beehive where we collected fresh honey. In the evenings, we would lay a quilt on the ground out back and gaze at the stars that passed over. I would point out the big dipper and little dipper, Cassiopeia, Andromeda, and the seven sisters, and told of their origins. We played games like Authors, and States and Capitols. They were very curious about my military time in France, and so I described the voyages over and back and how I was sprayed with ice cold water to get rid of the lice that roamed freely. I told them how we walked for miles and miles every day through the war-torn French countryside, stayed in barn lofts in the small villages, with only straw as a mattress, and as the ration supplies dwindled, horse meat became the only meat available. On occasion, I would show them the hard tack biscuit that I brought home, and I explained that it was just as hard then as it was now.

I was given two weeks off a year, and so every summer, we would go to my parent's farm where they experienced true rural living with no electricity or indoor plumbing. Once chores were done, I would lead them on walks to collect arrowheads and good skipping rocks and to see the whitened skulls of dead animals. On occasion, my father would take the old farm truck to the Oklahoma border (I never owned a car), where we watched the Indian Stomp Dance with its huge campfire and beating drums, and Indians chanting magically as they circled the fire.

*1931 Epperson family in front of 344 South Hamilton. Left to right: Joan, Orval, Billy, Therese, Tirzah.*

## THE GREAT DEPRESSION

Financial depressions hit us hard in the heartland. In fact, there were two depressions. One that ended just after WWI when troops returning home created a surge in the civilian labor force. Stocks fell dramatically and, under the gold standard, significant inflation of bank credit and paper claims followed. But, that was not the biggest depression to hit. On Black Thursday, October 24, 1929, the stock market crashed as panicked investors lost faith in the economy. An even bigger depression began.

There were many things that contributed to the global Great Depression, not one single event. One cause in Europe was that the Nazis came to power in Germany, sowing the seeds of WWII. Another was the overproduction of consumer goods, followed by a fall in demand. Half of all banks failed. People were stunned to find out that banks had used their deposits to invest in the stock market. They rushed to take their money out, but those runs forced even good banks out of business. Housing prices plummeted, and international trade collapsed. The Dust Bowl drought destroyed farming communities in the Midwest. It lasted ten years, too long for farmers to hold out, so prices for agricultural products dropped to the lowest since the Civil War. Unemployment rose to twenty-five percent, and homelessness increased as farmers left in search of work moving into shantytowns.

We were not immune to the savages of the Great Depression and took extreme measures to make ends meet. I had to sell off the back acre that we once used for geese and bees and tree swings. The *Neosho Times*, October 22, 1936 reported, "Real Estate Transfers, filed within past week. Orval W. Epperson to M. L. Davis, lot 10 in blk. 12, Zig Zag Hgts, addition to Neosho, for $1."

Our children did their part in helping out. Joan and Billy sold flowers, mainly peonies and lilies that grew in our backyard. My father-in-law, Eli DeBrosse, tended to them daily. But even before the Depression hit, in order to make ends meet we rented out bedrooms. Therese advertised in the Classified Want Ads section of the *Neosho Daily Democrat*, on May 20, 1925.

*Joan and Billy selling flowers, 1920s*

FOR RENT – Apartment; furnace, fireplace, kitchenette with four-burner oil stove; southern exposure 344 South Hamilton St. Phone 238.62.imo.

Peonies and roses for sale. Phone 238.344 South Hamilton. 88-5t.

By the 1940s we had multiple boarders living with us. We had trailers throughout the yard, and had rented out all the bedrooms. We even rented out the living room and dining room as bedrooms. In order to get to the kitchen, we had to go outside and around the house. The children slept in the bedroom next to ours, and although living quarters were tight, it allowed my storytelling to continue deep into the night. The only two rooms that were heated were the bathroom and kitchen, so we spent family time around the small kitchen table, while Therese and her mother cooked.

And life went on in our little town. In 1932, I was given a watch from the Bank of Neosho for 25 years of service. I remained active with my WWI veterans and the *Joplin Globe* reported on September 3, 1933, "Orval W. Epperson has been elected commander of Clyde Burdick post, American Legion, at Neosho. An installation will be held jointly with the auxiliary this month." I was on the Board of Education for the Neosho school system for many years, including a stint as President, so I was able to present each of my children their high school diploma.

*1932. Orval William Epperson holding watch given for 25 years at the Bank of Neosho.*

*1933. O.W. Epperson, Commander of American Legion, meritorious military medals.*

*1940s Neosho Board of Education. O.W. Epperson, second to the last on the right.*

Our children were involved in their schooling and community. Joan was an exceptional pianist, and a very good artist (she painted a mural of Missouri farm life that hung in the upstairs hallway). She won countless awards, was crowned Ozark Smile Girl, and Harvest Queen of Newton County. Just after earning her Journalism degree at the University of Missouri, she was asked to be the editor-in-chief for the college edition of the *Mademoiselle Magazine* in New York.

Billy was a very talented violinist and won statewide competitions. Together, Billy and I were in boy scouts; I was a troop leader and Billy went on to become an Eagle Scout. He was chosen to attend Boy's State during its inaugural year and because of his leadership qualities became a senator for the founding class. He was fair and well liked and was voted president for both his high school class and his junior college class. He had started engineering at the University of Missouri before he enlisted in the Army Air Corp.

Tirzah was very smart. She once wrote an essay on our national defense, and it was selected to represent Missouri in the national contest. She attended Girls State years younger than the other attendees. She was salutatorian for her high school graduating class, and was also the commencement speaker. Tirzah was a talented violinist and vocalist, performing in many recitals. She was active with the USO during the war and graduated with a Speech degree from Webster College in St. Louis.

*1943. Tirzah, Billy, and Joan.*

# Our Son Billy

Billy had finished junior college and one semester at the University of Missouri when he joined the Army Air Corps to do his part in the second World War. He became a bombardier. That war began 21 years after the end of the Great War that I fought in. At the age of twenty-one he followed in my footsteps to fight in the same European theatre that I fought two decades earlier. I was very proud of him, and he was the apple of Therese's eye. No one made her happier. We both wrote to him, but Therese wrote to him nearly every day and prayed constantly for his safety. Our beloved son was killed as a young man, barely old enough to experience his manhood.

When Billy was stationed at the Aviation Cadet Center in Uvalde, Texas, we were able to visit him, taking the 14-hour bus ride from Neosho to the Del Rio station. Tirzah, in high school at the time, made the trip with us. Therese's cousin Marie DeBrosse lived near the San Antonio base, and Billy had written home about meeting her for the first time in March of 1943.

*Billy home on visit. Left to right: Joan, Billy, Therese, and Tirzah.*

*1943 Orval William (O.W.) wearing WWI American Legion cap and Orval Wilford (Billy) wearing WWII uniform.*

```
Aunt Marie finally got to see me by driving out Sunday. She's the picture
of Aunt Blanche and a mix of all our French relatives. They drove me all
over S.A. and really seem to like me very much. They are very nice people.
```

We did not travel much, so the 1943 San Antonio trip was a big deal, and seeing her cousins, Marie and Louise made the trip even more special. The *Neosho Daily Democrat* July 7, 1943 reported,

> Mrs. O.W. Epperson and daughter, Miss Tirzah Epperson returned Saturday from San Antonio where they spent some time with Aviation Cadet Bill Epperson who has been in pilot training, and is now training in Navigation. Mr. Epperson accompanied his family to Texas, and Lt. Epperson was transferred from Uvalde to San Antonio. Mr. Epperson returned home at the end of a ten-day's visit, and Mrs. Epperson and daughter remained for a week longer, spending a delightful time in the southern city.

*June 20, 1943, Uvalde, Texas. Tirzah, Billy and Therese at City Hall Lawn.*

## SAFE AS IN GOD'S POCKET

On April 9, 1944, while at Ardmore Army Air Base in Oklahoma, Billy wrote a letter. It was similar to most of his letters, describing how his day went with training and classes and flying and any news he heard from friends at other bases, but this letter ended differently. Therese must have written to him about her concerns as his overseas departure date drew nearer, and so he wrote back to tell her not to worry, "I'm as safe as in God's pocket."

> Dear Folks,
>
> Today the rest of our boys came in from Salt Lake. And yesterday a class shipped out for combat. Things are being speeded up all over it seems for the big push. This much I will tell you. If I don't see you before Joan's birthday, then it will be after 25 missions.
>
> It's very warm here the last few days and cloudy. We haven't flown much for the last few days, but we have to stay at the line in case it clears up. If I could have contacted you that night, I might have met Joan at the station in Ardmore. I was in town that night. Some of our boys got up as far as Springfield the other night, but we haven't been scheduled for a navigation mission yet. Don't worry, you'll know when I fly over by the roar of the engine. You'll probably think that we're making a crash landing. Joan should have asked for more - especially in war time. No doubt she could have got more. And I wish she would write sometime. It will take a lot longer to reach me in another 5 weeks. Would you mind telling her? Baby graduates from high school next month, doesn't she? Almost a grown young lady already! Time will always fly, I guess. I appreciate her letters very much-as she would also appreciate mine.
>
> Please don't worry about me mother! I know I don't write often as I should, but I've always been that way. If anything happens you'd hear immediately.
>
> Well, thumbs up. I'm as safe as in God's pocket. I've been living right!
>
> Love, Bill

**ARDMORE ARMY AIR BASE**
ARDMORE, OKLAHOMA

Dear Folks,

Today the rest of our boys came in from Salt Lake. And yesterday a class shipped out for Combat. Things are being speeded up all over it seems for the big push. This much I will tell you. If I don't see you before Joan's birthday — Then it will be after 25 missions.

It's very warm here the last few days and cloudy. We haven't flown much for the last few days, but we have to stay at the line in case it clears up.

If I could have contacted you that night, I might have met Joan at the station in Ardmore. I was in town that night.

Some of our boys got up as far as Springfield the other night, but we haven't been scheduled for a navigation mission yet. Don't worry, you'll know when I fly over by the roar of the engines. You'll probably think that we're making a crash landing.

Joan should have asked more — especially in war time. No doubt she could have got more. And I wish she would write sometime. It will take a bit longer to reach me in another 5 weeks. Would you mind telling her?

Baby graduates from high school next month doesn't she? — Almost a grown young lady already! Time will always fly, I guess. I appreciate her letters very much — as she would also appreciate mine.

Please don't worry about me mother! I know I don't write often as I should, but I've always been that way. If anything happens you'd hear immediately.

Well, thumbs up. I'm as safe as in God's pocket. I've been living right!

Love,
Bill

*April 9, 1944 letter from Billy Epperson. Safe as in God's Pocket.*

## MOTHER'S DAY NOTE FROM BOMBARDIER SON

On a beautiful Sunday afternoon, Billy flew over our home and dropped a Mother's Day note that landed not far from the house. The crew had flown from Ardmore, Oklahoma, and as they neared Neosho, Billy attached a note to a small steel door handle and fashioned a handkerchief to it as a makeshift parachute. Then, while 30,000 feet in the air, using precise calculations, he dropped it with a note that read,

```
May 14, 1944
1:10p.m.
Dear Folks,
I can't land or get home, but I can at least fly over. I'll write a
letter tonight.
We thought we'd get 3 days off, but this is the air force. Also, this
is the army. I'm wondering how my aim is with this thing? The crew all
say hello.
Love, Bill
```

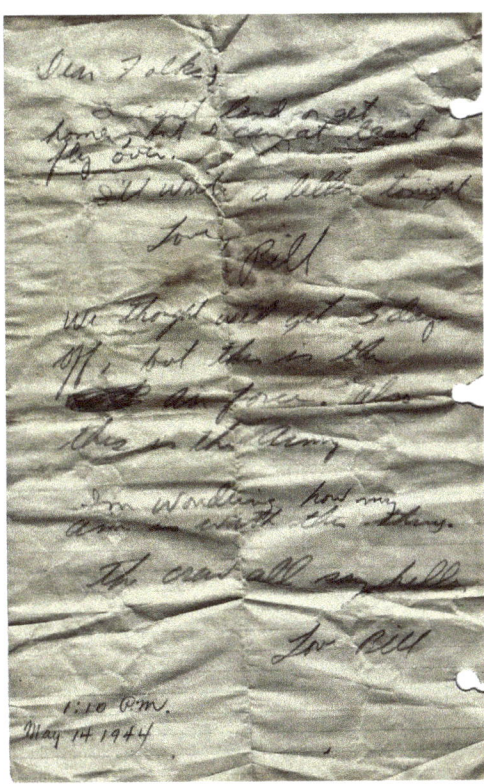 

*May 14, 1944, Mother's Day Note from Billy Epperson*

The *Neosho Daily Democrat* reported,

AIRMAN GREETS MOTHER WITH PARACHUTE NOTE

Lt. Wm. Epperson, son of Mrs. O.W. Epperson of 344 South Hamilton street, stationed at Ardmore, Okla., was on a routine flight yesterday and flew over Neosho in a Flying Fortress shortly after noon. His training as a bombardier evidently is good, for he sent down a handkerchief-sized parachute to which Mothers' Day greetings to his own mother were attached, and the tiny 'chute' landed within a few feet of the Epperson home on South Hamilton street.

## KING AND QUEEN OF ENGLAND VISIT KIMBOLTON

By June 1944, Billy had been shipped to Kimbolton, England, and was preparing for his first bombing mission. He wrote a letter home about a visit from the King and Queen of England, dated, July 6, 1944, but it had been missent, so by the time it reached Neosho, Billy was already missing in action.

```
Dear Folks,

Days pass and little out of the ordinary happens. However, the King and
Queen of England and eldest daughter, Elizabeth attended one of the
briefings. I sat just two rows in front of them during the briefing.
The king is really a good looking man. The Queen is an extremely nice
looking woman, and believe it or not, she's quite friendly. One boy had
a "Queenie" on the back of his leather flying jacket-and she stopped to
talk awhile. The princess had little to say, but appeared quite poised
- and had a sweet look about her. Naturally, there were a few generals
and staff also. Perhaps you'll see their picture in the newsreel by one
of our planes!!

We've been resting mostly these last few days, although we flew a
couple of days ago. We'll probably fly a lot-even more than we sleep
from on.

The mail has been held up again. None of us receiving any for the last
three days. It should be in tomorrow. I think we'd all rather be here
doing our part. It wasn't a pleasant feeling running around over the in
the states not having done anything.

I think I'll go to town tomorrow night to have my battle jacket made.
One finds it easy to save money here-nothing for which to spend it. I
may send a little home next month.

Love,

Bill
```

July 6, 1944 letter from Billy Epperson about King and Queen of England.

## BILLY AND CREW MISSING IN ACTION

Orders came at 3:00a.m. on a Sunday morning, July 9, 1944. The weather was cloudy and unsettled in England, and there was a notable lack of sunshine. The crew struggled to find a plane that was in worthy flying condition, and when they finally took off in the Pansy Yokum B-17, they could not find their assigned formation, got lost over the English Channel, and never returned to the airbase. It would be 15 days later before the next of kin were notified.

On a warm summer Monday morning, July 24, 1944, at 8:13a.m., a telegram arrived at 344 South Hamilton. I was just leaving for work, and Therese and Tirzah were planning to walk up the high hill to attend Mass at St. Canera. Instead, a knock came at the front door, and a telegram was delivered. No one wanted to receive a telegram during the war.

*Billy MIA Telegram July 24, 1944. Western Union. KAG41 43 Govt=Wux Washington DC 24 849a (1944 July 24 am 813). ORVAL W. EPPERSON=344 South Hamilton St. The Secretary of War desires me to express his deep regret that your son Second Lieutenant Orval W. Epperson has been reported Missing in Action since nine July over France if further details or other information are received you will be promptly notified=ulio the Adjutant General.*

A vision of Therese grasping the telegram, crumbling it in her hands, and falling to the floor in agony, is etched in my mind.

It became our sole purpose to find our son. We wrote to as many people as we could, trying to find his whereabouts. All our letters were nearly the same script, begging, pleading to those who could help, and reiterating the information that had been discovered. Since the military was not forthcoming, we hung on every detail, every rumor, verified or not, and we shared those reports with the crew's family members.

We wrote to the Queen of England, the International Red Cross, and Provost Marshall General in Washington, D.C., American Prisoner of War Information Bureau Section of the Provost, the Headquarter Army Air Force, Assistant Chief for Air Staff Personnel, Personal Affairs Division, Adjutant General in Washington, D.C., *Stars and Stripes Newspaper*, and the *St. Louis Post Dispatch* War Correspondent, Virginia Irwin. It was all-consuming.

February 1, 1945

To the Crew

Last week a friend of my son's happened to visit us. He had just come home to Neosho on a month's furlough - having completed his mission in the European theatre - and will probably remain in the States as Instructor. He was a navigator on a B-17 flying Fortress, arriving in England about a month after our crew. He brought with him a large map of that part of England where their bases were. Our crew's base was at KIMBOLTON, which is located about 40 miles north of London, about 40 miles southwest of Norwich and about 40 miles east of Birmingham. This navigator's base was about 10 miles north of Kimbolton at a place called Polebrook. These bases are not shown on the map of Europe but from the above description you will be able to know pretty clearly just where the base was.

While over there, he had access to the confidential files, but so far they have not been able to learn anything definite. He thought it most likely that the rumor about them being late getting gassed up and probably tagging on to another squadron the most logical. As I remember it, this information was first imparted by "Reggie."

This navigator cited several POSSIBILITES. The popular opinion being that - since it was pretty bad weather that day - their ship got lost in the clouds, and probably - due to some instrument error - wandered away from England. Now that could mean any number of things could have happened. Here are some opinions he gave:

"Their instruments could have gone out, and, since there is always a strong wind from a westerly direction, they might have been blow out over the North Sea and, eventually, when they found that they were over the Sea and were running short on gas, they turned Eastward, knowing that they would hit land in a short time. At that time a big part of France was still under Jerry's control, so they would have had to land or bail out over enemy territory. That sounds the most logical, knowing as I do, from experience, how very difficult it is to keep located over this part of the world and judging from a navigator's standpoint, the most logical thing to do in a case like this. Then it is possible that they wandered out over the Channel, and some Jerry fighters shot them up a bit, in which case they would still make for the nearest land. I do not believe myself that they would have had to land in the North Sea because land is too close on each side of the Channel to risk landing in the Sea. My personal opinion is that they just got away from England and had to land in northern France or Holland or maybe even Germany.

They might also have hit Norway on account of the almost continuous strong westerly winds that might have blown them out over the North Sea.

His latest report from the crew's base and my latest report from the War Dept. still lists them as missing.

Hugh E. Frye 2nd Lt. Pilot

Chester B. Stoupe 2nd Lt Navgt.

Victor B. Gluckman 2nd Lt Co-Pilot

O.W. Epperson 2nd Lt Bombardier

Tommy Kunrod Pvt. Ball Tur.

Lawrence Eiler Cpl. Tail Gun.

Harry Crites Sgt. Radio

Ronald Mackenzie Sgt. Waist Gun.

Robert Davids Sgt. Engineer

*Pansy Yokum crew. Lt. Orval Wilford Epperson (tall one standing center back row.)*

One of the first letters we received was from Lt. Reg Todd, a fellow bombardier and friend to the crew, in October 1944, three months after their MIA. In that letter, he discussed how difficult it was for them to disclose military operations with civilians, and how he was now in trouble for doing so. "I did an awful wrong by writing Joanne (friend of Lt. Frye), for I violated every rule of security ever given us. Please understand that the Security Curtailment keeps us from telling all we have scraped up, and put into the jig-saw puzzle."

That did not deter us, and we continued letter writing. We never gave up hope, even though Billy was never found. Eventually, a General was commissioned to travel to Neosho to console us personally, informing us that no more information on the whereabouts of our son was available.

Even after the presumption of death documents arrived with his life insurance, Therese never gave up hope. She wrote a letter to her dear cousin, Fr. John LaVelle, who was the superior of the Vincentian House of Studies in Washington, D.C. at the time.

```
I met a priest from Boston whom I had addressed at St. Anthony's
Shrine in New York City. I met him when I was there in May 1946. I
sent him information about Billy - similar to the enclosed ones to
you, only I enlarged on it and said Billy might even be in the bread
lines at St. Anthony's sometime and gave a thorough description and
enclosed a picture. Do you think, too, that Billy might be the victim
of amnesia, and would you deem it advisable to report all this to the
war department? An answer from a priest in Toledo said he thought it
was fantastic and thought someone was lying.
```

Many years later, while at an airport, she heard an announcement for a Billy Epperson. Shocked and driven, she sought out airline officials to determine if that announcment was indeed for her son. It was not, and for many years after, she prayed that perhaps he had amnesia and was still alive somewhere.

## BILLY AND THE SACRED HEART OF JESUS

Therese had a special devotion to the Sacred Heart of Jesus that began decades earlier during her First Holy Communion. She kept a small 4 x 6 picture of the Sacred Heart of Jesus on the living room mantle. Tucked into the back of the small frame was the MIA Western Union telegram, slightly torn and crumbled. She dedicated the return of our son to the Sacred Heart of Jesus and placed the telegram close to His heart as a reminder.

Therese made donations to St. Canera Catholic Church to have the 8:00a.m. weekly Friday Masses offered for Billy. The church bulletin read, "For the intentions of E." It privately stood for Epperson, and in particular for Billy Epperson, but no one ever knew what it meant. The church bulletin notifications began the year he went missing and continued throughout her life.

She stored her most precious notes and letters in the little study off the kitchen. She read from the bible every day jotting down any verse that spoke to her. She even made up her own prayers among them were "Having Prayed," and "Our Home." There were two letters that Therese wrote on Billy's twenty-fifth birthday. One addressed to Billy and the other to the Sacred Heart of Jesus. Those letters remained hidden for the rest of her life.

**HAVING PRAYED**

*Having prayed, lead thou me on,*
*Shall I feel terror of the dawn?*
*Having prayed, show me the way,*
*Shall I be fearful of the day?*
*Having urged, guide me aright,*
*Shall I go trembling toward the night?*
*No! He to whom I pray will hear,*
*Believing this, I have no fear.*

**OUR HOME**

*May this home stand out*
*As a bright light*
*Shining toward Heaven*
*In an appeal*
*That men may not*
*While engaged in the struggle of the street*
*Forget their God.*

Dear Billy,

I dreamed of you last night. You were sitting in the dining room by the table and I was so happy to have you home that I began planning a big party. I called up Kenton among the first and said I would have the party at our house. He had been planning one at his. You looked just like you did during high school days, young and school boyish – not like the soldier you were when you left. Among the names on the list for the party were the two Tarvin girls, and I was having difficulty figuring out their names. I do not remember much else about the dream but it was a very happy one and I grieved to part with it.

We were going to have a dance and play games, monopoly, jig-saw puzzles, etc. I thought, 'Won't the town be excited when they hear about it?'

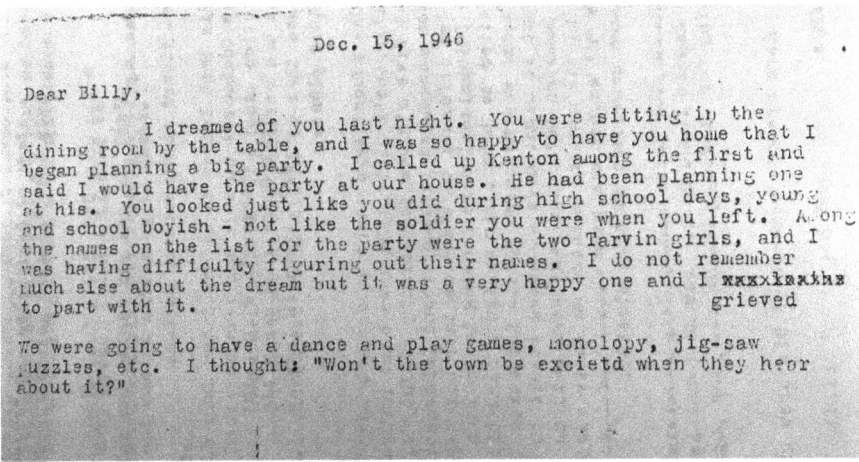

*December 15, 1946. Therese's letter to our son, Billy on his 25th birthday.*

Dear Sacred Heart of Jesus,

Please Sacred Heart of Jesus, on this day the 15th of December, the birthday of my only son, whom you gave to me 25 years ago, please hear me Dear God through your Divine Son. Wherever my son is (only you, Dear God, know) please be with him perpetually. Guard him, guide him, save him, and give him Thy protection and peace and happiness ALWAYS. He came from Thy Almighty Hand and only in Thy Hands is he secure.

In the letter I wrote him before he went overseas I said, 'Dedicate your each and every mission to the Sacred Heart of Jesus. He will guide your going out and your coming in and will bring you back safe. And don't forget to thank Him when you return.'

I want to always feel that you are keeping him safe, Dear Lord. Give me the faith and the hope and the trust that he is. Speak to him for me this day, dear Lord, and tell him I wish him the HAPPIEST Birthday he has ever had and that I love him very, very, very much, and that I wish, with all my heart, I had been a better mother to him. Please dear Mother Mary, you had a Son, and he was missing for only 3 days. My son has been missing almost 3 years. You know what a sinking feeling I get every time I think of it. My throat all chokes up. My eyes fill with tears. My whole world turns black. But I MUST trust to God's Ways. I don't believe He has let my son down.

Another thing: My son was wearing a St. Anthony's ring – St. Anthony holding the Christ Child. Somehow I believe that as long as he was wearing that ring he just COULDN'T get lost – or if he did, that he would be found SAFE. This is a long time to wait. But I MUSTN'T complain. God does not like people to worry or to doubt. I suppose St. Anthony did come through and I am not worthy to know it. Whatever the reason, please dear God, keep my son in your tender care perpetually, for who has You wanteth nothing. And Mother dear, perpetually intercede for my son.

Dear St. Anthony, I did believe in you. Help me to regain that confidence by believing even though I do not have evidence.

A happy, happy, birthday, dear Billy. I LOVE YOU WITH ALL MY HEART.

# Correspondence with Romere Martin

Although I never much spoke about the loss of our only son, it was deeply felt, and on occasion I would indulge my pain, and acknowledge the hurt. In 1974, I wrote to a friend named Romere Martin, who was an Indian living in Tiff City. She had just lost her brother.

*Romere Martin*

```
February 14, 1974

Dear Friend:

I am sorry to learn that your brother passed away. It is
sad when a middle-aged person is taken from his family.
It is even more depressing when a teenager is suddenly
taken, when he could normally expect many years of life
ahead of him.

We lost our only son when he was just out of his teens.
He was bombardier on a B-17 in World War Two. The whole
crew was lost and all were in their early twenties. I
served my time in Europe in WWI and in the same area in
which that crew was lost.

War is cruel and never solves problems for any great length of time. It
does work many injustices as when the American Indians were driven from
their homes and murdered when they resisted, to protect themselves and
their rights…...
```

Romere was once a celebrated Native American movie star, but she chose a simple life in a small Missouri town and while there started a charity for American Indian children. In addition to the shared pain of losing a loved one, she and I had more in common. I thought that I had some Indian blood in me from my mother's side (my great-grandmother's name was Buzzard, a known Indian name), and because Romere lived in the same town as my grandfather George Washington Epperson, I had hoped that by my candid description of him she would share what she knew about the man.

The *News-Dispatch*, Sept. 1977 in an article, *Remembering Romere Martin*, stated,

```
RoMere was a former Hollywood actress and performer who ultimately
made her home in Tiff City, on the Missouri-Oklahoma line, and spent
```

her latter days doing good. RoMere was born on the Pottawatomie Indian Reservation in Jackson County, Kansas, on July 20, 1911. Her father was Pottawatomie and her mother was Chippewa. Her birth name was actually Rosa Marie Grinnell, but she changed it to RoMere Darling when she moved to Hollywood to pursue a dancing and acting career. While a teenager, then living in Arizona, she had won a Miss Original America contest. As an attractive young actress, RoMere had a number of minor roles in several films, playing Native American or foreign character parts, in the 1930s and 40s. She also toured with Tex Ritter performing traditional Native American dances. She met and married fellow thespian Harold Rogers, a Seneca-Cayuga born near Tiff City, and they lived in Hollywood until he was killed in World War II when the B-17 bomber he helped crew as a tail gunner was shot down over Europe.

She next married Julius Martin, and they moved to Tiff City around 1950. RoMere retired from acting and stayed in Tiff the rest of her days. Although no longer on the silver screen, RoMere taught Native American dances to local schoolchildren and 4-Hers [4H Club], resulting in some national recognition, for which she supported them monetarily and in other ways. Soon after moving to Tiff City, RoMere employed local Native American women in making native handicrafts, which she sold in a gift shop in Tiff.

Perhaps what RoMere is most well-known for, however, is her Box 14-A charity (Box 14-A was simply her post office box). This was set up to benefit area Native American families in need, and provide them with a good Christmas. The charity became rather famous in its day, and RoMere even received a letter of commendation from President Richard Nixon for her good works among the Native American population in the Four-State area.

She was known for her generosity, and not just with the Box 14-A project.

RoMere quickly responded to my letter on stationary with smoke plumes coming off a mountain range with the words SMOKE SIGNALS FROM BOX 14-A. She did remember George Epperson, and in fact, she had acquired a piece of furniture from him; a safe for the kitchen. It was in poor condition with broken glass, gnawed shelves, and multiple coats of paint. Her husband brought it to the Crowder prison where he worked and had the inmates painstakingly restore it to its original beauty. We corresponded for years, mainly around Christmas when we donated to her charity.

December 19, 1973

Dear Mrs. Martin,

Mrs. Santa Claus tells me that she has misplaced one of her Christmas commitment lists. She found Box 14-A on it when it was located. Herewith is enclosed a little contribution to your worthy project.

You may or may not know that my grandfather George Washington Epperson was at one time a leading citizen of Tiff City. Around the first years of this century, he and his wife Laura operated a general store in Tiff City about a block west of where your store now stands. They did quite well for several years - UNTIL- evidently he became too ambitious for his wellbeing, or overestimated his business acumen. He was President of the Bank of Tiff City and owned the only automobile in town. It was the kind with wheels about the size of buggy wheels and traveled fairly well on the series of mud holes that were called roads at that time.

He bought his daily bottle of red-eye from John McKinney who owned the drug store. They dreamed up a plan to make a lot of money in the wholesale grocery business. Neosho Wholesale Grocery, was incorporated with grandfather as president and John as manager. It enjoyed a substantial volume of business but did not make money fast enough to suit them. John thought he could buy up all the navy beans in the country and force up the price, and make a killing. His plan backfired when he had his warehouse filled with navy beans and about a train load of freight cars on his railroad spur - and the beans were still coming in—and no money to pay for them, and all the cars costing huge demurrage while on his spur. To make matters worse the price of beans kept dropping and when the smoke cleared the company was out of business. A short time later the Bank of Tiff City closed its doors and grandfather's store burned down with all its contents lost including his records of who owed him and how much. Worst of all, he had no insurance. To top it off he had a sizable investment in a bank in Seneca when it failed.

Grandfather spent his last years as an invalid living in his own home just across the street, south of where your store stands and his funeral was held in the church just east of your store. When his estate was settled my father's inheritance was $100. This will demonstrate the ups and downs of life in these United States, 'The Land of Opportunity.' One person may seize an opportunity at the right time and succeed, another may grab a bear by its tail at the wrong time and meet disaster.

We extend to you our best wishes and kindest regards and hope your health improves so you may continue your pet project of helping the Indians. Incidentally, I, too, have some Indian blood. My great-grandmother was a 'Buzzard' from the Seneca area.

O. W. Epperson

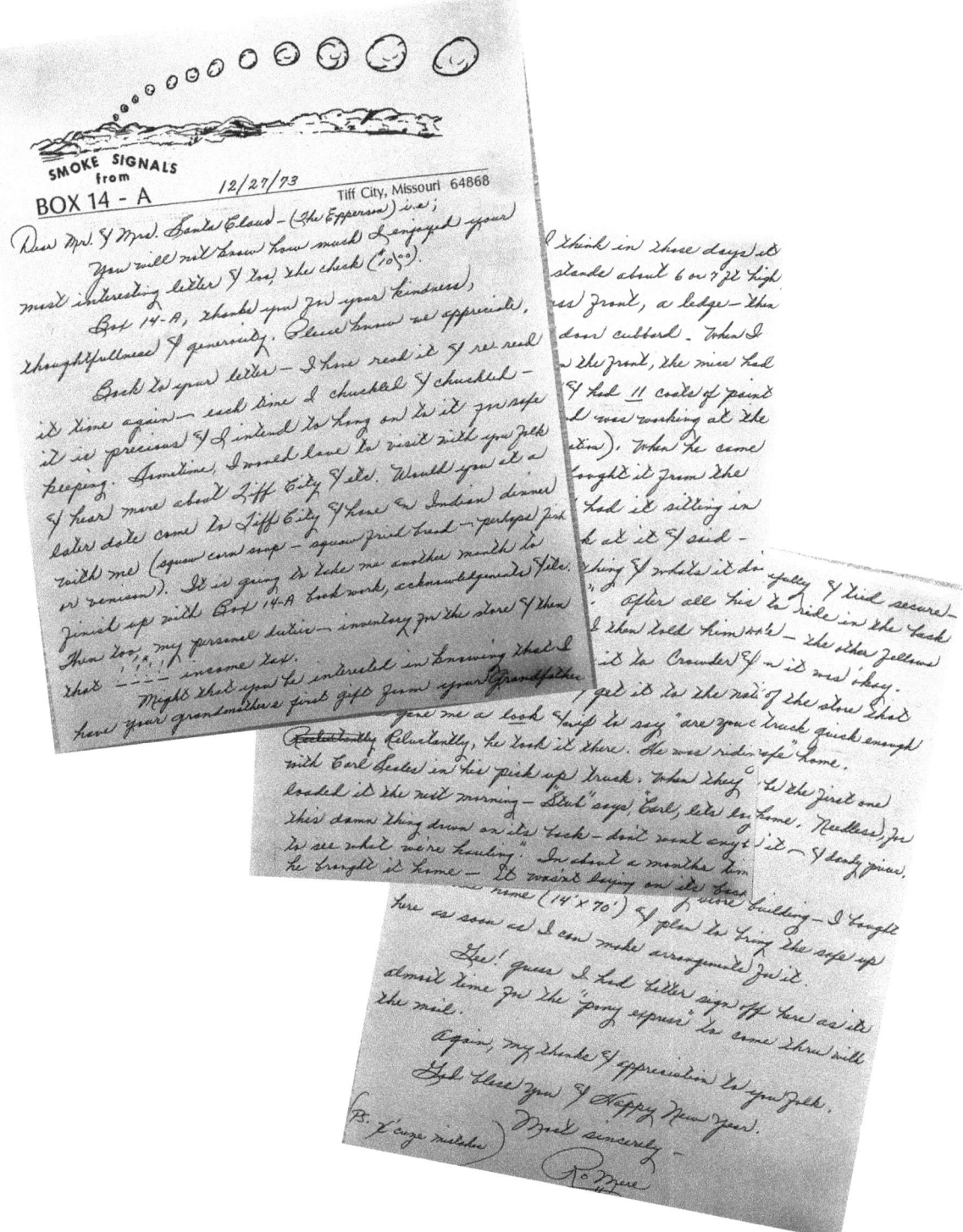

*1973 Letter to Orval from Romere Martin.*

Romere Martin letter to Orval Epperson:

December 27, 1973

Dear Mr. and Mrs. Santa Claus (The Eppersons),

You will not know how much I enjoyed your most interesting letter and too, the check $10. Box 14-A thanks your kindness, thoughtfulness and generosity. Please know we appreciate.

Back to your letter-I have read it and read it time again-each time I chuckled and chuckled. It is precious and I intend to hang on to it for safekeeping. Sometime, I would love to visit with you folks and hear more about Tiff City, etc. Would you at a later date come to Tiff City and have an Indian dinner with me? (Squaw corn soup, squaw fried bread, perhaps fish or venison.) It is going to take me another month to finish up with Box 14-A bookwork, acknowledgements, etc. Then too, my personal duties-inventory for the store and then that #$@&# insane tax.

Might you be interested in knowing that I have your grandmother's first gift from your grandfather after they were married. I think in those days it was called a 'safe.' It stands about 6 or 7 ft. high, two upper shelves with glass front, a ledge, then drawers and below a two door cupboard. When I got it, it only had one glass in the front, the mice had gnawed and gnawed on the shelves and had 11 coats of paint on it. Julius "Stub", my husband was working at the D.B. at Fort Crowder (prison section), when he came home the evening that I had bought it from the Shaver's and brought it home and had it sitting in our store. He took one look at it and said, "What the hell is that damn thing and what's it doing in here? Get it out of here!" After all his steam was over and calmed down, I then told him what I had in mind; that he take it to Crowder and have the prisoners work on it and get it to the natural wood. He gave me a look as if to say, "Are you crazy?" Reluctantly, he took it there. He was riding with Carl Seales in his pickup truck when they loaded it the next morning. Stub said, "Carl, let's lay this damn thing down on its back, don't want anybody to see what we're hauling."

In about a month's time, he brought it back home. It wasn't laying on its back; it was upright and padded carefully and tied secure. In fact, I think "Stub" wanted to ride in the back with it to make sure it was safe. The other fellows that he was riding with assured him it was okay. When he pulled up in front of the store that evening, he couldn't get out of that truck quick enough to let me know he had brought the "safe" home.

It is beautiful. "Stub" would be the first one wanted to show it off after we got home. Needless for me to say-how many offers I've had for it-and dandy prices, I just tell them it's not for sale.

I no longer live in my store building. I bought a mobile home (14'x70') and plan to bring the safe up here as soon as I can make arrangements for it.

Gee! Guess I had better sign off here as its almost time for the 'pony express' to come thru with the mail. Again, many thanks and appreciation to you folks. God Bless and Happy New Year.

Most Sincerely, Romere

Orval Epperson letter to Romere Martin, continued....

You once mentioned that you had the 'safe' that grandfather George gave my grandmother. My own mother had a 'safe' just like it. The Mrs. Epperson you knew was grandfather's wife Number Three. My blood grandmother was wife Number One and my father was her first born.

As I have mentioned, the Buzzards in my mother's ancestry furnished some Indian blood. My father's first [step]mother may have been part Indian also, as my father said her name was Meador, or possibly Meadow, as in those days a meadow was called Medder or Meador. It may have been Indian in name like Sitting Bull in a Sunny Meadow by a Running Water, etc.

My grandfather George W. Epperson was of German descent and "EPPER" in German means 'wild boar', and from what I have heard, he lived up to the name in his younger years. My father was very young when his mother died and since she could neither read nor write, he had no information as to her ancestry. She did give grandfather George three children in rapid succession before she died. Then wife Number Two gave him two more before she died. Laura, the Mrs. Epperson you know, seemingly domesticated the 'wild boar' and they have no children.

Well enough of my family history which probably tiring you, so I will bring this to a close with kindest regards from Mrs. Santa Claus and myself, and hope that your pet project will continue, after you leave it, as you have given it a good start and may go ahead on the momentum.

O.W. Epperson

# Grandfather George Washington Epperson

My grandfather George Washington Epperson was a successful businessman. He became director of the Bank of Seneca, owned a general store, and started the very first bank in Tiff City (although it was only as big as a small kitchen). Still, an impressive resume for a man with no formal education. It was generally believed, however, that he had a helping hand getting these ventures started.

George was born on October 19, 1848 in Marion, Illinois, the youngest of six children to Aphrey and Elizabeth (Hire) Epperson. His siblings were: Sarah, Emily, Martha, Martin Van Buren, and Hezekiah.

According to the census figures of 1860, my great-grandfather Aphrey Epperson, (George's father), had $3,000 in real estate and $1,000 in his personal estate, just before the Civil War. Aphrey had originated from Smith County, Tennessee (where the balance of the Epperson clan lived) but left to homestead in Marion, Illinois. Over the years, he had prudently purchased good farming lands, improved them, and sold the lands for a profit. In 1879, Aphrey died, and by the next year, his youngest son, George, claimed $4,000 in personal property, a large amount for a young man and the exact sum that Aphrey had amassed.

On September 27, 1867, the 19-year-old George married a 20-year-old Nancy Poe (my grandmother). They were married for 10 years before she died, and their oldest child was my father, William Stanley Epperson. His two brothers were Charles Newton and Edward Lihue. George married again to Lucinda Meador, a distant relative, and they had three more children, Henry, Marietta, and Wesley (who died an infant). My father, William Stanley was then raised by his stepmother Lucinda, who died the year I was born. At age 50, George then married a third and final time to Laura Clemons, who was twenty years his junior.

Years later I found out that my real grandmother, Nancy Poe, whom I never met, came from North Carolina with her family. After her parents died, the children were separated, and she along with her younger brother, Joshua, became wards of the J. Miller family in McDonald County. Some of her siblings followed the Oregon Trail to California and landed in Healdsburg Northern California as ranchers, but she stayed in Missouri, unable to read or write (per the 1860 census), and by the time she married George, her name was Hamlin, although no marriage record was found.

Part VI. The Married Years 183

*Vibrator thresher, Nichols-Shepard tractor, and high wheeler car.*

As a successful farmer and businessman, my grandfather George purchase 260 acres of fine land just south of Anderson where he owned a saw grist mill, threshing machine, and a Nichols and Shepard separator and tractor engine. He would thresh wheat up and down Indian Creek for a fee. His general store and bank were right on the Oklahoma border, and he loaned money to the Indians who lived there. With the profits, he purchased a high wheeler car with a chain drive, becoming the first person in Tiff City to own an automobile.

*Goodspeed Publishing for McDonald and Newton County 1888* wrote a short biography on him.

George W. Epperson, a well-to-do farmer of McMillen Township, McDonald Co., Mo., is a native of Marion County, Illinois, born on October 19, 1848. His father, Ashrey [sic] (Aphrey) Epperson, was a native of Tennessee, who brought his family to Missouri in 1855. He first located in Newton County, but came to McDonald County two years later. Here, he spent the remainder of his life. George W. Epperson was reared on his father's farm, and secured a limited education in the common schools. Since reaching his majority he has been engaged in farming for himself and has been successful. He is the owner of 260 acres of fine land under a fair state of cultivation. Besides his farming interests he has for several years been managing a threshing machine, and now a Nichols & Shepard separator and tractor engine. He also owns and operates a saw mill. Mr. Epperson has been twice married. His first wife, Nancy Poe, to whom he was married in the spring of 1867, died in 1877, leaving three children: William, Charles, and Edward. He was next married in the fall of 1878 to Hannah Meador, a daughter of Joel Meador, of Pineville Township, McDonald County. Two children have been born to this union, Henry and Marietta Ann. Mr. Epperson is one of the substantial citizens of the county, and is a member of the Farmer's Alliance.

*George Washington Epperson and 3rd wife, Laura Clemons.*

## EPPERSON VS. EPPERSON

There was conflict among two of the adult Epperson brothers, Martin Van Buren and George. *Reports of Cases Determined in the Supreme Court of Missouri* published in 1901, Vol. 161, October Term 1900, Division One, March 29, 1901, Appeal from McDonald Circuit Court Hon. J.C. Lamson, Judge, reported a lawsuit, *Epperson vs. Epperson*, which went to the Supreme Court of Missouri. It appeared that a section of the farm that Aphrey gave his son, George Washington, was now disputed by another son, Martin Epperson. George had recently sold the tract to Ozark Orchard Company, and in doing so, Martin found a discrepancy in the original title and sued for ejectment.

Twenty-six years earlier, on January 1, 1870, Aphrey Epperson and his wife Elizabeth had deeded the land, tracts and parcels situated in McDonald County to George, but when they wrote the tracts of land, they repeated a section description, which made a mess when George sold the property to Ozark Orchard in 1896. His brother Martin, acting on behalf of their deceased father, Aphrey, claimed the deed was not valid due to statute of limitations.

As part of their defense, George and Ozark Orchard asked the court to declare it a mere clerical error and to disregard Martin who sought to take advantage of the mistake made 26 years earlier and recover an undivided fifth of the real estate. The court said that it was evident upon the face of the deed that the grantor (Aphrey) intended to convey five tracts of land, all in section 13, township 22, range 33 and containing 189.38, but by repeating the description of one of the tracts (southeast quarter of the southwest quarter) he conveyed only 4 tracts, and 149.38 acres. The supreme court ruled there was no grounds for invoking the statute of limitations.

It was never clear why there was contention between the brothers. My grandfather George had at one time written a deposition testifying that his older brother, Martin Van Buren, had in fact fought in the Civil War and was due compensation. Martin had been married to a woman named Malinda (last name unknown), said to be a Cherokee Indian, from 1860 to 1894, and they had 11 children together. The year after her death, the 50-year-old Martin married again to a 33-year-old Demarcy Vashti Davis, who took on the responsibility of raising the children. Demarcy and Martin then had five children of their own. In 1896, the year the lawsuit began, their firstborn child, Goldie Mae had died at a year old, and another child, Leander "Lee," was born soon after. Perhaps Martin, as he struggled to feed his large family, felt he was owed something. In 1903, Martin moved to Benton County, Arkansas, owning 127 acres there and died on March 15, 1906 at the age of 66.

## G.W. EPPERSON IN TIFF CITY

In the small town of Tiff City (less than 100 residents), Grandfather George was an important man with close friends. Two of them were Dennis Burns and John McKinney. The local newspaper photographed George and his friends in front of his home as he stood above all the others. He appeared somewhat portly with a nice head of hair and a large bushy mustache, and he looked on with authority as he rested his left hand on his lapel and neatly tucked his right hand in his suit pocket.

George Epperson and Dennis Burns owned separate general merchandise stores in town, and John McKinney owned the drug store. Every morning the three of them would meet at John's drug store where George was known to drink a whiskey highball as his "eye-opener." There, the three successful men would hatch money making ideas and surely thought, "We're making good here in Tiff City. Let's go bigger, to Neosho, and really coin money."

So, in 1908, they formed the Neosho Wholesale Grocery Company and built a warehouse next to the train tracks in the county seat. That building, at the corner of Washington and East Brook Street in Neosho, Missouri, still stands today, and can be found in the National Register of

*Neosho Wholesale Grocery Company, 224 N Washington, Neosho, Missouri.*

Historic Places and the County Recorder's office. It was to be the beginning of a long and prosperous business venture.

But it wasn't meant to be. They decided to speculate in navy beans, and they put all their savings into it. John was the manager and decided that navy beans were going to make money that year, so they bought several carloads at about 8 or 9 cents a pound, figuring that the value would at least double in the future as demand for beans increased.

Their agreement to sell beans at a predetermined price at a specific time in the future was risky. They hedged that the price they bought the beans was low enough and would increase enough to make it worth their while, and it would have to happen before the freight trains arrived in Neosho. Once they found a buyer they would then just re-route the freight train full of navy beans to the new location, never taking them off the track. It was just paperwork. They would acknowledge receipt of cargo, make out a new bill of lading for shipment, and then pocket the profits.

### RESIDENCE OF G. W. EPPERSON.

*Grandfather George Washington Epperson in front of his home on Seneca Street in Tiff City, Missouri with friends. George W. Epperson is in the center, standing tall with a bushy mustache and left hand resting on his lapel.*

But the market didn't move fast enough, buyers weren't interested, and they couldn't cover the difference, so they got caught in the pinch. Their bet that the price of navy beans would increase was called because that year there was a boom crop of beans, and the price actually sank below what they had paid. It wasn't much of a margin, but it was still more than they could afford.

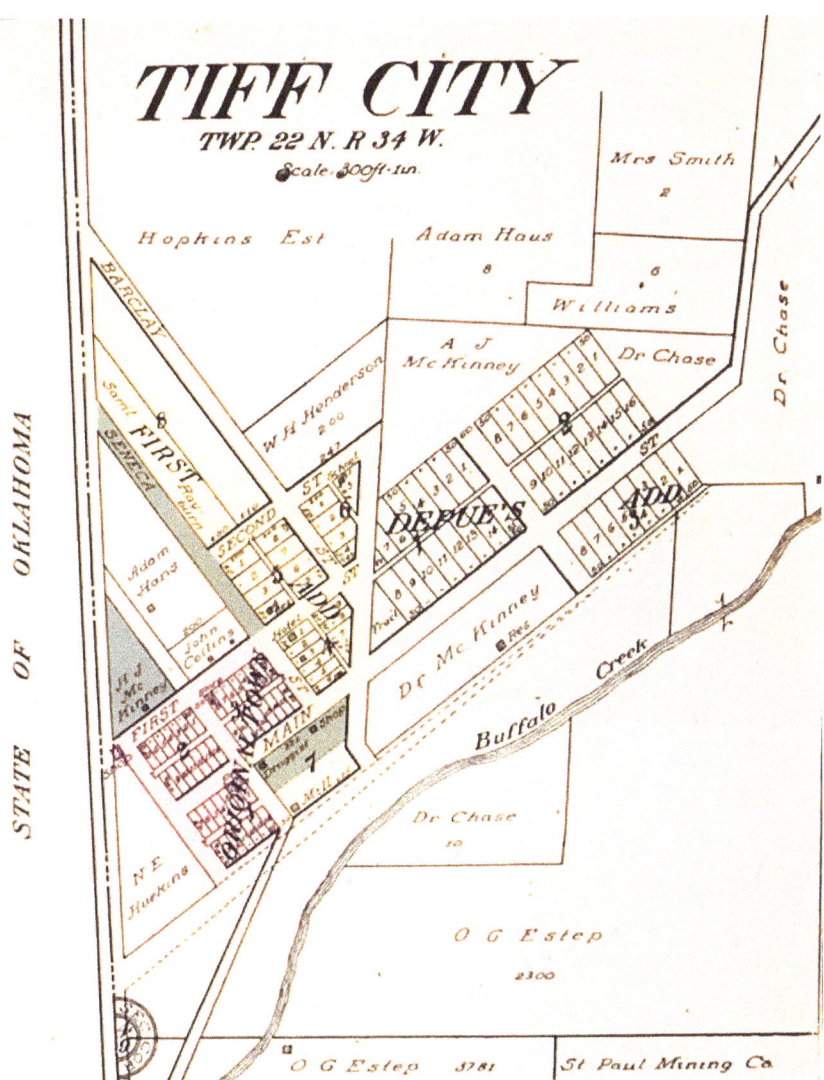

*1909 Map of Tiff City. Grandfather George Washington Epperson lived on Seneca Street (left side of map, highlighted). G.W.'s friend, John McKinney's grocery store was the triangular corner lot (highlighted) closest to the Oklahoma border, and friend Dennis Burn's drug store (highlighted) was on Main street next door to Dr. McKinney's residence.*

Well, here came the carloads of beans and no buyers. They filled up the new building with sacks of beans and about fifteen railroad cars full of beans on the KCS siding auxiliary train track, waiting for payment. Since the cars remained on the track for over twenty-four hours, they were then assessed demurrage (a charge payable to the owner of the railcars for failure to unload the shipment within the agreed time).

At first, they tried kiting checks (a type of bank misuse that took advantage of the float between banks). It was not illegal at the time. The common practice was generally thought of as harmless IOU's with zero collateral. It became known as flying a kite, as there was nothing to support the loan besides air, but by the 1920s the practice was deemed fraudulent.

Grandfather George had accounts at the Bank of St. Louis, the Bank of Tiff City, and Neosho Savings (Neosho Savings was a different bank from the Bank of Neosho, where I worked.) He would write a check for a carload of beans from the St. Louis bank account, then he would draw a check on Neosho Savings, and deposit that into the Bank of St. Louis to cover. Before the original St. Louis check was returned for insufficient funds, he would deposit a check from the Bank of Tiff City, into the Neosho Savings, in an attempt to keep ruse going until he could find buyers. He hoped that he could sell enough beans to cover the deficit, but he went the limit.

They finally had to borrow $30,000 on the building from the Nevada Building and Loan Association, never having even made the first mortgage payment. The Nevada Building and Loan eventually sold the Neosho Wholesale Grocery Company to a man named Fred North for $10,000. The building wasn't easily adaptable to just any kind of use, and wasn't easy to sell. They lost it all, went bankrupt, and had to liquidate the business.

The Bank of Tiff City had a little over $5,000 by then. Mary Poland had a $5,000 timed deposit in the bank, and when she died it all came to a head. They had to use that money, with interest, to settle her estate and didn't have enough to continue operating the bank, so it closed. Eventually, in the 1930s, the Bank of Seneca also closed. On top of it all, Grandfather George's general store burned down, and he never carried insurance on it.

Towards the end of his life, Grandfather George was said to have become an exemplary husband, devoted father, and a patient sufferer. He had become senile and had succumbed to his illness on November 30, 1933. *The Anderson Review*, December 7, 1933 posted the obituary.

> George Washington Epperson was born in Illinois October 19, 1848 and departed this life at his home in Tiff City, Mo at 2:00 pm, Nov. 30, 1933 at the age of 85 years one month and eleven days.
>
> He came with his parents to southwest Missouri when a child and grew to manhood in the community. He was married to Nancy Poe in 1867. To this union three sons were

born, two died many years ago–one Will Epperson, lives near Tiff City. Nancy his wife died in 1876. About two years later he married Hannah Meador, three children blessed this union; Henry Epperson of Omaha, Nebr., and Mrs. Anna Wilson of Anderson; Wesley died in infancy. His second wife died April 3, 1891. July 20, 1898 he married to Laura Clemons who survives him.

Besides these he leaves to mourn his departure a nephew and niece, Mr. and Mrs. Abe Tharp, thirteen grandchildren, other relatives and a host of friends. Mr. Epperson was an exemplary husband and devoted father and a successful business man. He had been postmaster in Anderson and Tiff City. During his illness he was a patient sufferer.

Mr. Abe Tharp that was mentioned in the Anderson Review obituary was the son of George's older sister Emily (Epperson) Tharp. Abe was an apprentice to George at his farm. It might be well to note that in those times it was customary to have young children, from age two up to be 'bound' as apprentices until they were twenty-one years of age to 'learn the art and mysteries of farming,' so it was assumed that the Shetleys and Abe Tharp were apprentices for my grandfather. When I lived with my folks near Anderson, Abe Tharp lived about a mile from us, and I enjoyed many of his watermelons and cantaloupes over the years, which we bought for five cents each.

*George Washington Epperson Death Certificate, November 30, 1933, age 85, 1 month, 11 days. Principal cause of death: Senility.*

# My Siblings and Parents Later in Life

After all the high life that my grandfather George lived, he died a common man and upon his death, my father only received one-hundred dollars. My father, on the other hand, lived as a simple farmer, and even with that small sum of inheritance he was very secretive about his finances. I do, however, recall him telling us once that he owned war bonds and hid money at the farm.

My brother, Graydon Love, told me that he saw large sums of war bonds, socked away in various hiding spots around the farmhouse on Patterson Creek. Jim, too, had apparently found money on the farm. He told Love that he went snooping through some books on the farm and had come across $1,000 in bills, tucked between the pages of some books that mother had hidden away. So, on one of my visits home, I intended to talk to my brothers about these findings. Jim was not around when I arrived, he was out on his milk route, so Love and I went over to the house, dug around a bit, but never found anything. After our father died, I checked with the Division of Bond and Currency to see if any bonds had been issued in the name of William Stanley Epperson, and all they recorded was $300 worth of registered bonds.

*Three generations of Epperson men. Left to right: Grandfather George Washington, standing, Orval William (me), and my father, William Stanley.*

As time went on, my family grew apart and although we were all born in McDonald County, Missouri, only my brother Jim stayed in Anderson. Graydon Love moved to Oklahoma, and Ina eventually to Kansas.

**James Edward** (1901-1963) was a milkman and also operated a filling station in Anderson for many years. In 1922, he married Clara Belle Johnson in Anderson, and had three children: James Lester, Ramona Joseph, and Dudley Eugene. He died in Anderson from coronary thrombosis.

**Graydon Love** (1905-1986) was a mechanic and in 1928 he married Hazel Mildred Betts. They had five children: Graydon Robert (Bob), Roy Allen Epperson, George, Anna Belle Kirby, and Jadeen Jane Osborn Stroud. He died at Grove General Hospital in Delaware Oklahoma.

**Ina Mildred** (1909-2008) married Lyman Fry in 1928 and had nine children: Colleen Mae, Tommy E, Donald Durwood, Arlene Jane, Orville W, Freddie Leon, Emelie, Linda Louise, Karen Sue. She died in Sharon Springs, Kansas.

On September 5, 1951, my mother, Emily Jane (Sellers) Epperson died at the age of 82 from cerebral hemorrhage after suffering for 2 days. Antecedent cause was arteriosclerosis for years, and cardiac decompensation for one year. She had been living with my brother, Jim for several years at that time, while my father remained living on the farm. In one letter to my daughter Tirzah she regretted that she had never attended any of her children or grandchildren's weddings. Her funeral was held at the First Baptist Church of Anderson, by the Rev. Paul Andrews and she was buried at the Anderson cemetery.

My father, William Stanley Epperson lived five years longer than my mother. He lived alone at his farm and died on May 14, 1956. He had stayed there even after my mother pleaded with him to sell it. But he was stubborn. His death certificate stated he was widowed living in rural McDonald County for 49 years. He died from a cerebral accident with antecedent causes of arteriosclerosis for years due to chronic myocarditis.

My father's funeral service was held at the First Baptist Church in Anderson, Missouri. Little did we know at the time that the Baptist faith he professed began in Virginia in the middle 1700s, with the first Anthony Epperson, and preached in Tennessee by his son, Anthony Epperson, Jr. (William Stanley's great-grandfather) during the early 1800s. It was also assumed to be the faith of Aphrey Epperson (his grandfather) in the middle 1800s, and son, George Washington Epperson (William Stanley's father), in the early 1900s. But it would end there with my father, and although I never converted to Catholicism, I attended weekly Mass with my beloved, Therese.

*Emily Jane Epperson Death Certificate September 5, 1951, at age 82, 2 months, 20 days. Condition directly leading to death: Cerebral Hemorrhage with antecedent cause due to Arteriosclerosis for years.*

*William Stanley Epperson Death Certificate May, 14, 1956 at age 87, 7 months, 6 days. Condition directly leading to death: Cerebral Accident with antecedent cause due to Arteriosclerosis for years and Chronic Myocardial.*

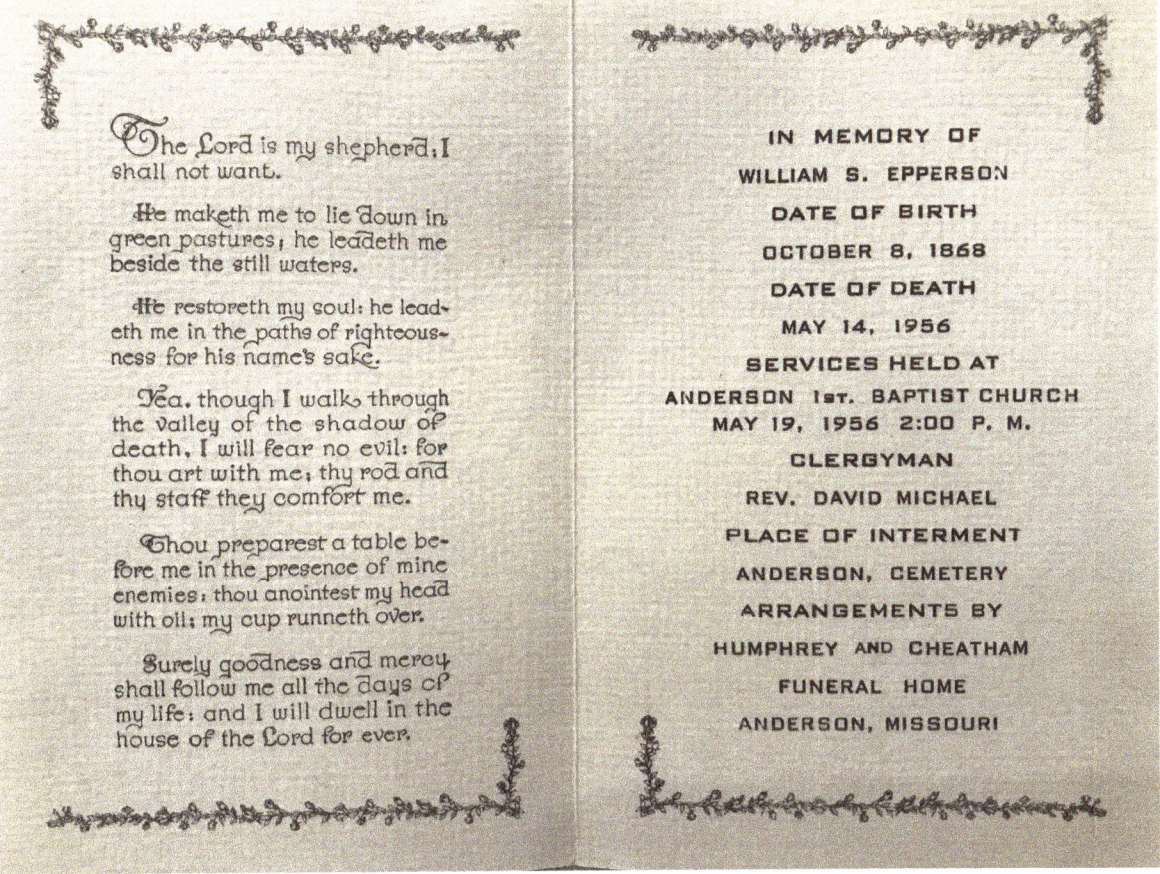

*William Epperson funeral prayer card, Psalm 23. In memory of William S. Epperson. Date of Birth – October 8, 1868, Date of Death – May 14, 1956, Service held at Anderson, 1st Baptist Church, May 19, 1956, 2:00p.m. Place of Interment – Anderson cemetery. Arrangements by Humphrey and Cheatham Funeral Home, Anderson, Missouri.*

# Our Children and Grandchildren and Golden Wedding Anniversary

Although our son died as a young man, our daughters grew to adulthood, married, and had children of their own, who called us Poppy, or Pop-pop, and Dede.

**Joan Rosalind Epperson Giles** *married James P. Giles and had three children: Christopher 'Cricket', William Epperson 'Eppy' and Allison Conrey 'Allie' Giles*

**Orval Wilford Epperson** *died in WWII over the English Channel, near La Havre, France. He did not marry and had no children.*

**Tirzah Madelon Epperson Federer** *married Richard L. Federer and had 11 children: Maria Therese 'Mimi', Katherine Jeanne 'Kathy', Richard Eric 'Rich', Elizabeth Ann 'Lisa', William Joseph 'Billy', Winifred Yvonne 'Winnie', Thomas Alexander 'Tom', Theodore Giles 'Ted', Constance Madelon 'Connie', James Robert 'Jim', John Michael 'John'.*

*1969 Left to right: Dick and Tirzah (Terry) Federer, Therese (Dede) and Orval (Poppy), Joan and Jim Giles.*

*1965 Giles and Federer visit to Neosho. Left to right: Dick Federer holding twin sons Tom and Ted. Standing: Rich, Mimi, and Kathy Federer, and Cricket and Eppy Giles. Sitting: Tirzah (Terry) Federer holding daughter, Connie. Dede and Poppy, Joan and Jim Giles. Sitting on ground: Lisa, Billy, and Winnie Federer, and Allie Giles.*

*1969 Federer visit to Neosho. Left to right: Mimi, Rich, Tirzah (Terry) holding baby John, Poppy and Dede, Billy, Kathy, Lisa, and Dick Federer. Front row: Tom, Connie, Winnie, Ted, and Jim.*

## GOLDEN WEDDING ANNIVERSARY

At our half century mark together, our daughter, Joan, planned a beautiful golden wedding anniversary celebration. The grand affair was coupled with the wedding of our oldest granddaughter, Christopher Giles, to Samuel Graham, even Tirzah and Dick with eight of their eleven children flew from St. Louis. The *Society Page of Pasadena, California*, Wednesday, August 20, 1969, reported,

> Golden Anniversary Feted with Giles Family Reunion.
>
> A golden anniversary celebration, a wedding, and a family reunion all in one week kept Mr. and Mrs. James P. Giles Jr. of San Marino busy recently.
>
> The anniversary celebrants were Mr. and Mrs. Orval W. Epperson of Neosho, Mo., Mrs. Giles' parents.
>
> The newlyweds are the Giles's' daughter, Christopher, and Samuel Graham.
>
> Among the reunion visitors were Mr. and Mrs. Jess N. Legg of Dallas, uncle and aunt of Mr. Giles of San Marino; Mrs. James P. Giles Sr., his mother and Mrs. Richard Federer of St. Louis, Mrs. James Giles Jr., sister. Out-of-town visitors, stayed at the Huntington Sheraton Hotel where many of the activities took place.

*Therese and Orval Epperson*

# My Investments

I started investing from scratch in the early 1950s and although I enjoyed it, and had some early successes, I had to stop for a while because I had accumulated some debts. It was nearly 10 years later before I could start it up again. I found that I had a bit of my grandfather George Washington Epperson in me, because I, too, speculated in futures. Not navy beans, like he did, but in butter and eggs, and I was a tad more successful.

I had been working at the Bank of Neosho for many years and quite comfortable in financial matters when I met a fellow at St. Canera's church named Dick Finucan, who worked at the Fish Hatchery. Together, we hatched up a scheme on eggs as futures, and we made a small profit.

When eggs were selling for 17 cents a dozen for a future delivery, we would put up a small margin, say $300 for one carload of egg futures, and by that future date, if the eggs went up to 19 cents, we would have made a profit of 2 cents per dozen, and at 360 cases of eggs in a carload, with 30 dozen to the case, we made a nice return, after we paid the broker's commission.

$.02 cents/dozen x (30 dozen to the case x 360 cases) = $216 profit.

The broker wouldn't accept any dealings from someone in a financial institution, so the eggs were all bought in Finucan's name, even though we both put up half of the money. In the end, we accumulated about $1,500 in profit, not a bad return.

*Bank of Neosho building. Bank of Neosho vault with Orval Epperson on right.*

Then we thought, what about the butter business? That could work the same way. Once we bought a carload of tub butter in July for delivery at the end of September. We thought we had most of September to decide who to sell it to but on the first day of September the broker wired us that the carload was delivered on the future's contract. This was nearly 30 days before we thought we would have to decide. The carload was sitting there in Chicago and the broker wanted to know what to do with it.

Finucan came rushing into the Bank of Neosho, all flustered, waving the telegram. "What does this mean? We have a carload of butter?"

I told him to relax, we would instruct the broker to sell the butter, before any demurrage charges were applied, which he did, and we lost $400 in the exchange. But that was not the only thing we lost. Our partnership dissolved, because finicky Finucan was not comfortable with the risks. He was eventually transferred back to New Jersey, and I never saw him again.

In 1960s, I started to buy and sell more frequently. I started with Goodyear stock at $42 per share and sold it at $55. That was the beginning of my successful stock dealings. I only bought a few shares at a time, nothing excessive. But in 1969, at age 78, I owned stock in both Goodyear, and B.F. Goodrich. I saw that Goodrich was paying more dividends, and the only difference was that the S & P rated Goodyear as A Grade, and Goodrich as B Grade, so I sold Goodyear at $55, and bought Goodrich at $45.

When Goodrich got up to $55, I thought that was a good enough profit, so I called the broker and asked, "What is quoted on Goodrich this morning?"

He said there was no market yet on Goodrich; no one was trading. But there was a rumor that Chicago Northwest Industries (C&NW), a railroad holding company from Chicago, was trying to take over Goodrich.

So I said, "Well, keep track of it, and if anything develops give me a call."

It wasn't but an hour later when he called me back with the news that Goodrich opened at $66. The attempt to acquire B.F. Goodrich was being fiercely defended, and they were thwarting the C&NW takeover. So I got out at $65. That wasn't the result of good management or insight, it was just perfect timing and a bit of dumb luck. I made $2,000 instead of $1,000 on my stock.

With the profits on B.F. Goodrich and Goodyear, and also what I had saved from various dividends, I thought I would buy 300 shares of Pet Milk at $25 per share. Pet Milk had a solid reputation and was paying good dividends. My initial investment of $7,500, turned into $10,500, when Pet Milk increased to $35 per share. I sold it and made $3,000. I was feeling pretty good with that trade, but if I had just held on to it a little longer, I could have made three times that amount. But that is the way the market goes, you can't get stuck on what ifs.

In 1974, I was 83 years old, and still working at the bank. The bank didn't press me with a lot of responsibilities, I was more of a consultant by then anyway, so I had time to dabble further in the market. I would move my investments into bonds when things got too high, then switched back and forth from bonds to stocks. It got to be where I could buy a few hundred shares at a time, and sell on a much larger scale. So I bought Swift, International Minerals, Woolworth, and Western Union.

I used to do all my trading with Merrill Lynch in Tulsa, and started letting Bill Mildren trade for me because of my friendship with his father, Bill, Sr. So, in that way, Bill, Jr. made a nice commission. One of my purchases totaled $60,000. Bill got a good commission that day.

Bill used to say, "Epperson comes here like he's going through the grocery store. He never asks the broker what to buy. He just scans the grocery shelves, and then places his order. Gives me 100 shares of this, and 100 shares of that, then sell 200 of this, and so on."

Every once in a while he would call to ask if I wanted to take some profits, and so I'd check the Dow Jones. If it weren't favorable then I would say, "No, I'll just hold on awhile and see what develops."

During the spring of 1976, I sold half a dozen shares, and made $16,000 profit. I could have made $50,000, had I sold the whole smear, but I didn't want to incur too much income tax in one year, and at the price that I had originally bought the shares, I would make a good amount at any time.

Recently, I sold Goodyear, Goodrich, Woolworth, and W.T. Grant, and I made a nice profit, with the exception of W.T. Grant. That company was a mass merchandising chain store that went belly up. It was the second largest bankruptcy in history, with the most apparent cause being the decision to extend credit to all customers without assessing their ability to repay. I didn't use my head on W. T. Grant when I bought the shares, but I only lost $1,000 when I sold. There were many other people, and banks, that lost much more. So, I guess didn't do too badly.

Over the years, I've bought International Minerals, Morton Salt, Western Union, Kansas City Southern, Woolworths, Swift & Co., Union Bank, to name a few. But I only bought oil stocks once and came out all right. So I guess you could say that I've scattered my shots. Not just in stocks, but of a wide variety of stocks. Timing in the marketplace is the essence to the game. And, of course, sometimes you get a winner and sometimes you get a goose.

# Orval the Fisherman

I guess I have always been a fisherman, ever since my mother and I fished for chub down on Indian Creek. For many years, George Tretbar, Bob Woods, Dee Haggard, and I were a fishing foursome. We used to go down to Grand Lake in Oklahoma, occasionally, bringing along one or two of George or Bob's boys.

We put up our tent, near the shoreline, and used that as our headquarters, where we slept, played cards, and cooked on a little stove. George, being a plumber, had a little container he used to heat lead in, and we used that as our cooking pot. I would cook our meals in it. The plumber's furnace heated lead quickly, which was necessary for their trade, but it cooked potatoes too fast, and I had a hard time keeping them from burning. No one complained, though. I guess they knew their turn to cook would eventually come. Sometimes, we cooked our fresh fish right there, sometimes we would bring the fish home, and sometimes, of course, we didn't catch anything.

*Orval Epperson, the fisherman*

There were times when we went down to fish just for the day or the evening. We didn't bring a tent then, and would sit in the little house structure on the dock, and fish out of the circular well that was in the center of it. During one of those times, we caught a right nice turtle. There were some folks fishing nearby who asked what we were going to do with the turtle. We said that we'd eat the legs and throw the rest away.

Oh no, don't do that," one woman replied, "We'd like it."

So they took the turtle, shell and all, cut it into about one-inch squares. and cooked it in a little pot all day, to make it tender. I never knew turtle shells were edible, but they were, and didn't tasted too terribly bad.

The *Kansas City Star Rod and Gun* and the *Joplin Globe,* Wednesday June 11, 1947 reported, A HAUL OF CATFISH FROM GRAND LAKE

These Neosho business men have returned from a four-day fishing trip on Grand Lake, which was quite profitable, thank you. They are left to right, George Tretbar, Dee Haggard, Bob Woods, and Orval Epperson.

Two hundred and fifty pounds of catfish were caught by trot line including two fish of 21 pounds each, one of 17, two of 13, two of 12, and one of 10 pounds shown in the picture. Rod and reel and cane-pole fishing landed several nice bass, crappie, perch, drum, and carp.

The men camped in Delaware County, Oklahoma, north of Zena, and fished in water usually too rough for successful trot line fishing.

They are all veterans of World War One and members of Clyde Burdick post, No. 163, American Legion, and all have served as commanders of the post. They have fished together many times and after good catches have donned aprons and cooked and served fish suppers to the Neosho Chamber of Commerce, of which all are members.

The *Neosho Daily Democrat,* June 7, 1949 reported,

Dee Haggard and Orville[sic] Epperson Give Fishing Lesson. Glen Morse of the U.S. Bureau of fisheries was guest of Dee Haggard and Orval Epperson for a weekend fishing trip to Grand Lake where the prized fish of their career was landed.

Glen was running the lines when this monster showed up, and becoming excited at the size of what he termed, 'an animal' called for help. He held on to it while Epperson placed the landing net under it and boated it.

When they returned to Neosho Monday afternoon and weighed the 'animal' it tipped the scales at 27 pounds. They evidently had hooked several larger fish than this one for several had broken away.

About two dozen fish of other varieties were caught, including a number of smaller catfish, drum, carp, and crappie, also two turtles and a gar. Glen's enthusiasm was expressed in these words, 'I have waited 50 years to go on a fishing trip like this. I did not know there was any place you could go to catch fish of this size, quality and variety.'

## FISHERMAN TALL TALES

All Fisherman are liars, but here are some true stories for your consideration.

I have been fishing all my life and have fished with the same good friends for many of those years. In fact, we have been fishing together since before Grand Lake formed. Lake O' the Cherokees became Grand Lake in the 1940s with the completion of the Pensacola

Dam, and we fished in those parts for decades before then. Together we pitched our tents on numerous weekends at many different places on some 1300-mile shoreline meandering through the foothills of the Ozark Mountains.

Our fishing equipment was rather skimpy. We had a small plywood row boat, several trotlines with a total length of about a half mile, and some 200 hooks for those lines.

When the legion post quit operating concessions at the Annual Harvest Shows in Neosho, two canvas backstops were salvaged from the doll-racks, and when faced together made a satisfactory tent, large enough to cover our four canvas army cots.

*Fishing at Grand Lake. Left to right: George Tretbar, Dee Haggard, Bob Woods, O.W. Epperson.*

Miners carbide burning lamps furnished all the light needed in our tent. A plumber's furnace for melting metal served to cook our food in double quick time. Four canvas chairs, a card table, and a pinochle deck were practically all the rest of our equipment.

In the hottest part of the summer days, we'd strip down to our shorts, and sometimes even took them off, too, and played pinochle in the shade of our tent until the cool of evening. Needless to say, we tried to pick places on the lake where roads made it difficult for the usual weekend fisherman to come or where the water was usually too rough for successful trotline fishing, and this enabled us to dress, or undress, just about as we liked without the probability of being disturbed, and also accounted for our unusual experiences and some large catches.

On a recent weekend, we boated about 250 pounds of catfish, besides several carp, bass, perch, and drum. The larger ones weighing twenty-one pounds each. Of course, an even larger one got away.

A three-pound catfish was caught on the original bait, and a larger one had swallowed it, but with the waves running about three feet high, the small boat had to be handled carefully. Just before the big one could be brought near enough for the landing net to be used, it disgorged the three pounder without getting hooked. The three-pound bait, however, furnished a nice dinner for us fisherman.

Another time, we put out our tent in the shade of four small persimmon trees a few steps from the lake at a point where the shallow water extended several hundred feet out. Along about dusk what appeared to be a fog began to rise from the surface of the lake and almost before we knew it, millions of what were called mayflies began settling on us, our tent, and the little group of trees, which were the only trees near the shore for a considerable distance in either direction. We hurriedly closed our tents, but all night it sounded like a strong wind blowing in the little trees. Within 36 hours the dead insects were more than two inches deep, by actual measurement, under the trees and for some distance around our tent, so we pulled stakes and went home.

Those flies were said to live forty-eight hours. After they came out from the mud at the shallow bottom of the lake and rose to the surface, they shed their skin and used it as a raft while they dried their wings enough to fly to the shore where they spent the few remaining hours of their life cycle breeding, and then died. A short time later, the newborn grubs made their way to the water and into the mud to grow until the time came to repeat the ancient performance.

That was a very long night. We could not sleep as hundreds of fish were splashing in the shallow waters eating the insects before they could shed their skins and fly to land. We tried all sorts of bait but could not get any to bite. Big fish, up to three feet long would be splashing around the water not more than one-foot deep and in desperation we waded in and tried to snare them with the landing net, which had a four-foot handle. It tried our patience to watch those big ones swim up to within eight or ten feet from us and then calmly gulp in an insect on the surface and move slowly on with its back fins above water. It looked very much like they were making faces in derision at our frustration. We finally did manage to net a few of those with our short minnow seine net, otherwise, we would have had to go home without any fish.

Of course, not all trips were as eventful as the one just described, but unusual things happened so frequently that the trips were never monotonous.

June 1, 1946, was an unusually cold day for fishing. While on the small row boat, we spotted some color in the distance and came across something special. We waded out to one of the small islands on the lake and picked several gallons of dew berries that grew wild there. It was so cold that day that we had to wear heavy coats all buttoned up to keep comfortable in the cold wind, which had been blowing for several hours, but the sweetness of the dew berries made it all worthwhile.

On another trip last summer, we did not catch a single fish, even though crawfish, minnows, worms and artificial lures were used. However, a two-pound bass jumped into the boat before we arrived at our normal honey hole, and when rowing back to our camp a three-and-a-half-pound bass jumped in also. Those were the only fish caught that trip. Twice as many voluntarily jumped into the boat as were caught by actual fishing.

In the hottest weather, we'd do our trot line fishing in water ranging from forty to one-hundred feet deep and weighted the line so it stayed at the bottom of the lake. We found that most of the catfish caught at that depth would be dead within two hours unless we ran the lines more often than that. They seemed to drown from either the water pressure or the lack of oxygen. We theorized that in the summer, the water at the surface received a fresh supply of oxygen from the waves and the wind. But being so hot, the fresh oxygen did not sink to the lower depths, and the water down deep became stagnant and drowned the fish when they were hooked and could not come near the surface to breathe after feeding a short time near the bottom.

Now all this may have caused some folks to say, "All fishermen are liars," but if Ripley or anyone else cared to verify the truth of the quote, "Believe-it-or-Not," it could be arranged. There was usually about three times during the summer when the phenomenon of the flies occurred, and the spot on the lake where the fish drowned could be proven in late July and August.

## FISHING PRANKS

Once George Tretbar and I went fishing at the Ponderosa (a dock at the Elk River area of Grand Lake). We fished all Saturday night with no luck. Lots of other people were there, too. Along about 7:00 a.m. the next morning, Lila Robison and her sister, began pulling them in directly where we had been fishing all night, but had moved because we weren't catching anything. So you just never can tell.

Larry Hoberock went with us once. Everyone was catching fish but Larry. So while he was away from his poles I hung a fish on his hook, as a prank. When Larry came back, he was so excited to see a fish that he began to pull it up. But somehow, before he could get it on land, he managed to lose that one, too. Larry just wasn't much of a fisherman.

Another time Guy Scott went with us to Shadowrock, near Grand Lake in Oklahoma. Although everyone was catching fish all around him, Guy wasn't catching any. At one point, when he left to go to the restroom, I hung a fish on his hook and dropped it back into the water. When Guy returned, I mentioned that something seemed to be fooling around with one of his poles. Guy looked at the pole, and then looked at me and said, "Yeah, and it's a two-legged something." He wasn't as easy to fool.

Once, John Kirsch was bemoaning the fact that he never caught any fish, even though he and Lewis Oldham went down to their own dock almost every weekend. I said that I had no trouble catching fish at the Colonial Height's dock at Grand Lake, and invited him to come down the following weekend with us.

So John did. He sat right across the well from me and sure enough, this time he caught twenty-seven fish. He couldn't get over it. However, in the same period of time, I caught one-hundred-and six. John couldn't get over that either.

You could fish with more than one pole on the dock if there wasn't a big crowd. I would often sit with two poles only a couple feet apart. And yet all the fish I caught on any given night would be from only one pole, even though the two were baited, and watched exactly the same. Who knew why? Maybe some submerged trees on one side had bugs on them; the minnows would come in and eat the bugs, and the big fish would come in and eat the minnows, and one line was in the right spot for them, and the other wasn't.

On that same trip, John complained that he wasn't feeling very well and when I asked why, he remarked that he was eighty-years-old.

"Why, I'm eighty, too." I added.

John was flabbergasted.

"When is your birthday? September?" I asked, "Well, mine is in October, so you are only a month older that me."

John couldn't get over that, but he did have heart trouble. He carried around some pills for it, and that was what eventually got him. One day, he went out walking his little dog, and when they found him he was in between the house and the hospital, on the sidewalk. I guess he was 82 when he died. Joyce came to settle the estate, and the house was sold to the hospital and became part of the parking lot.

## I CAUGHT A SHARK

My oldest daughter, Joan and her family lived in California. One summer we went out to visit them and went fishing. The *Joplin Globe*, Tuesday, August 6, 1968 reported,

> Orval Epperson, Neosho Banker, has a bottle of shark teeth to remind him of a midsummer fishing expedition off Catalina Island in Pacific waters. The accompanying photo, however, shows the banker and his catch – before the 101-pound trophy was reduced to mere teeth.
>
> Let me tell you the banker's fishing story – as it happened.
>
> Using a monofilament leader with five hooks – about a foot apart – the Neosho adventurer was fishing with 1,000 feet of 20-test line. He and his party were fishing for codfish about 300 feet down. Epperson reports that while bringing a cod to surface, a little shark snipped at the bait and took it off. The skipper of the 'Harbor Patrol,' the speedy little craft from which the party was fishing the Pacific waters, started up the motor and gave Epperson a helping hand in tiring out the big fish.
>
> The banker told me he had the drag on the reel set for 10 pounds and the big fish made three runs, once with the end of the line coming up on the spool, and 30 minutes after hooking the shark more than a half-mile from where the fish bit off more than he could chew, Mr. Shark was boat side.
>
> This, too, is almost another story. Suddenly, it seems there was no gaff with which to lift the hefty one into the boat. What to do? Epperson didn't want to lose his big fish. Well, a couple of members of the party grabbed the shark by the tail and flung it to the bottom of the boat and after the slashing shark calmed down- stabbed it with a butcher knife.
>
> After grand illusions of shark steaks, one of the party told him it would be like eating leather. So, the Neosho angler decided he had to have something to show for his angling adventures and asked if the shark's teeth might be cleaned off the meat (by boiling).
>
> Later it was found there was no jaw bone – just gristle and in the process of boiling the meat off, the only thing left was the teeth. And that's what Epperson has to show for his big shark.
>
> Then there's another angle to this fish story, too. After the shark had been conked out with the butcher knife, it was discovered that two of the original five hooks had been bitten off by the ravenous fish, and three remaining barbs had been caught in the shark's belly–that's how close (among other things) my Neosho banker friend came to losing his biggest fish.

Joining in the exciting expedition with the Neoshoan were James P. Giles, Epperson's son-in-law and president of the American Cement Co. in Los Angeles; 'Eppy' Giles, grandson of the Newton County banker, Bob Vickers, skipper of the boat, and Butch Rhinehart, superintendent of the American Cement Co. quarry on Catalina Island.

Oh yes, neighbor, the party caught other fish, too, in addition to the exciting adventure with the shark. Fish like codfish, Bonita, kelp bass, sheep-head, sculpin, perch, grouper, halibut, barracuda, etc. etc.

Incidentally, the shark was six feet, two inches long.

Anyone for a bit of quiet bass fishing in the Ozarks?

*August 6, 1968. Orval Epperson, Neosho Banker's Catalina Shark Catch.*

# PART VII
# THE LAST YEARS

*MR. BANKER AT BANK OF NEOSHO*

*THE MAPLE TREE POEM*

*ORVAL AND THERESE DEATHS*

*RESEARCH ON SELLERS AND SHERER*

*EPPERSON BRIEF FAMILY LINEAGE*

# Mr. Banker at Bank of Neosho

**NEOSHO BANKER ORVAL EPPERSON PASSES HALF-CENTURY IN CAREER**

The *Neosho Newton County Missouri News*, Friday, January 24, 1958 reported,

*Orval Epperson, Neosho Banker.*

> Starting now on 51 years of service to a community as a banker is the record of O. W. Epperson, assistant cashier and assistant trust officer of the Bank of Neosho, who, December 7, rounded out the half-century mark.
>
> It was on this date that Mr. Epperson started with the local bank. Back in 1907 all of the bank's work was done by the cashier, assistant cashier and one bookkeeper. Willie Wills, then cashier of the bank, hired Orval to run errands and assist the bookkeeper with the pen and ink postings. The new employee was not able to amass much capital from his $6.00 weekly wage after paying for board, room and other necessities.
>
> By the time he was 21 he had saved enough money to make a down payment on 10 shares of bank stock, which he was permitted to buy from J. M. Ritchey, president of the bank. At that time the board of directors had to give written consent before any bank stock could be sold to a new stockholder.
>
> At the next annual meeting of stockholders, Epperson was elected to the board of directors, appointed secretary of the board and made assistant cashier. In 1918 he took a leave of absence and went overseas with the 338th Machine Gun Battalion, 88th Division. When the Armistice was declared, he was participating in the drive on Metz. After being discharged from the Army in June 1919, he returned to his work at the bank.

Epperson was elected Cashier of the bank in 1921 following the death of Willie Wills. He served in that capacity until he sold his stock to John E. Wagner, who had become president of the bank.

Since that time, he has served in an administrative capacity and has given much of his time to civic affairs.

In the Newton-McDonald County Bankers Association he has filled all of the offices from the president down; in boy scout work, served as chairman of the Newton-McDonald District and a member of the Mo-Kan area council board; as Commander Adjutant and Finance Officer of the local American Legion post; holds offices in the 15th district Legion Association; has held various offices in the local Masonic bodies and presently is treasurer of Neosho Lodge #247; a member of the Neosho Chamber of Commerce: served as secretary, treasurer and director of Neosho Community Sales, Inc. and also Neosho Recreation Company, which among other things acquired and sold to the Neosho School District, for a nominal sum, the C.R.C. building and its grounds.

He was president of Neosho Board of Education for 10 years of the 15 years he served on that board and it was during his tenure of office that the land was acquired for the present high school site on highway 71.

In 1921 he was elected to the Board of Directors Neosho Building and Loan Association, serving continuously, since that time and is also treasurer of the association. In recognition of his 50 years of service the bank presented Epperson with an Elgin Shock Masters wrist watch, appropriately inscribed.

## NEOSHO BANKER ORVAL EPPERSON IS A GOOD CITIZEN

The *Neosho Newton County Missouri News*, Friday, January 13, 1961 reported on Orval Epperson,

> I was born October 13, 1891. Retiring at 65 did not appeal to me because I believe that working for more than fifty years in the Bank of Neosho has given me some valuable experience, and the bank is justly entitled to the benefit of that experience for as long as they think my salary is being earned. I enjoy having my friends bring me their problems and quite often have been able to prevent their making serious mistakes.
>
> I also believe my patriotic duty to work as long as my health permits so I can pay income taxes, for if I should retire and draw social security and disability pension for military services, I would be drawing from, instead of paying into, the United States Treasury.
>
> Finally, I like to work and would prefer to "wear out" and not "rust out.

## ORVAL EPPERSON DAY FEBRUARY 17, 1967

The *Neosho Newton County Missouri News*, February 17, 1967 reported,

>Orville [sic] Epperson could be described Neosho's 'Mr. Banker.'
>
>If Orville [sic] Epperson, assistant cashier at the Bank of Neosho were to be given a nickname it would be "Mr. Banker." Mr. Epperson has been with the Bank of Neosho since December 1907, nearly 60 years. In fact, it has been the only job he has ever known.
>
>"I came with the bank when I was 16," Mr. Epperson said, "and have been here ever since. I once sold all my stock and didn't expect to stay long, but it didn't turn out that way. I'm still here."
>
>He became assistant cashier when he reached his 21st birthday. "I started at 16 and did a little bit of everything. Then when I became 21, they made me assistant cashier. That was when Willy Wills was cashier."
>
>Mr. Epperson also revealed that he was at one-time secretary to the board and cashier. But when he sold his stock, he then reverted back to assistant cashier, a position he still holds.
>
>To look at Mr. Epperson, one would not think that he was 76 years of age. In fact, he doesn't look that much over 60. He attributes this to "not worrying, three good meals a day and a lot of exercise."
>
>When he says exercise, he means just that. Mr. Epperson walks to and from work each day, rain or snow, "except when it's raining too hard, I take a cab."
>
>The banking business has undergone a number of changes the past 60 years. "When I started," Mr. Epperson said, "We did our posting on the old Boston ledger. All by hand and had to be balanced each day. Then we went to silicate slate, and it was a lot easier but we still had to do it daily and sometimes when erasing we would erase someone else's balance and then we would have to start all over again."
>
>He continued, "Now we have a proof machine that takes care of everything. Things are a lot easier than they used to be. In the old days we used to count each person's deposits and add up each check. Now all we do is count the cash and let the proof machine take care of the rest."
>
>The loan business has also changed. "Back in those days we had mostly unsecured loans, no chattels, and as a result we had quite a few losses. But today we have chattels and the borrowers know that if they don't pay their loans they stand to lose something."

In 1907, when Mr. Epperson started with the Bank of Neosho, deposits totaled $300,000 and nearly one-half of that was in stockholders' accounts. Now the deposits at the bank total a little more than $12 million.

"It was virtually a one or two-man operation in 1907, and now we have many employees," Mr. Epperson said.

"And are you a married, man?" Mr. Epperson was asked.

"I guess you could say I'm married. I have 13 grandchildren," Mr. Epperson replied. He and his wife, Therese have 2 daughters - Mrs. Joan Giles of Los Angeles, and Mrs. Tirzah Federer, St. Louis.

"We used to all get together each summer," Mr. Epperson recalled, "But now it's just too many for our house. You know 13 grandchildren in one house at one time can be a problem."

Mr. Epperson is a native of McDonald County, being born in Anderson and then came to Neosho for high school where he attended until he started in the banking business.

"I wouldn't live anywhere else except Neosho," He said, "Things have changed a lot in the past 60 years, but it's still the best place to live."

*1967 Orval Epperson Day*

# The Maple Tree Poem

Poppy loved to fish and garden and do all things in nature. He would often spend time in silence outside with his eyes closed rocking on the wooden bench swing in their backyard, listening to the birds and humming along. Every opportunity he had, he would find a lake or stream and fish, and if he wasn't fishing, he was gardening. When his grandchildren came to visit, he would teach them to fish and garden as well.

In one of his letters to his granddaughter, Lisa (Tirzah's daughter), on May 14, 1974, he wrote about two birds who took up residency in a tree next to their bedroom window and named them after Therese and himself.

> The two lovebirds are chirping to each other as usual. Also, Poppy bird manages to bring home a few worms for Dede bird to arrange attractively before him at meal time.
>
> You should see our garden now. It is not at all like it was at Easter. The irises on each side of the walk to the sidewalk make a lovely sight. The peonies are almost shoulder high by the asparagus bed and have the most blossoms they have ever had and in such a variety of colors. It's just about time to mow down the jonquils and plant the marigolds and zinnias. They are coming up thick as hair in our little plot where we raised them up for transplanting time.
>
> The fish were still biting last Saturday down on the lake and I hooked eleven nice crappies, two lineside bass, and two rock bass, so I was pretty well pleased with the results.

*Poppy with grandsons Rich (Tirzah's son) and Eppy (Joan's son) after a fishing trip.*

Later on in his life, he wrote a poem about a maple tree that his children nurtured from a seedling. As his children grew up, he taught them to respect the land just as he had learned. As the seasons turned and the years passed, the maple tree had some years of struggle, but through it all, the tree and Orval survived, and it became a trusty old friend.

*Dede and Poppy in the backyard of 344 South Hamilton.*

# MEMORIES

*My friendly Maple waves to me*
*When summer breezes blow*
*And hints of comforts, only we*
*Are privileged to know.*

*Above me stretch her verdant arms*
*Inviting me to share*
*The soothing solace of her charms*
*And gently stirring air.*

*In Fall kind nature tints her hair*
*With colors gay and bright*
*And people drive for miles to share*
*This lovely God-made sight.*

*When winter whips with ice and sleet*
*Her neighbors cower in fear.*
*Staunchly she stands on sturdy feet*
*A crystal chandelier.*

*Comes Spring, our grandchildren abound*
*And furtively they peek*
*As squirrels scamper up and down*
*And birds play hide-and-seek.*

*One day when Tirzah, Bill and Joan*
*Played on our garden wall*
*They spied this seedling, all alone,*
*Then only inches tall.*

*Smothered by grass and choked by weeds*
*It barely was alive,*
*It sorely craved its sunshine needs*
*If it were to survive.*

*"Come, Mom and Dad, join in our plot*
*You're kind to things, we know.*
*Let's move it to a sunny spot,*
*Give it a chance to grow."*

*As time moves on – in future years,*
*You'll sit beneath this tree*
*Recall, perhaps, through misty tears,*
*The foresight of YOUR THREE.*

*With Therese watching by my side*
*They worked with hoe and spade,*
*And made a bed, with youthful pride,*
*In it the waif was laid.*

*A graceful Maple here now stands,*
*God's son, his rain and air*
*Have fruited what six little hands*
*Began with tender care.*

*The years have passed and God above*
*Has called Bill to his home,*
*He there awaits with tender love*
*Till we no longer roam.*

*Tirzah and Joan, unite as one*
*Though living far apart*
*And 344 South Hamilton*
*Is always in each heart.*

*Therese and I, alone abide,*
*Enjoying Maple shade.*
*From cups of memories, with pride,*
*We sip those dreams THEY made.*

*Their prophesy about their tree*
*Was made with hearts afire.*
*Now, dreams and memories, have we,*
*What more could one desire?*

# Orval and Therese Deaths

In July 1974, Orval began feeling unwell. He thought it was perhaps an old hernia acting up, but it was cancer, malignant melanoma, and within two years, he would be gone. Dede wrote a letter, dated February 21, 1976, to her granddaughter, Lisa, that prayers and chemotherapy would beat it.

*Poppy and Dede.*

> Dear Lisa – you precious one,
>
> It was wonderful to hear you put us first in your prayers for Poppy's healing. I know your prayers will be heard for they come from the heart. Please don't let up on them, we both need your intercession. I was numb when I first learned the news but with much prayers and your mother coming, we got a needed lift. She has been so wonderful. The first time she came your brother, Billy was with her. Next time, your older brother, Dickie, who worked the whole time he was here installing a mount wall faucet in the kitchen. It is lovely. Last Sunday, February 15 your mother and Winnie came and we went to Springfield. We thought we'd be there until Friday, but the doctor let us return on Tuesday. Your Poppy is being treated by chemotherapy and was given a special injection last time plus a new drug that has not yet been released to the public. At the end of three weeks we are to return to Springfield for checkup and treatment. That will be March 8. Your mother is usually only here for one night.
>
> For a long, long time we've had beautiful, warm days with bright moonlight nights. But on Friday the 20th there was a change. Last night there were several tornados not far away and today's temperature is below 40. Maybe winter is to return just at the time when our jonquils and white lilacs are about to burst out in bloom. The tall rubber plant is also thriving. I give it a drink occasionally. Lisa, dear, please

keep us in your prayers as you are in ours, and I hope you can make it to Lourdes while over there. Maybe, bring back some Lourdes water?

I'll try to write oftener.

Love you so much!!

Poppy and Dede

During his illness, Poppy's oldest daughter, Joan, would travel from California to Neosho to spend weeks and months with them. She kept his mind off the cancer by having him recount his life, recording it all. She would transcribe her notes for a book one day, but after Poppy's death, Dede told her to destroy the tapes. Joan had written down some of his memories which we now have today, and which are the basis for this book.

Poppy died as he lived, gracefully and without complaint on Saturday, November 20, 1976, at the age of eighty-five. They had been married 57 years. At the funeral home, in front of all their children and grandchildren and great grandchildren, Therese flung her arms over Orval's body and buried her head into his chest, giving out a loud and agonizing cry. He was gone, and she was alone.

*1975 backyard swing at 344 S. Hamilton. Left to right standing: Dede, Joan Giles, Poppy, Chris (Giles) Graham.*

*Orval William Epperson Death Certificate, November 20, 1976, age 85. Immediate cause of death: Malignant Melanoma for 1 year.*

The *Joplin Globe,* Sunday November 21, 1976 reported,

> Neosho, Mo. – Orval W. Epperson, 85, 344 S. Hamilton Ave., died at 7 a.m. Saturday at his home after a one-year illness. He was born Oct. 13, 1891, in Anderson, Mo. He moved to Neosho in 1907 and attended Neosho High School. In December of 1907, he started a 69-year banking career at the Bank of Neosho and worked there as assistant cashier and trust officer until his death. In 1918, he served with the 338th Machine Gun Battalion of the 88th Division in World War I.
>
> From 1937 to 1952, he was a member of the Board of Education, serving as board president for 10 of those 15 years. He was a former member of the Neosho Community Sales, serving as its secretary-treasurer and director. He was past commander, finance officer, and adjutant of the Clyde Burdick American Legion Post. Mr. Epperson also held offices in the 15th District Legion organization. He was past chairman of the Newton-McDonald County District of Boys Scouts and past member of the Mo-Kan Area Council Board. He has held, at different times, all offices in the Newton-McDonald County Bankers Association. He was currently a member of the Neosho Chamber of Commerce and secretary of the Board of Directors of the Neosho Building and Loan Association, having served since 1921.
>
> He is survived by his wife, Mrs. Therese Epperson; two daughters, Mrs. J.P. Giles, Claremont, Calif., and Mrs. Richard Federer, St. Louis, Mo., a brother, Love Epperson, Grove Okla.; a sister, Mrs. Ina Fry, Sharon Springs, Kan., and 14 grandchildren and four great-grandchildren.
>
> Services will be at 10 a.m. Monday in St. Canera's Catholic Church with Father James J. Unterreiner officiating. Burial will be in Neosho IOOF Cemetery under direction of the Clark Funeral Home. Pallbearers will be James Giles, Dick Federer, Epperson Giles, and Oliver Clerc Jr. The family will receive friends at the funeral home from 5 until 7 p.m. today. Mr. Epperson's body will lie in state at the funeral home until 9 a.m. Monday.

Therese lived just over fifteen years longer. She kept the large house, and walked up the hill to attend Mass. She didn't cook much, but lived on canned soups, garden vegetables, and later, meals-on-wheels. She read the paper, including the *Wall Street Journal,* kept track of all her stock investments, and wrote letters to her daughters and their children. Some of her grandchildren (Lisa, Bill, Tom, Jim, and John) would visit her in Neosho as a halfway stop as they drove to and from college in Dallas, Texas. Tirzah's daughter, Lisa, lived with her for a year while teaching at the local high school.

Fifteen years and one month later, Therese DeBrosse Epperson died of heart failure on Thursday, December 19, 1991, at Sale Hospital. Her daughter, Tirzah, who traveled nearly every weekend to Neosho was at her side, cradling her head as she quietly left this world to join her husband, son, sisters, and parents. She had lived a long and abundant life to the age of 98.

The *Joplin Globe*, Friday, December 20 1991, reported,

> Therese Epperson. Neosho, Mo. – Therese DeBrosse Epperson, 98, 344 South Hamilton St., died at 6:02 a.m. Thursday at Sale Hospital after a six-month illness.
>
> She married Orval W. Epperson on July 4 1919, in Neosho. He died Nov. 20, 1976. Surviving are two daughters, Tirzah Federer, St. Louis, and Joan Giles, Claremont, Calif., 14 grandchildren and 38 great-grandchildren.
>
> Funeral Mass will be held at 1:30 p.m. Saturday at St. Canera's Catholic Church. The Reverend John Harth will officiate. Burial will be in Neosho IOOF Cemetery. Grandsons will serve as pallbearers. A wake service will be at 7 p.m. today at St. Canera's Catholic Church. Visitation is scheduled afterwards. Arrangements are under direction of Clark Funeral Home, Neosho.

The interesting lives of Orval and Therese Epperson (born 1891 & 1893 respectively) offer us a remarkable window in time of southwestern Missouri on the frontier border with the Indian Territory after the Civil War. Their joys and hardships…their rewards and challenges, in fact, how they lived their simple humble lives are truly inspirational and worthy of a nearly inexpressible pride in our heritage and an acknowledgment and gratitude for God's blessings, in the past, the present, and for generations to come.

+++AD MAJOREM DEI GLORIAM +++

*Therese Gertrude (DeBrosse) Epperson Death Certificate, December 19, 1991, age 98. Immediate cause of death: Heart Failure for years.*

## PARABLE OF A MOTHER

Dede always loved a good story or clever poem. She would retype and store them with her other precious letters in the little room off the kitchen. This poem was among them and summed up how she felt about motherhood and her beloved family.

> The young mother set her foot on the path of life, "Is the way long?" she asked.
>
> And her guide said, "Yes, and the way is hard, and you will be old before you reach the end of it. But the end will be better than the beginning."
>
> But the young mother was happy, and she could not believe that anything could be better than these years. So she played with her children and gather flowers for them along the way, and she bathed them in the clear streams, and the sun shone on them and life was good. The young mother cried, "Nothing will ever be lovelier that this."
>
> The night came with storms, and the path was dark and the children shook with fear and cold and the mother drew them close and covered them with her mantle. The children said, "Oh Mother, we are not afraid for you are near, and no harm can come." And the mother said, "This is better than the brightness of the day for I have taught my children courage."
>
> And the morning came, and there was a hill ahead, and the children climbed and grew weary, and the mother was weary, but at all times she said to the children, "A little patience and we are there." So the children climbed, and when they had reached the top, they said, "We could not have done it without you, Mother." And the mother, when she laid down that night looked up at the stars and said, "This is a better day than the last for my children have learned fortitude in the face of hardship. Yesterday, I gave them courage, today I have given them strength."
>
> And the next day came with strange clouds which darkened the earth. Clouds of war and hate and evil, and the children groped and stumbled and the mother said, "Look up, lift your eyes to the light." And the children looked and saw above the clouds and Everlasting Glory, and it guided them and brought them beyond the darkness. And that night the mother said, "This is the best day of all, for I have shown my children, God."

And the days went on, and the weeks, and the months, and the years, and the mother grew old and she was little and bent. But her children were tall and strong and walked with courage. And when the way was rough, they lifted her, for she was light as a feather, and at last they came to a hill, and beyond the hill they could see a shining road and golden gates flung wide.

And the mother said, "I have reached the end of my journey, and now I know that the end is better than the beginning, for my children can walk alone, and their children after them."

And the children said, "You will always walk with us, Mother, even when you have gone through the gates." And they stood and watched her as she went alone, and the gates closed after her. And they said, "We cannot see her, but she is with us still. A mother like ours is more than a memory. She is a living presence."

# Research on Sellers and Sherer

Orval began investigating his mother's side of the family in the early 1940s, and his daughters, Joan and Tirzah continued the research for many years afterwards.

His grandmother Emaline grew up in Seneca, Missouri, on the border of Indian Territory. Her parents, Edward and Elizabeth (Buzzard) Sherer, were pioneers from Ohio and one of the founding families that established Seneca. Elizabeth (Buzzard) Sherer was the old woman that Orval thought to be Indian and smoked a little clay pipe by the fireplace, which she lit from live coals dug out of the burning embers with her bare hands.

Her father was the renowned Captain Jonathan Buzzard from the Black Hawk War who in the 1830s led the pioneering group down the Ohio and Mississippi rivers on homemade flatboats, to Van Buren County, Arkansas, and finally overland to Missouri, carrying few household goods and implements to start their new lives.

Just before the start of the Civil War, Orval's great-grandfather, Edward Sherer was murdered by bushwhackers while on his way home from Neosho. The widowed Elizabeth (Buzzard) Sherer, then ran the farm alone and lived through the atrocities of the Civil War. She had one son who fought for the Confederates and one son who fought for the Union.

In the Fall of 1861, over 200 southern rebel sympathizers stole her cattle and forced her and her remaining children to leave their homestead. With what little she had left, Elizabeth (Buzzard) Sherer set off for Ft. Scott, Kansas, with her daughters, Sarah and Emaline (Orval's grandmother), and her twelfth child, James. Once again they were set upon by marauders, this time Indians, who took their oxen and left them helpless in the road. John Reding, a family friend, owned a mill (Reding's Mill), and although he had southern sympathies, he took them in for a while. A neighbor named Lee gave them some cornmeal, and they found abandoned houses to sleep in. James, the youngest, later wrote that they were so poor, he had to chop wood for fire in his bare feet. The next year, they spend the winter in a stone barn of a farmer named Ritchey. It was the very homestead where the Battle of Newtonia had taken place just months before. Emaline Sherer met Nathaniel Sellers because he was in the same Union Company as her brother, Daniel Sherer, and they married soon after the war, on December 30, 1865 in Newton County, Missouri.

Orval's grandfather Nathaniel Sellers came to Missouri with his family from McMinn County, Tennessee. But before he turned twenty, he and his older brother John Connaway

Sellers (J.C. Sellers) joined hundreds of other young men for the California Gold Rush. They made their money, not from gold, but from cutting cord wood for the mine tunnels and for the pop-up towns that grew around the mines. It was nearly as profitable because wood was more plentiful than gold. They returned home by way of a clipper ship through the Drake Passage and around Cape Horn, where the waters were known to be the most dangerous at the southernmost tip of South America. When they arrived back in Tennessee, their father was dead, and so they moved the family to McDonald County, Missouri.

Nathaniel, along with two brothers, Silas and George joined the Union army (Kansas 2$^{nd}$ Cavalry Regiment Company K) while brothers John Connaway, Wylie Blount, and William Sellers fought for the Confederates. Nathaniel fought in only one battle, the Battle of Newtonia, before he was injured and discharged for disability. He was a blonde-haired, blue-eyed, light-skinned man at 5'10".

After they married, Nathaniel and Emaline moved from Lost Creek Township, in Newton County to the vicinity of Anderson. Nathaniel, or Lee, as he was known, had little property and so the farmland known as Home Place was purchased from his wife's inheritance.

In the Missouri State Census of 1876, Nathaniel Sellers (age 43) and his wife Emaline (age 36) could both read and write. Nathaniel owned 1 horse, 13 cattle, 14 sheep, 18 hogs, 124 bushels of wheat, 500 bushels of corn, 40 pounds of wool, 1 ton of hay, and 50 gallons of molasses. They had 12 children in 18 years, but as a middle-aged father, he died tragically while hauling lumber from the Ozark hills. Most of their children lived long lives with many children of their own. Some stayed in Missouri while others moved to Texas.

*Nathaniel Sellers' younger brother, George W. Sellers Since there is no known photo of Nathaniel Sellers, a photo of his younger brother George W. Sellers (1910 in Bilby, Oklahoma), may show a likeness.*

*Sarah Matilda (Sellers) Chapman/Weaver*

**Sarah Matilda (Sellers) Chapman/Weaver** (1862-1943) first married Henderson W.C. Chapman in Anderson and had one child, Ellege O. Chapman. After her husband died in 1884 she married W.F. Weaver (he had one child from a previous marriage with Mariam Elliff who died in 1883, named Clara B. Barnett.) Sarah Matilda (Tilda) and W.F. Weaver had two children: Roy Weaver and Emily Bell Weaver Guess. Matilda and her husband moved to Bell, Texas in 1910 where she was affectionately called grandma Weaver by all the Vontress community of Haskell County, and where she operated a general store for many years, and was postmistress for the town post office. She was a devoted Christian and died from pneumonia and senility in Haskell, Texas.

**Mary Armetta (Sellers) Chapman** (1866-1952) married Jefferson Harrison Chapman in 1885. Lived in Anderson, Missouri in a large home near the cemetery where they spent their entire lives. Her husband was a produce merchant and they had seven children: Artie (1886), Amy Lois Eppard (1890), Ethel (1891), Ruth (1895), Hubert (1897), May (1900), Roxy (1910). Their son, Hubert was the cousin that would train hop and frog gig on Indian Creek with Orval. Mary died in 1930 from pulmonary hemorrhage.

*Mary Armetta (Sellers) Chapman*

*Margaret Elizabeth (Sellers) Wallace*

**Margaret Elizabeth (Sellers) Wallace** (1867-1948) married Ross August Wallace in 1884. Their children were: Perry, Leona, Hesler, Henry, Lilian, Gladys, Francis. In 1900, they moved to Milam, Texas about the same time as her older sister Matilda and husband W.F. Weaver, left. Afterward they moved to Cobb, Oklahoma, and then finally returned to Bell, Texas (where her sister lived) and where she died from an infection and arthritis of the spine.

**Emily Jane (Sellers) Epperson** (1869-1951) Orval's mother who married William Stanley Epperson in 1894. They had four children: Orval William, James Edward, Graydon Love, Ina Mildred Fry. They moved to Adair, Oklahoma for a few years, then back to farm near Anderson, Missouri. She died from cerebral hemorrhage with arteriosclerosis and cardiac decompression.

*Emily Jane (Sellers) Epperson*

**Silas Elicord** (1871-1896) married Henrietta (Etta) Victoria Higgs, in March 1893. He died young (age 25) from cancer of the neck, and Orval recalled seeing the large sores on his neck. Silas and Etta had one child, Roy E. Sellers.

**Daniel Marion Sellers** (1873-1930) and wife Ora Clark (pregnant with son Daniel), and Margie. He was known as Bull of the Woods, had several illegitimate children including: Mae Webb and Bessie Mitchell. In 1919, at the age of 46, he finally married Ora Clark, age 19. In 1920, he and his wife, Ora were living at the farm of his younger brother, Jim Sellers, but by the 1930 census, he was a berry farmer. He and his wife, Ora, had three children: Margie F., Daniel J., Betty Lou.

*Daniel Marion Sellers*

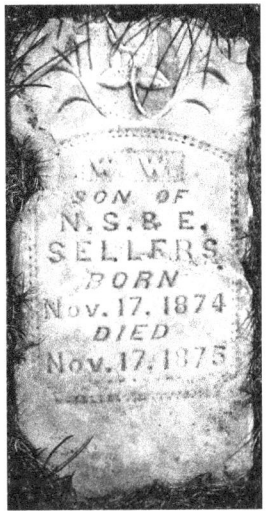
**Baby Willy Sellers**
*(November 17, 1874 – November 17, 1875) died on his first birthday.*

**Baby Willy Sellers** (November 17, 1874 – November 17, 1875)

**James David (J.D.) Sellers** (1876-1943) on right. Married in 1903 to Ruth Ball, who died six years later in 1909. They had three children: Carl, Marvin, Lorine. He and his brothers were known as 'holy terrors' in southwest Missouri. (Daniel Sellers in photo on left)

**Joseph Alonzo (Lon)** (1879-1962) married a fiery redhead named Blanche Maybelle Parsons and had no children. His wife put a bullet in his leg when she caught him making moonshine.

**Martha May (Mae)** (1881-1971) married Tyra E. Bell. They had two children: Clifford and Denna May. They lived as farmers in Anderson, Missouri.

*James David J.D. Sellers on right, Daniel Sellers on left*

**Wilford Lawton (Lawt)** (1882-1936) married Molly Pierce in 1905. They had four children: Raymond, Violet, Basil and Leslie Wells. They spent their years farming in Anderson, Missouri. Wilford was also the middle name that Orval chose for his son, Orval Wilford Epperson.

**Ethel Maud (Sellers) Roark** (1883-1956) married Tom Roark and lived at the edge of Anderson. They had two children: Thomas Elijah and Reeta R. Her husband was first a poolroom keeper, then an oil driller, and then a bookkeeper for public road construction. Orval recalled that her favorite treat was raw onions, slightly cooked bacon, and cornbread, and when she ate it, tears rolled down her cheeks.

*Ethel Maud (Sellers) Roark*

# Epperson Brief Family Lineage

Orval Epperson began extensive research on the Epperson family. His daughters, Joan and Tirzah, continued the research, but they only got so far. The Epperson lineage is believed to have begun in France in 1554, as **Épernon**.

**Jean-Louis de Nogaret de la Valette**, duc d'Épernon, (1554-1642) was closely connected to the kings of France. He was a loyal catholic to King Henry III, Admiral of France, Governor of Normandy, Caen, and La Havre, First Gentlemen of the King's Chamber, Chevalier de l'Ordre du Saint-Esprit, and many more. He and his son Bernard's stories are historical and extensive.

**Bernard de Nogaret la Valette,** 2nd duc d'Épernon (1592-1661) was installed as a chevalier in the Ordre du Saint Esprito. He was commander of the French Army but was so disliked by Cardinal Richelieu that when he refused to lead the charge in the Battle of Fontarabie, because he believed it an ill-fated attack, he was accused of treason. Bernard fled, and his death sentence was carried out in effigy (that is still reenacted today). He met Antoinette Faudoas while exiled in England, and she bore a son, John Épernon.

**John Épernon** (1638-1689) was the first to immigrate to America in 1671. He married twice. His first wife, Sara Fondan Ramon died, and his second wife, Elizabeth Beard, was the mother of Thomas Epperson.

**Thomas Epperson** (1685-1712) born the youngest in Virginia. He had three siblings and three half-siblings. He married Elizabeth (unknown), and they had one child in their short lives, named William Apperson. The names Epernon, Apperson, and Epperson were all interchangeable during those years because not many could spell.

**William Apperson/Epperson** (1708-1768) married Anne Perault and lived in Goochland County, Virginia where they had six children, and belonged to a French Huguenot parish (French Calvinist Protestant), called King William Parish, Virginia. Their second oldest child, Anthony Epperson is our ancestor, but their two youngest children, Littleberry and Elizabeth were bound out to the church of Southam Parish because William neglected to take proper care of them.

**Anthony Epperson** (1730-1814) born in Goochland County, Virginia, baptized Anglican, was widowed and then married a Quaker, named Susannah Holland, whose father owned extensive lands in Bedford County, Virginia. Anthony also was an extensive landowner, and was said to have been on the wrong side of history during the American Revolution. He was jailed for high treason and sedition and soon after left Virginia for Tennessee, joining the Baptist movement with his four sons, including son, Anthony Epperson, Jr.

**Anthony Epperson, Jr**. (1771-1839) born just before the American Revolution, left with his father and family for Tennessee, first to Washington County and then to Smith County. Anthony married Ellender Divers and they had eleven children. He became a Tennessee Primitive Baptist Minister at Kendrick's Creek and Buffalo Ridge and was known to be a strong preacher of the true pioneer spirit, more inclined to do evangelistic work than to be pastor. The other families that pioneered from Virginia to Tennessee with the Eppersons were Hire and Meador. Those three families soon intermarried and joined in our Epperson family lineage.

**Aphrey Epperson** (1806-1879) married Elizabeth Hire, whose family had deep German roots and strong German Reformed beliefs. Her father and uncles were storied Revolutionary patriots and other family members were captured by Indians. They took their six children and left the Tennessee homestead for Marion, Illinois, where he farmed and improved the land. He sold his lands in Marion and moved to McDonald County, Missouri where he was a successful farmer even through the Civil War, with real estate value of $3,000 and personal estate of $1,000.

**George Washington Epperson** (1848-1933) lived in Tiff City, Missouri and became a wealthy, prominent businessman, and bank owner. He married three times and his first wife, Nancy Poe, was mother to William Stanley Epperson.

**William Stanley Epperson** (1868-1956) was a farmer in Missouri, who married Emaline (Emily Jane) Sellers and they had four children, their oldest was Orval William Epperson.

**Orval William Epperson** (1891-1976) became a banker, married Therese DeBrosse and had three children: Joan Rosalind, Orval Wilford (Billy) and Tirzah Madelon.

There are many descendants from Joan Epperson and James P. Giles, and Tirzah Epperson and Richard L. Federer.

```
                    Notes pertaining to ancestry of O.W.Epperson.
                    * * * * * * * * * * * * * * * * * * * * *
Census of 1860 showed in Newton County, Missouri, Lost Creek Township.
Page 18.        John Sellers  Age 36  Farmer  Born, Tenn. Property $765.00.
Household 117.  Nathaniel         26  (my grandfather) brother of John.
                Silas             24  another brother of John and Nathaniel.
                William           13
                Samuel            20  Note: my mother says grandfather's
                Rebecca           40  name was Nathaniel Simmons Sellers
                Matilda           27  but was usually known as LEE SELLERS.
                Lamina            22
                Washington         9.
Household 121  Daniel Shearer   22. Farmer. Born Missouri, Property  $300.00.
                Martha           18.        do
House    122.  John Shearer    24  Farmer   do                       $300.00.
                Mary            27           do
                Thomas           3           do
                John             1           do
House    125   Elizabeth Shearer 48    Born Ohio Personal property $391.00.
                (My Great Grand Mother.)    Real Estate valued at 5,460.00.
                Martin           20  Farmer
                Emeline          16  (my grandmother) Born Missouri.
                Sarah            15.                 do
                Mary             13.                 do
                James             6.                 do
                Jonathan Mitts   22. Farmer (probably a hired hand. Born, Tenn,
         Note.  Nathaniel Sellers married Emeline Shearer Dec 30, 1865
                by Rev. George Britton, Minister.
                It is my understanding that John Sellers married Sarah Shearer,
                the sister of Emeline, and Silas Sellers married another
                Sarah Shearer, so the Rebecca Sellers, age 40 in the household
                of John Sellers, age 36, must have been an older sister. My mother
                always referred to the two Sarahs as Aunt Sarah John, and Aunt
                Sarah Sile.
                Nathaniel Sellers and Emeline moved from Lost Creek Township,
                in Newton County to the vicinity of Anderson in McDonald County,
                and there William Epperson married Emily Sellers.
Census of 1880. Pineville Township, McDonald County Missouri showed.
Page 8 House 75 Lee Sellers  Age 47. Farmer Born. Tenn. His Fr. Born Tenn .Mot.Tenn.
                Emeline (wife)   40       Born Mo.  her Fr.  Ohio. Mother Ohio
                Sarah            18            Mo             Tenn         Mo.
                Mary A           14            Mo
                Margaret E       12            Mo.
                Emilia J         11            Mo   (My mother)
                Silas E.          9            Mo
                Dannie            7            Mo
                James             4            Mo
                Joseph            1            Mo

Note. It would appear that Nathaniel (or Lee) Sellers had very small chance
of inheriting any property, so the extensive real estate my grandmother
owned must have been inherited from her parents. The first I remember of
her, she was a widow, as my grandfather was killed in an accident (a log
rolled off a wagon and crushed him) when I was only a year or so old and
my great grand mother lived with my grandmother and smoked a little clay
pipe, which she would light by picking up a live coal from the big fireplace
and placing it on her filled pipe, with her bare hands.
```

*Notes pertaining to ancestry of O.W. Epperson as written by Orval William Epperson.*

Notes pertaining to the ancestry of O.W. EPPERSON.
\*\*\*\*\*\*\*\*\*\*\*\*\*\*\*\*\*\*\*\*\*\*\*\*\*\*\*\*\*\*

Goodspeed's History of McDonald County, at page 1060 shows that GEORGE WASHINGTON EPPERSON, was born October 19, 1848 in Marion County Illinois. His father as shown was ASHREY EPPERSON, who was born in Tennessee.

First wife of George W. Epperson was Nancy Poe, whom he married in 1867 and she died in 1877. leaving her children William Epperson, (my father) and Edward Epperson and Charles Epperson.

Second wife was Hanna Meador, daughter of Joel Meador. She left two children Henry and Marietta Ann.

Eppersons in Illinois as shown in Census of 1850, Marion County.
Household No. 1033.  ALFRED Epperson Age 43, Farmer Born Tennessee.
                     Real Estate held valuation $800.00.
          Elizabeth- wife Age 40     Born Tennessee.
          Milla, Daughter age 15 (Attended School) Born Illinois.
          Martha        do     13     do            do
          Martin VanBuren Epperson, Age 10  do      do
          Hezekiah   (Not in school)  6               do
          George Washington Epperson  2               do

Household No. 1034.  ESSEX Epperson, Age 43 Farmer Born Tennessee.
                     Probably a twin brother. Land Valuation $800.00.
          Mary. wife Age 34           Born Virginia.
          Napoleon, son      14       Born Tennessee.
          Josephine,         12       Born Tennessee.
          Louise              3       Born Illinois.
          Mary.     six months old    Born Illinois.

Eppersons in McDonald County as shown by Census of 1860. Rutledge Township.
Page 11. House 75.   APHREY Epperson, Age 53,  Personal Property $1,000.00.
                     Elizabeth Age 40.         Real Estate       3,000.00.
                     Shown both Aphrey and Elizabeth Born Tennessee.
          George W. Epperson, Age 12, Born Illinois.

Eppersons in McDonald County as shown by Census of 1870. Pineville Township.
Page 11 House 81.    EPHREY Epperson, Age 63, Property $300.00. Personal. Born Tenn.
                     Elizabeth, Epperson, Age 61.           Born Tennessee.
Page 11. House 82.   George W. Epperson, Age 22. Property $4,000.00. Real Estate
                     Nancy Epperson, Age 22.               1,800.00. Personal.
                     William Epperson, Age 2 (My Father) Born, Missouri.
                     Notation says that Nancy cannot read nor write and that both
                     George Was born in Illinois and Nancy born in Tennessee.
                     Other members of house 82 were Andrew Shetley Age 14,
                     John Shetley Age 9 and Abe Tharp Age 9, all born in
                     Missouri and listed as Farm Laborers.

It might be well to note here that in those times it was the custom for the young children, at ages from two up to be "bound " as apprentices until they were 21 years of age "to learn the art and mysteries of farming", so it is assumed that the Shetleys and Abe Tharp were "apprentices" to my grandfather. It should be further noted that the 1860 census showed Aphrey had property to the total of $4,000.00. and the 1870 census showed he had only $300.00. valuation. Possibly the Civil War wiped out his assets, but there is no explanation of where George W. at age 22 had accumulated $5,800.00. in assets. I have heard my father say that George W. had the only threshing machine in McDonald County and also owned the grist mill at Anderson for a long time as well as a sizable acreage just South of Anderson, which would explain the nature of his assets and need of "Apprentices" but still would not explain WHERE he raised funds to purchase. Abe Tharp lived about a mile from us when I lived East of Anderson, and I have enjoyed many of his watermelons and cantalupes which we bought for five cents each. It might also be worth while to note that a large portion of the population could neither read nor write and undoubtedly the census takers did not write very well, and when their census sheets were copied on the master census records what might have been originally intended for ALFRED, could be misread as ASHREY, APHREY, or EPHREY. However, the other things indicate that they were all meant to be the same person, and my father said he had always heard of him as APHREY EPPERSON.

*Notes pertaining to the ancestry of O.W. Epperson as written by Orval William Epperson.*

www.ingramcontent.com/pod-product-compliance
Lightning Source LLC
Chambersburg PA
CBHW061128170426
43209CB00014B/1706